FILM AND VIDEO

CAREER
DIRECTORY

Inside

Visible Ink Press proudly presents the first edition of the *Film and Video Career Directory*. The hallmark of this volume, part of Visible Ink's Career Advisor Series, is the essays by active professionals. Here, industry insiders describe opportunities and challenges in many areas of film and video, including:

- Motion picture producing
- Screenwriting
- Independent filmmaking
- Documentary filmmaking
- Internships
- Acting

- Stunt performing
- Animation
- Corporate video production
- Multimedia/interactive video production
- Art directing
- Lighting design/technology

In fully up-to-date articles, they describe:

- What to expect on the job
- Typical career paths
- What they look for in an applicant
- How their specialty is unique

Provides Excellent Job Hunting Resources

Once this "Advice from the Pro's" has given you a feel for film and video, the *Directory* offers even more help with your job search strategy:

- **The Job Search Process** includes essays on determining career objectives, resume preparation, networking, writing effective cover letters, interviewing, and auditioning. With worksheets and sample resumes and letters. **FEATURES:** Resumes are targeted to the realities of film and video careers.

- **Job Opportunities Databank** provides details on hundreds of companies that hire at entry-level. **FEATURES:** In addition to the entry-level information, entries also include information on all-important internship opportunities.

- **Career Resources** identifies sources of help wanted ads, professional associations, employment agencies and search firms, career guides, professional and trade periodicals, and basic reference guides and handbooks. **FEATURES:** Resource listings include detailed descriptions to help you select the publications and organizations that will best meet your needs.

Master Index Puts Information at Your Fingertips

The *Directory* is thoroughly indexed, with access to essays and directory sections both by subject and by organization name, publication title, or service name.

FILM AND VIDEO

CAREER DIRECTORY

A Practical, One-Stop Guide to
Getting a Job in Film and Video

1ST EDITION

**Bradley J. Morgan and
Joseph M. Palmisano, Editors**

Diane M. Sawinski, Associate Editor

DETROIT • WASHINGTON, D.C. • LONDON

CAREER ADVISOR SERIES

FILM
AND VIDEO

C A R E E R
D I R E C T O R Y

1st Edition

A Practical, One-Stop Guide to Getting a Job in Film and Video

Published by **Visible Ink Press**™
a division of Gale Research Inc.
835 Penobscot Building
Detroit, MI 48226-4094

ISBN 0-8103-9492-8

Art Director: Cynthia Baldwin
Cover and Design: Mary Krzewinski
Career Advisor Logo Designs: Kyle Raetz

Printed in the United States of America

Contents

PART ONE

Advice from the Pro's

PART TWO

The Job Search Process

Acknowledgments

The editors would like to thank all the "pro's" who took the time out of their busy schedules to share their first-hand knowledge and enthusiasm with the next generation of job-seekers. A special thanks to Kathleen M. Daniels, Assistant Director of the Career Planning and Placement Office at the University of Detroit Mercy, who provided much needed help with the job search section.

Thanks are also owed to the human resources personnel at the companies listed in this volume and to the public relations staffs of the associations who provided excellent suggestions for essays. Debra Vodenos of *InMotion* magazine deserves special mention.

Introduction

Getting and keeping a job these days can be a demanding proposition. Despite an economy that is finally recovering from the latest recession, many firms are still downsizing and are reluctant to increase staff levels. As for "show business"—well, everyone knows how hard it is to break into this competitive field.

What this means is that the job search is an increasingly challenging process. To beat the competition, job seekers need information. By utilizing the *Film and Video Career Directory*, job seekers gain all the information they need to make the best possible decisions about their job search. The *Directory* is a comprehensive, one-stop resource that includes:

- Essays by industry professionals that provide practical advice not found in any other career resource

- Job search guidance designed to help you get in the door in film and video

- Job and internship listings from leading companies in the United States

- Information on additional career resources to further the job hunt

- A Master Index to facilitate easy access to the *Directory*

The *Directory* is organized into four parts that correspond to the steps of a typical job search—identifying your area of interest, refining your presentation, targeting companies, and researching your prospects.

Sidebars located throughout the *Directory* are intended to amplify the text or provide a counterpoint to information presented on the page. They'll help you build a context for your career and job-search efforts by bringing you discussions of trends in the book publishing industry and the business world, labor statistics, job-hunting techniques, and predictions about our future worklife. These and other tips and tidbits were gleaned from a wide range of sources—sources you can continue to draw upon for a broader understanding of your chosen field and of the job-search process.

Advice from the Pro's: An Invaluable Tool

Instead of offering "one-size-fits-all" advice or government statistics on what the working world is like, the *Film and Video Career Directory* goes into the field for first-hand reports from experienced professionals working in many segments of film and video. This "Advice from the Pro's" is offered by people who know what it's like to land that first job and turn it into a rich and rewarding career. Learn about:

- what it means to be a creative motion picture producer from Buck Houghton, best known as the producer of the first 100 *Twilight Zone* episodes and author of *What a Producer Does: The Art of Moviemaking (Not the Business)*
- opportunities in documentary filmmaking from Jon Wilkman, President of the International Documentary Association
- how to break into a career in animation from John Cawley of the International Animated Film Association
- and nine other areas of specialization, including:

Screenwriting	Corporate video production
Independent filmmaking	Multimedia/interactive video production
Internships	Art directing
Acting	Lighting design/technology
Stunt performing	

The essays cover the most important things a job applicant needs to know, including:

- What college courses and other background offer the best preparation
- Specific skills that are needed
- What organizations look for in an applicant
- Typical career paths
- Salary information

The Job Search Process: Making Sense of It All

What is the first thing a new job-hunter should do?
What different types of resumes exist and what should they look like?
What questions are off-limits in an interview?

These important questions are among the dozens that go through every person's mind when he or she begins to look for a job. Part Two of the *Film and Video Career Directory*, **The Job Search Process**, answers these questions and more. It is divided into five chapters that cover all the basics of how to aggressively pursue a job:

- **Getting Started: Self-Evaluation and Career Objectives.** How to evaluate personal strengths and weaknesses and set goals.
- **Targeting Companies and Networking for Success.** How to identify the companies you would like to work for and how to build a network of contacts.
- **Preparing Your Resume.** What to include, what not to include, and what style to use. Includes samples of the three basic resume types and worksheets to help you organize your information, and covers the auditioning process and use of head shots.

- **Writing Better Letters.** What letters should be written throughout the search process and how to make them more effective. Includes samples.
- **Questions for You, Questions for Them.** How to handle an interview and get the job.

Job Opportunities Databank: Finding the Job You Want

Once you're ready to start sending out those first resumes, how do you know where to start? The **Job Opportunities Databank,** Part Three of the *Directory,* includes listings for more than 210 major film and video production companies, post-production facilities, and other companies providing services allied with film and video in the United States that offer entry-level jobs. These listings provide detailed contact information and data on the companies' business activities, hiring practices, benefits, and application procedures—everything you need to know to approach potential employers. And since internships play an increasingly important role in the career research and employment process, information on the internship opportunities offered by the companies listed is also included.

It should be noted that the companies found in the *Directory* are primarily involved in some segment of the film and video industry. Since there are many other smaller companies that also provide jobs for film and video professionals, students should not limit their job or internship search to the companies listed, but instead, should investigate all companies of interest.

For further information on the arrangement and content of the **Job Opportunities Databank**, consult "How to Use the Job Opportunities Databank" immediately following this introduction.

Career Resources: A Guide to Organizations and Publications in the Field

Need to do more research on the specialty you've chosen or the companies you'll be interviewing with? Part Four of the *Directory*, **Career Resources**, includes information on the following:

- Sources of help wanted ads
- Professional associations
- Employment agencies and search firms
- Career guides
- Professional and trade periodicals
- Basic reference guides and handbooks

Listings contain contact information and descriptions of each publication's content and each organization's membership, purposes, and activities, helping you to pinpoint the resources you need for your own specific job search.

For additional information on the arrangement and content of **Career Resources**, consult "How to Locate Career Resources" following this introduction.

Master Index Speeds Access to Resources

A **Master Index** leads you to the information contained in all four sections of the *Directory* by citing all subjects, organizations, publications, and services listed throughout in a single alphabetic sequence. The index also includes inversions on significant keywords appearing in cited organization, publication, and service names. For example, the "International Television Association" would also be listed in the index under "Television Association; International." Citations in the index refer to page numbers.

Information Keeps Pace with the Changing Job Market

This first edition of the *Film and Video Career Directory* contains essays in the **Advice from the Pro's** section that were contributed by leading professionals in the film and video industry on subjects of particular interest to today's job seekers. All employers listed in the **Job Opportunities Databank** were contacted by telephone or facsimile to obtain current information, and **Career Resources** listings were obtained from selected material from other databases compiled by Gale Research Inc.

Comments and Suggestions Welcome

The staff of the *Film and Video Career Directory* appreciates learning of any corrections or additions that will make this book as complete and useful as possible. Comments or suggestions for future essay topics or other improvements are also welcome, as are suggestions for careers that could be covered in new volumes of the Career Advisor Series. Please contact:

Career Advisor Series
Visible Ink Press
835 Penobscot Bldg.
Detroit, MI 48226-4094
Phone: 800-347-4253
Fax: (313) 961-6815

Bradley J. Morgan
Joseph M. Palmisano

How to Use the
Job Opportunities Databank

The **Job Opportunities Databank** comprises two sections:

Entry-Level Job and Internship Listings
Additional Companies

Entry-Level Job and Internship Listings

Provides listings for more than 210 major film and video production companies, postproduction facilities, and other companies providing services allied with film and video in the United States. Entries in the **Job Opportunities Databank** are arranged alphabetically by company name. When available, entries include:

- **Company name.**
- **Address and telephone number.** A mailing address and telephone number are provided in every entry.
- **Fax and toll-free telephone number.** These are provided when known.
- **Business description.** Outlines the company's business activities. The geographical scope of the company's operations may also be provided.
- **Corporate officers.** Lists the names of executive officers, with titles.
- **Number of employees.** Includes the most recently provided figure for total number of employees. Other employee-specific information may be provided as well.
- **Average entry-level hiring.** Includes the number of entry-level employees the company typically hires in an average year. Many companies have listed "Unknown" or "0" for their average number of entry-level jobs. Because of current economic conditions, many firms could not estimate their projected entry-level hires for the coming years. However, because these firms have offered entry-level positions in the past and because their needs may change, we have listed them in this edition.
- **Opportunities.** Describes the entry-level positions that the company typically offers, as well as the education and other requirements needed for those positions.

- **Benefits.** Lists the insurance, time off, retirement and financial plans, activities, and programs provided by the company, if known.
- **Human resources contacts.** Lists the names of personnel-related staff, with titles.
- **Application procedure.** Describes specific application instructions, when provided by the company.

Many entries also include information on available internship programs. Internship information provided includes:

- **Contact name.** Lists the names of officers or personnel-related contacts who are responsible for the internship program.
- **Type.** Indicates the type of internship, including time period and whether it is paid, unpaid, or for college credit. Also indicates if a company does not offer internships.
- **Number available.** Number of internships that the company typically offers.
- **Number of applications received.** Total number of applications received in a typical year.
- **Application procedures and deadline.** Describes specific application instructions and the deadline for submitting applications.
- **Decision date.** Final date when internship placement decisions are made.
- **Duties.** Lists the typical duties that an intern can expect to perform at the company.
- **Qualifications.** Lists the criteria a prospective applicant must meet to be considered for an internship with the company.

Additional Companies

Covers those companies that elected to provide only their name, address, and telephone number for inclusion in the *Directory*. Entries are arranged alphabetically by company name.

How to Locate
Career Resources

The **Career Resources** chapter contains six categories of information sources, each of which is arranged alphabetically by resource or organization name. The categories include:

▼ **Sources of Help Wanted Ads**

- **Covers:** Professional journals, industry periodicals, association newsletters, placement bulletins, and online services that include employment ads or business opportunities. Includes sources that focus specifically on film and video concerns, as well as general periodical sources such as the *National Business Employment Weekly.*
- **Entries include:** The resource's title; name, address, and telephone number of its publisher; frequency; subscription rate; description of contents; toll-free and additional telephone numbers; and facsimile numbers.
- **Sources:** *Job Hunter's Sourcebook* (published by Gale Research Inc.) and original research.

▼ **Professional Associations**

- **Covers:** Trade and professional associations that offer career-related information and services.
- **Entries include:** Association name, address, and telephone number; membership; purpose and objectives; publications; toll-free or additional telephone numbers; and facsimile numbers. In some cases, the publications mentioned in these entries are described in greater detail as separate entries cited in the Sources of Help Wanted Ads, Career Guides, Professional and Trade Periodicals, and Basic Reference Guides and Handbooks categories.
- **Sources:** *Encyclopedia of Associations* (published by Gale Research Inc.) and original research.

▼ **Employment Agencies and Search Firms**

- **Covers:** Firms used by companies to recruit candidates for positions and, at times, by individuals to pursue openings. Employment agencies are generally geared towards filling openings at entry- to mid-level in the local job market, while executive search firms are paid by the hiring organization to recruit professional and managerial candidates, usually for higher-level openings. Also covers temporary employment agencies because they can be a method of identifying and obtaining regular employment. Includes firms that focus specifically on film and video concerns, as well as some larger general firms.

- **Entries include:** The firm's name, address, and telephone number; whether it's an employment agency, executive search firm, or temporary agency; descriptive information, as appropriate; toll-free and additional telephone numbers; and facsimile number.
- **Sources:** *Job Hunter's Sourcebook.*

▼ Career Guides

- **Covers:** Books, kits, pamphlets, brochures, videocassettes, films, online services, and other materials that describe the job-hunting process in general or that provide guidance and insight into the job-hunting process in film and video careers.
- **Entries include:** The resource's title; name, address, and telephone number of its publisher or distributor; name of the editor or author; publication date or frequency; description of contents; arrangement; indexes; toll-free or additional telephone numbers; and facsimile numbers.
- **Sources:** *Directories in Print* and *Video Sourcebook* (published by Gale Research Inc.) and original research.

▼ Professional and Trade Periodicals

- **Covers:** Newsletters, magazines, newspapers, trade journals, and other serials that offer information to film and video professionals.
- **Entries include:** The resource's title; the name, address, and telephone number of the publisher; the editor's name; frequency; description of contents; toll-free and additional telephone numbers; and facsimile numbers. Publication titles appear in italics.
- **Sources:** *Gale Directory of Publications and Broadcast Media* and *Newsletters in Print* (published by Gale Research Inc.) and original research.

▼ Basic Reference Guides and Handbooks

- **Covers:** Manuals, directories, dictionaries, encyclopedias, films and videocassettes, and other published reference material used by professionals working in film and video careers.
- **Entries include:** The resource's title; name, address, and telephone number of the publisher or distributor; the editor's or author's name; publication date or frequency; description of contents; toll-free and additional telephone numbers; and facsimile numbers. Publication titles are rendered in italics.
- **Sources:** *Directories in Print, Video Sourcebook,* and original research.

ADVICE FROM THE PRO'S

Internships in Film and Video

John Holderried, Office Manager, Sanborn Perillo and Co.

We all know that the shortest distance between two points is a straight line, but when *Point A* is your film or communications degree, and *Point B* is the film or television job of your dreams, the line may not be so direct. An **internship** may be just what you need to test the waters of film and video production, learn about your own abilities, and develop contacts that might lead to a permanent position.

Wouldn't it be great if someone could tell you all that you'll need to know in order to find and land that perfect internship—and turn it into a full-time job? Well, I can't do that. However, I can explain a bit about what a production company might look for in an intern, what it expects from interns, and what an intern should and shouldn't expect from the company in return.

Getting Started

Usually, the best place to start is at your school—and the best time to start is now. If your school has an internship office devoted to helping you find a position, you're in luck. If not, don't worry. You can do your own search. You'll need a book like this one (or Peterson's *Internships*) listing all the available opportunities. Many colleges use these guides or maintain their own listings. If all else fails, you can use a production guide (such as the NYPG for New York), but keep in mind that because these guides sometimes charge for listings, not every production company in an area may be listed.

Once you have a large list of production companies, you'll need to narrow the search. You may want to focus on your local area, or one particular city, once you know what your postcollege plans are. Knowing what type of productions you want to work on is also a great help, enabling you to concentrate on, for example, music video production in New York, or animation production in Los Angeles. The more specific

1

you can be, the more you'll increase your chances of getting the most out of an internship.

Prepare yourself to spend a couple of hours on the telephone at this point. Call each of the companies on your list, and ask for details on their internship programs. Here are some important questions to ask:

- Is the internship paid or unpaid?
- What is the length of the internship?
- What are the required working hours or days per week?
- What are the duties and responsibilities of an intern?

If you are in the same city as the companies you are calling, you can attempt to set up interviews during these phone calls, or you can ask to drop off your resume.

If you're calling from out of town, these calls will save you valuable time and postage. Send a resume and cover letter to those companies that have met all your criteria so far. Be sure to get the name of the person you spoke to at each company, and mention your phone conversation in the cover letter. If you plan to be in their city at some point, you can suggest potential interview dates in the letter.

Wait a week or so, and then be sure to follow up. Keep in mind that some of the people you spoke to are flooded with resumes, and may not have time to respond to them all. In these cases, only the persistent get interviewed.

The Interview

At this point, the internship search is largely out of your hands; who you see depends on who wants to interview you. As you answer the calls to schedule interviews, be sure to leave yourself ample travel time between appointments, especially if they're in an unfamiliar city. It goes without saying that you should dress well and show up on time, but beyond that, you may be wondering what else you can do to prepare.

One thing you can bring is your student films if you have them. It's not necessary, but it couldn't hurt. Be sure to bring backup copies on VHS if your originals are in another format, just in case. Also, bring another copy of your resume in case your original was lost in a busy office. You may want to have several different versions of your resume on hand, each tailored to a different aspect of production (i.e., an office work resume, a production resume, etc.).

At this point, you should already be familiar with each company's type of work, so you can begin to think of ways that your previous experience relates to their work. You'll want to list all of your skills on the resume, and be prepared to talk about how you will put them all to work for whoever hires you. Following is a partial list of the skills that an interviewer may be looking for:

- Previous office experience—the basics (filing, typing, phone work).
- Previous production experience—mention any directing or producing on the college level, as well as any work (even production assistant work) on a professional level.
- Experience with film or video editing.

- Experience with computers—be sure to specify Apple Macintosh, IBM, or both, and what specific programs you are familiar with.
- Any work related to scripts, budgets, or grants.

Having a college degree is important, but if you don't have your degree yet, be sure to include the name of your school and the expected date of your graduation.

One major ingredient in a successful interview that many overlook is a good speaking manner. A comfortable manner during the interview suggests a comfortable phone manner, and an interviewer may be more likely to hire an intern who will speak for the company in a positive way. Use your experience and your attitude together to sell yourself.

What's Next?

If you don't get the internship, keep looking. If you do get the internship, keep looking anyway. It's important to have a backup in case the first falls through. Or, you may find another internship that you like better or where you think the opportunities or benefits are better. After all, people don't stop job hunting just because they have a job—they're always looking for something better!

Employment of Women in the Film Industry

1990-91 percentage of women employed in the film industry by occupation.
1. Production Associate, with 78%
2. Associate Director, 39.8%
3. 2nd Assistant Director, 38.0%
4. Stage Manager, 27.1%
5. 1st Assistant Director, 24.7%
6. Technical Coordinator, 18.2%
7. Unit Production Manager, 15.6%
8. Director, 10.2%
Source: *Premiere*

Practical Advice

A few things to keep in mind, particularly if you take a nonpaying internship or choose to travel to another city:

Have a source of income! It may take a long time for your internship to develop into a paying job, so get a second job that lets you work around your internship schedule so you'll be able to pay your bills.

If you're coming from out of town, finding a place to stay is usually your responsibility. This may seem obvious, but once in a while an intern will show up at a company on the first day and ask for help finding an apartment. Needless to say, this does not impress an employer.

Similarly, feeding yourself is your responsibility as well. Most companies will provide lunch for the crew on a shoot day, but don't expect it on a regular basis. Also, keep in mind that interns and production assistants usually get the shortest lunch breaks. Basically, you can't survive only on production meals.

Food, shelter, money—get these basics out of the way so you can concentrate on your internship!

Your Responsibilities as an Intern

These duties vary from company to company, but an office intern is usually called upon to be part secretary, part receptionist, part researcher, and part personal assistant. Of course, this is by no means a complete list.

The duties of a production intern are quite different, and may involve dubbing tapes, messenger jobs, painting sets, picking up props, etc.—similar duties to those performed by paid production assistants. While on the set, the duties may be defined as anything that the producer or production manager needs done. (Some internships may combine both sets of tasks, or a little bit of each.)

Tasks can sometimes be tailored according to the abilities of the individual. For example, I worked with an intern who had previous experience with grants, and he was given the assignment of researching all the potential grants that the company might be eligible to apply for.

Attitude

On the job, your attitude is just as important as your performance. An intern should be eager and willing to do whatever comes up, though it may not be a particularly glamorous task. An intern who constantly gripes and complains does not stand a good chance of being kept on in any capacity, as employers may prefer to hire people whose company they enjoy.

If a task arises that you don't understand, there should be no shame in asking for an explanation. In general, it would be worse to go ahead with a task without completely understanding it. If you need a job explained to you, be sure to pay attention so you won't need to ask again.

In a word—volunteer! The staff may not know that you can handle a certain task unless you tell them. Make yourself available and be ready to work—you never know when you might be asked to "fill in". The more responsibilities you take on and perform well, the more indispensable you become to a company.

Behind the Scenes

Once you've got your foot in the door at an internship, you have a chance to observe what goes on behind the scenes, and decide in what direction you want to take your career. Take some time to acquaint yourself with the different positions in the production office and the different jobs on the set. Observing the specialists on the set can help you determine what production positions you would like to hold in the future.

If a position interests you, talk to the person who holds that position. Compliment their work, and ask them to explain more, or show you a little about how it's done. (Make sure not to do this on a busy set—wait until a break.) You can also ask if they need any help—but be sure not to neglect the tasks already assigned to you.

Volunteering whenever possible on the set is the best way to develop the skills that will get you hired for more production work. After you've worked as a production assistant (PA) a few times, you can start to specialize. Some PAs are hired to work in positions like props assistant, (PA) script supervisor, and lighting assistant after they've performed similar tasks as a PA. In order to get those offers, though, you'll need to network.

Networking

Networking can be as simple as letting everyone you encounter know that you are available and willing to work. It can be as complicated as maintaining a list of names and numbers of producers, and making a round of phone calls once a month. It's important in this case to let everyone know your skills—a producer might have a long list of PAs, but a short list of script supervisors or props assistants.

Yes, free-lance producers keep lists, too. Getting yourself on them not only increases your chances of getting work, but also enables you to work for many different companies, which could help you find companies that are looking for full-time production or office staff. Ideally, each production job should lead you to more contacts, which can lead to more production jobs, which leads to more contacts, and so on.

Down the Road

Let's assume you've networked yourself pretty well into the world of film and video production. Where can you expect to be in five or ten years time? A successful office intern could be offered a position as an office assistant, with the ultimate goal of becoming office manager. A successful production intern could, through networking, get enough production work to become a professional PA, or develop the skills necessary to hold one of the following positions:

- props assistant, and eventually prop manager or art director
- camera assistant, and eventually cameraman or director of photography
- grip or lighting assistant, and eventually key grip or lighting designer
- sound assistant or boom operator, and eventually sound mixer

Your salaries at any of these positions will be determined by your experience, the importance of your contacts, and the type of production (union or nonunion), as well as the state of the industry.

Miscellaneous Tips

Here are some odds and ends you may end up discovering for yourself the hard way. They may not all apply to your particular situation, but those that do can help you avoid some common mistakes.

1. Keep the company's money separate from your own.
2. Always get a receipt.
3. Learn to make good coffee—you're going to be doing it all the time.
4. Never transport master videotapes by subway or in a car trunk—the electric fields could erase the tapes.
5. Whenever possible, turn off machines (computers, video decks) before plugging or unplugging cables.
6. Wear old clothes on the set and be prepared to do physical labor.

7. Don't fawn over celebrities on the set. At the most, say "I admire your work" and leave it at that.

8. Don't badmouth anyone's professional work on the set—you don't know who's worked with whom.

9. Don't get involved in office politics—you don't know who's dating whom.

10. If you're the one with the keys to the production vehicle, be on time.

I'd like to think that these tips can put you one step ahead of the game.

In closing, I'd just like to bid you welcome to the world of film and video production, and wish you success in your internships and in your career afterward.

▼

JOHN HOLDERRIED has been office manager for two years at Sanborn Perillo and Company, where he began as an intern five years ago. He has handled all of the administration of the company, including the hiring and supervising of interns. He has also been production manager on several projects, including the opening logo for the PBS series *Behind the Scenes*. In addition, he has worked as office assistant and billing manager for Ice Tea Productions.

Mr. Holderried has just begun working as assistant to animator Bill Plympton, for whom he plans to produce animated and live action feature films.

Mr. Holderried was born and raised in Westwood, MA, and received his BFA in film and television production from New York University in 1989.

CHAPTER TWO

You Are Entering Another Dimension: How to Become a Screenwriter

Harvey Ovshinsky, Screenwriter

When I was 13 years old I wrote to my hero and favorite screenwriter, Rod Serling, asking him for his advice on how to become a **writer**. Mr. Serling wrote back and warned me that, while he was happy to respond to my list of questions, he was also reluctant to counsel young writers on their careers because there "just aren't any magic rules."

That's the first rule. There are no magic rules or secret shortcuts when it comes to learning how to navigate a successful career in screenwriting. Writing for the big (or small) screen can be both an exhilarating and excruciating roller coaster ride. But if you are someone who loves going to the movies and you have a passion for writing and telling stories, a career in screenwriting, even with its share of bumps and curves, may be a ride worth taking.

Now is the best time to start out. Ours is an audio visual culture where television and movies have become the primary source of entertainment and literature. With the advent of the 500-channel fiber optic highway and high-definition satellite distribution of movies to the theaters, the demand for screenwriting is expected to grow. The only way all those blank movie and television screens are going to be filled is if writers fill their blank pages and computer screens with words and images. No matter how digitized or computerized our culture becomes, some things will not change: no words, no story. Thank God.

Learning the Job

The best way to learn how to write screenplays is to go out and watch as many movies as you can and then make a point of watching your favorites again to break down and analyze how each element of the story's screenplay contributes to your viewing pleasure. It is also helpful to borrow from the library or purchase a few of the fine anthologies of scripts and screenplays now available. Just don't be intimidated by what you see. I don't know anyone who actually enjoys wading through all the strange margins, borders, and separation of action and dialogue that are essential to the screenplay format. Movies are great to watch in a darkened room or theater, but on the printed page, they can be a very tough read.

There are literally hundreds of fine "How To" books, but my favorites are *The Art of Dramatic Writing* by Lajos Egri, Michael Hagues's *Writing Screenplays That Sell*, Jurgen Wolff and Kerry Cox's *Successful Screenwriting*, William Froug's *Screenwriting Tricks Of The Trade*, and any of the Syd Field books. I also recommend *The Art Spirit* by the great painter and teacher, Robert Henri. This book has absolutely nothing to do with movies or scriptwriting, but what Henri teaches us about craft and the creative process is as inspirational as it is nourishing to the heart and soul.

A word of caution about screenwriting books: although many are certainly instructive and supportive, and offer helpful advice on how to find an agent and when you have to join the Writers Guild of America, reading too many "How To" manuals can waste valuable time and energy better spent in doing the actual writing. Read a couple of books, take a couple of classes and workshops, and then write. Just do it. Put aside some time, find your own space to work, and just write your heart out. And don't stop until you've completed at least a first draft.

▼

Writers Guild of America, West

1990-91 percentage of women writers employed by the major studios.
1. Disney, with 25%
2. Hollywood Pictures, 24%
3. Paramount, 20%
3. Columbia, 20%
4. Tri-Star, 18%
5. Fox, 16%
6. Universal, 15%
7. Warner's, 12%
8. MGM, 11%
Source: *Premiere*

Don't worry if you have another job or you can't write full time right now. It took me almost three years of waking up at 5:30 in the morning and writing only an hour or two each day before I completed my first screenplay. Juggling the "real world" demands of family, work, or school is never easy, but whenever I got discouraged I recalled Rod Serling's advice to me. "You must practice your craft diligently. Writing involves rigid discipline. You learn how to write by writing, writing, writing."

My hero.

A Screenwriter's Education

What about attending college or film school? Absolutely, if you can do it. The more formal education you can get the better. Just watch out for taking too many film or screenwriting classes for their own sake. "The main thing to remember," Mr. Serling warned me, "is that writing mirrors life which encompasses so many things; therefore the standard rule to observe when you begin your education is to consider a 'whole' education. Don't limit yourself in the subjects you take. Don't simply take 'writing' per se, because you don't write about just writing, you write about the world and everything in it. Cram every bit of knowledge into your head. Ultimately, it will be grist for your writing mill."

Breaking Into the Business

Don't hold your breath waiting for someone to hire you to write a script. It doesn't work that way. New screenwriters break in by first writing their scripts on "spec," without ever being asked and without being paid first.

These spec scripts are important because they show potential producers that you not only have what it takes to endure the writing process, but that you also have the talent to actually write a good script. Don't laugh. It's difficult enough just to write a movie, any kind of movie. Coming up with a really good screenplay is a rare and precious thing even for experienced writers. And don't be surprised if it takes at least a dozen drafts to get it right. That's how hard it is. Just ask David Mamet who wrote seven drafts of *The Untouchables* for Brian DePalma and producer Art Linson. Or Steve Martin who, rumor has it, wrote ten drafts of *Roxanne* before he even showed it to anyone.

The path to writing a fine screenplay is the same road talented musicians must travel if they want to get to Carnegie Hall. Practice, practice, practice.

Do I Have to Live in Los Angeles?

It takes more than a couple of wonderful spec scripts under your belt to break into the screenwriting business. Talent is important, but aspiring screenwriters must also know how to cultivate a network of contacts and relationships with industry professionals who are in a position to read, evaluate, or even produce their scripts.

If you can move to Los Angeles, then do it. That's where the meetings and the important contacts and relationships are. Although most movies are no longer made in Hollywood, most of the deals certainly are, especially the development deals. But if you can't make the move, don't beat yourself over the head. Some of the most successful Hollywood screenwriters don't live anywhere near L.A. Just ask my Michigan neighbors Kurt Luedtke (*Out of Africa*, *Absence of Malice*), Jim Cash (*Top Gun*, *Dick Tracy*, and *Legal Eagles*), Jim Bernstein (*Renaissance Man*) and the great mystery novelist and screenwriter Elmore "Dutch" Leonard. The only exception is if you want to write for episodic television. It's almost impossible to write for a series and not be in L.A. for all the creative meetings and rewrite sessions.

What It Takes to Become Successful

Although talent and skill are important, your success as a screenwriter will also depend on one other key ingredient—your personality. Do you have what it takes to endure both the creative process and the business of writing? No glass jaws, please. A thick skin is mandatory if you hope to survive the inevitable, intermittent waves of loathing and self-doubt that come from unreturned phone calls and the seemingly endless number of rejections and rewrites.

Remember that filmmaking is a collaborative process, and that your script is only the first stop on the assembly line. Your job is to supply the blueprints. It is the job of the producer and director to actually build the house. If you want to call the shots, you may want to rethink your decision about becoming a screenwriter.

The Good News

If a career in screenwriting is so frustrating and difficult, then why even consider writing for television and the movies? The easy and obvious answer is that the work pays so well. Screenwriters can earn anywhere from $50,000 to $500,000 per script depending on the quality of the work and the writer's reputation in the community. Not to mention the revenues you can expect from rewriting and polishing other writer's scripts. Although it isn't as satisfying, script doctoring can be even more lucrative than writing your own material.

For many of us, the money is only part of the story. We write because we have no choice. Words on paper is our passion, our path, our calling. We're storytellers. Writing helps me understand and define myself, it's my way of checking myself out and trying to appreciate and accept who I am and where my place is in the vast blank pages of the universe.

And if there's a remote chance that even the smallest part of our vision (and version) of reality will end up on the screen, then we go for it. Because in the end, truly successful screenwriters understand that we don't just write for the movies, we also write for ourselves. And to not write is more painful and unbearable then anything they can do to us along the way.

▼

The Detroit News describes Michigan-based screenwriter **HARVEY OVSHINSKY** as "one of the country's finest storytellers." Mr. Ovshinsky has taught undergraduate and graduate students at Wayne State University. His popular workshops and groups, *Introduction to Screenwriting—A Survival Course* and *How to Complete Your First Movie Script In 6 Months* continue to motivate and inspire aspiring screenwriters. In addition to writing screenplays, Mr. Ovshinsky is also an award-winning documentary producer and director. His many awards include a CINE Gold Eagle, two Ohio State Awards, a Gold Plaque from the Chicago International Film Festival, and a national Emmy and a Peabody Award, two of the most prestigious awards in broadcasting.

The Art and Business of Screenwriting

James A. Mac Eachern, Free-lance Screenwriter

The hardest trade in the world is the writing of straight, honest prose about human beings.

—Ernest Hemingway

Mr. Hemingway expressed a basic truth about the difficult and lonely task that faces every writer who sits down at his or her desk and confronts a blank piece of paper. The **screenwriter** must face this moment of truth like all other fiction writers. If the reader is not already aware of this fact, let me make it crystal clear—writing a screenplay *is* writing. In order to be a good **screenwriter**, you must be first and foremost a good **writer.** This may seem painfully obvious, but there is good reason to say it. In the past, the craft of the screenwriter has not been held in high regard—in literary circles or in Hollywood. However, in recent years, with record fees being doled out to screenwriters like Joe Eszterhaus, who was paid $3 million for his script *Basic Instinct* and Shane Black who made a hefty $1.75 million for *The Last Boy Scout*, there has been a deluge of scripts from aspiring screenwriters pouring into Hollywood hoping to cash in on the big money.

Writing Is Work

Most of the scripts that are submitted to agencies and studios are unprofessional and badly written. Why is this? The problem is at least partly a get-rich-quick mentality that afflicts so many in our culture, and partly the mistaken impression that writing a screenplay is an *easy* endeavor. People who would never dream of sitting down to write a book or a play are somehow convinced that they can write better scripts than what they see on television or at the movies. While it is all too true that there is a lot of poor quality work being produced on television and at the movies, the same can be said of books and plays. For whatever reason, the mistaken impression that screenwriting is not *hard work* persists and is a notion I hope to dispel in this essay.

Screenwriting is an art, a craft, and a business, and unless you are committed to learning, practicing, and perfecting the skills necessary to write a good script, you will never rise above the fierce competition and claim the potentially huge rewards of a Joe Eszterhaus or Shane Black. For those of you who are willing to pay the price and are determined to become screenwriters, there are many practical considerations you should be aware of in preparing to enter the profession.

Where to Get the Tools You Need

Film School

In recent years, many of the top young screenwriters in the business have come out of such big film schools as the University of California, Los Angeles (UCLA), University of Southern California (USC), and New York University (NYU). Talented writers like John Singleton (*Boyz N the Hood*) are also directing their scripts. Mr. Singleton, along with Spike Lee, is a film school graduate who is carrying on the tradition of other film school successes like Francis Ford Coppola, Brian De Palma, Paul Schrader, Martin Scorsese, and George Lucas. These well-known industry leaders are not the only ones who find success right out of school, however. Hollywood's obsession with youth has meant that agents and producers keep a sharp eye trained on the big film schools ready to spot a talented writer and/or director. Current UCLA, USC, and NYU students and recent graduates are routinely employed in the industry—but there is a catch. Film school degrees have become the MBA's of the '90s, and the competition for admission is *fierce*. In the past five years or so, for example, it has become harder to get into the top film schools than it is to get into Harvard. USC and NYU accept only six percent of the applicants to their program and UCLA accepts a paltry three percent. By contrast, Harvard admits 14 percent of their applicants.

College/University

Although attending and excelling at one of the *top* film schools can be a fast track into the industry, the aspiring screenwriter can get the basic education needed to become a good writer at almost *any* college or university. The fact is that the notable film school successes I have mentioned are the *exceptions* rather than the *rule*, and most of the writers in Hollywood and New York got their education and training where they could find it—and then made the most of it.

The aspiring screenwriter should obtain a strong liberal arts education at a local college and take as many courses in dramatic writing as possible. Classes in literature and film are essential, but knowledge of history, politics, sociology, and psychology can provide a wealth of knowledge to draw from for the rest of your life.

Writing the Script

When you write, you lay down a line of words. The line of words is a miner's pick, a woodcarver's gouge, a surgeon's probe. You wield it, and it digs a path you follow. Soon you find yourself deep in new territory.
—Annie Dillard in *The Writing Life*

A young writer should study the basic three-act structure and look for stories he or she wants to tell within this structure. Every writer should be familiar with Aristotle's *Poetics* and Lajos Egri's *The Art of Dramatic Writing*. The first script *I* wrote in college was an autobiographical piece called *Fathers and Sons*. I was a graduate student at the time and I drew on my knowledge of dramatic writing, which has as its basis an understanding of conflict, and applied this knowledge to a disturbing life experience.

You should also read some of the many screenplay anthologies that are available. I would suggest reading the scripts of Horton Foote, Ingmar Bergman, and Woody Allen. No one can teach you how to write, but a good teacher can clarify some of the basic rules of dramatic structure and give you guidance in constructing a strong plot with compelling characters. One of the best pieces of advice I've ever received was an elaboration on the obvious rule that a story must have a beginning, middle, and an end. My teacher told me, "You should tell them what you are going to tell them, tell them what you are telling them, and tell them what you told them." It's also important for screenwriters to keep in mind Jean Luc Godard's advice that "a film must have a beginning, middle, and an end, but not necessarily in that order."

Finding an Agent

Before you approach an agent, you should have at least two well-written scripts that are professionally formatted and ready for sale. One good script is not enough because the agent may like your writing but doesn't think the script you've submitted will sell. In that case, you must have another script ready to demonstrate that you are taking your writing seriously and to show that the first script wasn't a fluke—or worse—that it was a *paint-by-number* job.

There is a catch-22 involved in finding an agent, however. If you really *need* an agent, it is almost impossible to find one. Conversely, if you somehow manage to sell or option one of your scripts on your own and therefore (at least in theory) *don't* really need an agent, they will be knocking your door down. You must remember that it is not enough to just find an agent—you must find a good one. The agent must love your work and have the time to promote you energetically. The relationship between a writer and his/her agent is like a marriage—and thus depends on mutual trust.

Finding Work

If you are determined to become a screenwriter, you are almost by definition going to be looking for free-lance work. The chances of obtaining a regular full-time position as a writer are slim. There are some staff writing jobs in movies and television, but they are few and far between. The staff jobs that are available are for the most part in episodic television, writing scripts for the soap operas, situation comedies, and weekly drama series (even some of this work goes to the free-lance writer). Gone

Use Industry Contacts When Seeking an Agent

The consensus is that the best way to get an agent is by referral. If you know someone who knows someone in the business—whether they are in the creative or technical end of the industry—by all means, try to connect with them. Under no circumstances should you submit material to an agent who charges a reading (or any other) fee. Chances are good that if an agent needs to charge a reading fee, they are not making a living representing writers, and are probably not going to be much help to you.

13

are the glory days of Hollywood when the studios had stables of writers and steady work was plentiful. Of course at that time, the writer was the low man on the totem pole and had very little influence on the final product.

Almost all feature film work today is free-lance. You will thus have to learn how to market yourself as a writer to become a success in movies. While writing talent is essential, success as a screenwriter in today's market depends just as heavily on three things: the way you present yourself and sell yourself to a prospective employer, willpower, and your drive to succeed. There are only a few hundred feature films made in this country each year and the competition for the plum assignments is obviously intense.

Of course, there is the large television market—both network and cable—and the large commercial video market to consider. There are more and more *movies of the week* on both cable and network television that provide opportunities for screenwriters to write and sell feature-length works that can eventually lead to film assignments. Perhaps the biggest market opening up for writers is the $4-billion-a-year commercial video market.

Commercial scriptwriting—writing scripts for nonfiction, information films, videos for corporate use, sales and training aids, and for the retail home video market—is a growing and lucrative field for writers. This work can serve as the day job for ambitious screenwriters who can still work on their screenplays at night. The average fee for a writer who fashions a 10- to 12-minute video script is about $2,000 and can go up to $3,500 or more. This will certainly not make you rich, but it can help pay the rent for the talented and energetic writer waiting for his/her big break.

Conclusion

The aspiring screenwriter should be aware of all the scriptwriting gurus who are hawking their formulas in books and seminars. A veritable cottage industry has sprouted up in the past decade of *experts* with a "new, easy-to-follow plan that just can't fail." While some very helpful books and teachers exist, there are many *more* charlatans making a lot of money selling phony formulas. Most of these formulas are gimmicks and only lead to a paint-by-numbers approach that produces cookie cutter scripts and films. If the movies you've seen recently all seem to hit the same notes, the emphasis on formulas is probably the reason.

Finally, it is important to remember that the purpose of any career should be the work itself. As I pointed out at the beginning of this chapter, there are far too many people writing screenplays for the wrong reasons. Those who pursue a screenwriting career only because it may make them *rich* or because they think it's *easy* are bound to fail. They will not succeed because they do not have that burning desire needed to become a good writer. Although the work is hard and the chances of grabbing that brass ring of success as a *big time* Hollywood screenwriter are slim, there are many opportunities more attainable in cable television and the booming commercial video market. For those of you with this desire, all you need to do is work hard at perfecting your craft and becoming the best writer you can be. If you accomplish this, you will prevail against the odds and become successful at doing what you love most in life.

Recommended Books

Walter, Richard. *Screenwriting: The Art, Craft and Business of Film and Television Writing* (Plume, 1988).

Hauge, Michael. *Writing Screenplays That Sell* (McGraw-Hill, 1988; Harper Collins, 1991).

▼

JAMES MAC EACHERN is an award-winning free-lance screenwriter with four feature and several short scripts to his credit. Mr. Mac Eachern received a Graduate-Drama (Tompkins Award) for his first short script while a student at Wayne State University in Detroit, MI. His first feature screenplay was completed with the help of a Creative Artist Grant from the Michigan Council for the Arts. Mr. Mac Eachern has been working as a writer for almost a decade and a recent documentary script he wrote was broadcast in the fall of 1993. He has published several film-related articles including resource guides on filmmakers Ingmar Bergman and Jean Cocteau.

Mr. Mac Eachern was born and raised in Michigan but lived for a time in Nova Scotia, Canada. He received his MA in radio-TV-film from Wayne State University.

CHAPTER FOUR

The Art of Movie Making: What a Producer Does

Buck Houghton, Producer

Editors note: This *essay* by Buck Houghton is a collection of writings he has issued through the years on what it means to be a creative producer—something Houghton knows well. Best known as the producer of the first 100 *Twilight Zone* episodes, Mr. Houghton has also written a book called *What a Producer Does: The Art of Moviemaking (Not the Business)* (Silman-James Press, distributed by Samuel French Trade). This essay is divided into two parts:

1. A letter Mr. Houghton wrote to the *Los Angeles Times* in June 1993 in reference to two earlier stories on producers.

2. An addendum to that letter written just for this directory.

It Really Only Takes One Producer to Make a Movie

The two articles that Sunday Calendar published regarding the multiplicity of *producer* credits in movies and television . . . didn't mention the several projects shooting today, smoothly and under a single producer—nor recall how well pictures were managed before the manipulators of today muddled up the scene. Carroll O'Connor never had it so good as when he was in *All in the Family* under the producer expertise of Norman Lear. O'Connor exposes another blind spot when he says of his show, "...what goes on that screen is 100 percent mine." There is no 10 feet of film, much less 5,000 feet, that is 100 percent anyone's.

Understanding why some operations work so well today and hodgepodge organizational practices don't lies in comprehending the following truism: Movie-making is a cooperative enterprise of skilled artists whose effectiveness, both in terms of high-quality results and prudent cost, depends on the strength of their cohesion to a concept and to one another. That cohesion is planned and engineered best by an equally skilled professional: the producer—a person with an overview, an overseer. And there is no better way to disrupt a tightly knit team than to assign several overseers or one overseer who is not their equal, professionally. There is no orchestra that could get through a symphony with two or three conductors (no matter how bright they are musically).

A good producer is a highly trained specialist (not a financier, a know-it-all player, or a power-juiced agent) with experience around stories and storytelling, budgets and payrolls, and a curiosity about how the movie crew accomplishes its miracles. With years of background, this person is qualified to be a creative administrator to those very geniuses—not to tell them how to do it, but to understand the range of their capabilities and push them to their best work. And, understanding the value of each job in the jigsaw puzzle, see it fully realized—maybe enhanced—as it goes through the hands of other geniuses toward the picture they all planned for.

This requires constant attention, not the spare-time focus of a player or a writer or a director. This is not a matter of titles; it is a specific function. When it is spread out, mistakes are made (for example, a "line producer" was not present when the tiny creative stroke of a red Rolls-Royce for the leading lady was decided upon—she's flamboyant; so the one in charge OKs a black Mercedes). Spreading the producer function around is costing management both money and quality; their product is becoming a committee-designed horse. (Remember the joke? You get a camel.)

Costs mount when crew members do not know who to turn to. If an important bit actor can't report tomorrow, do you reschedule and face the resulting turmoil and wait for the actor? Or recast?

Can't ask the player-producer busy shooting an important scene. Can't ask the associate producer or the co-executive producer, for they're never around and wouldn't understand the implications of the problem if they were. Money will be wasted by procrastinating and, perhaps, the right actor for the part will be lost.

There are other important matters on a producer's desk that others do not know about—but it took me 200 book pages to cover what I'm trying to say here; I only hope that it becomes clear that the muddle that Welkos and Willens reported on so well is a farce that will soon correct itself. There are plenty of highly qualified or soon-to-be qualified producers out there.

To Students With a Motion Picture Career on Their Minds

The previous letter I wrote to the *Los Angeles Times* defines, in broad terms, what a producer does. In my view, it is a good idea to be familiar with a producer's goals, no matter what part you play in the movie or television production team—the producer is your flagpole.

Preparatory Education

It is good to have some familiarity with bookkeeping—the juggling of figures to keep the total about the same. The more familiarity with English literature and drama, the better. Have a grasp of the difference between novel story-telling and dramatic story-telling. This may be classwork, or it may entail reading extensively and studying one or two of the several books about screenplay writing.

Career Paths

Get a job on a production crew—gofer, coffee boy, laborer, assistant director trainee (the Screen Directors Guild siphons successful applicants into their studio training program). See how the set works, day to day. Roam the studio lot to see how the various departments do their work. Wander into the a dubbing session and listen in on the process of putting the music, dialogue, and sound effects tracks together.

Another path: Get a job reading and reporting on story material. Agents have readers to cover their clients' submissions; studios have big story departments who assess what's out there for sale.

Then, the trick is to switch from the first path that came your way to the other. Shift from production and money to stories . . . because it is the combination of these two backgrounds that solidifies your producer capabilities.

As I have stated in the *Los Angeles Times* article, the producer must know what the artists who make up the crew can do (you have watched them do it); the producer must know if real costs are running even with the guess figures (the budget).

With this background, you can start to search for a producer role. Get your hands on a good script somehow—from an idea of your own . . . from a good story you read . . . from a good friend of yours in the agency field (you will have cultivated a few) who leads you to one of his/her clients . . . from *your own* writing. With your background, you've got a good shot at producing the picture that this certain script proposes. At least, the project will not fail because a studio or financial banker feels that you're unqualified.

There are occasions when a project (script, interested studio, or actor) needs a producer to round out the proposal. There are occasions when a script is all set to go—actor aboard, enthused director, etc.—now who's going to mind the store . . . administer these assets? You're the qualified person to try for it.

No one can tell you for sure how to get any of these jobs. A friend of a friend, a relative, a chance social encounter, sheer persistence with the personnel department . . . these are all possibilities. Most important is a willingness to start low. In short, it's like any other business with a pot of gold at the end of its rainbow—hard to get started.

I got started as a mailboy at a big studio. In two years, I was in the budget bureau. Then came World War II, and upon return, I got a job at a big studio story department. Then a big spender who got a television series sold without knowing a camera dolly from a lawn mower accepted my credentials . . . and I was off!

Salary potential in this business is quite high. Mail clerks probably get $200 per week—a producer of a television series will probably get $10,000 per episode.

I would recommend college through your 20th or 21st year, only because of the breadth of view that four years of academia can give you. And, if you're a producer

Most Profitable Movie Companies

Ranked by: Five-year average return on equity, in percent.
1. General Cinema, with 36.5%
2. Paramount Communications, 26.2%
3. Walt Disney Co., 24.5%
4. LIVE Entertainment, 20.8%
5. Handleman, 18.3%
6. Commtron, 13.5%
7. Time Warner, deficit
8. Orion, deficit
9. AMC Entertainment, deficit

Source: *Forbes*

who puts together a picture about logging in the Northwest one year, and a picture about the Knights of the Round Table the next . . . you'd best be capable of shifting to one area of intensity and then another—just like college.

CHAPTER FIVE

Independent Filmmaking

Douglas A. Grossman, Independent Filmmaker

o paraphrase an immortal writer, being an independent filmmaker is the *best* of times and the *worst* of times.

The most general definition of independent filmmaking is producing a film outside the studio system—and therein lies the paradox. On the one hand, the filmmaker has no outside interference in the creative process. On the other hand, he/she cannot tap into the already established studio support systems (i.e., prop, wardrobe, set construction, pre- and post-production, promotion, screening, transportation, etc.). The independent filmmaker starts from scratch on each new project and is responsible for putting all the necessary elements together to make a successful film. Before we examine the *hows* of making an independent film, let us discuss some of the ways one might receive the *training* to become a filmmaker.

Career Preparation

The independent filmmaker is responsible for delivering a completed film for distribution. The more he/she knows about the various jobs and positions on a film, the better that completed film will be. There are a number of outlets where the individual can go to receive the needed experience.

Not everyone has the opportunity to attend film school, and it is not imperative that you do to become a successful filmmaker. An alternative is to get a job on *any* type of production, whether it be a commercial, television show, or feature film. Don't be picky about what type of job it is or how much money you make. The objective is to get on the set, where you can observe and learn. Once on the set, you can find out what each crew member's function is and how they fulfill that function—don't be afraid to ask questions. This type of experience is invaluable whether you have gone to film school or not. It is very important to know how a set functions—and practical experience cannot be beat.

If film school and practical experience is not within your reach, simply going to the movies or renting videos is another alternative. Study the films. Look for technique, how the filmmaker brought out performances, the use of locations, the photography, the sound, the pacing and editing, and how music affects the scenes. Watch your favorite films over and over. You will be amazed at the things you missed the first time you screened them. Book stores and libraries are another good source of knowledge. They are filled with books and articles on the ins and outs of filmmaking.

Making Your Own Film

The Creative Side

The first element you need is a script—this is where it all begins. Many independent filmmakers write their own scripts. A few recent examples would be: Spike Lee's *She's Gotta Have It*, *Do the Right Thing*, and *Jungle Fever*; the Coen brothers' *Blood Simple*; and John Singleton's *Boyz N the Hood*. If you have a story to tell and feel you are best qualified to tell it, then sit down and write the script. If you are not familiar with the screenplay form, there are many helpful books on the market. One of the best is a book by Syd Field titled *The Screenplay*. However, you do not have to write an original screenplay to qualify as an independent filmmaker. You can purchase someone else's screenplay and work with the writer to develop a final draft.

The next step after you acquire the screenplay is to assemble the creative elements—the director and cast. Most independents direct their own films, including the writers mentioned above. The reasons for this are simple. First, *you* control all the creative aspects and decisions associated with the movie. This includes casting, appointing the director of photography, the production designer, the editor, and making the final cut of the movie. Most independent films are low budget, and a tremendous amount of money can be saved by personally doing as many jobs as you can. Lastly, you want people in the industry to appreciate your creative skills so that they will hire you or help finance your next film. That is the beauty of making an independent film. John Singleton was 23 years old when he made *Boyz N the Hood*—because of its success, he was able to secure a deal with Columbia Pictures for three additional films.

Casting the film is usually contingent on finding actors and actresses who like the script and feel comfortable with the director. For distribution purposes, it helps if at least one of the featured actors is reasonably well known.

▼

Why Should I Attend Film School?

Film schools are a great place to learn about filmmaking. Most schools have production courses where students get to direct, shoot, and edit short films. The students also learn how to budget and schedule a shoot and work with others to form a crew and cast. Besides learning the technical aspects of filmmaking, film school is valuable because you are surrounded by like-minded students who you can exchange ideas within a creative atmosphere.

The Business Side

That covers the creative side of the process, but without money, none of the above is going to happen. You must be able to raise the money to make the film. To do this, you must start with a budget. If you are unable to personally put a budget together, hire a production manager to assemble one. The fee is reasonable and should not exceed a few hundred dollars. Once the budget is in place, you must find the money it will take to make the movie. You can act as the sole producer, which means it is your responsibility—and yours alone—to raise the entire budget. You can co-produce, sharing the responsibility with others, or you can let others produce, freeing yourself to concentrate on the more creative aspects of the film—directing and/or writing.

There are many ways to raise the money. One of the most popular is friends and family. They tend to trust and believe in you, but be imaginative. Robert Townsend used his credit cards to finance his first film. The director of *El Mariachi* was the subject in a medical test program. He used the $7,000 he was paid to produce his film. If you really want to get your film made, you will find a way to raise the money.

After the film is finished, the object is to see that it is distributed. The ultimate goal is theatrical distribution, meaning the film is released in movie theatres. However, films may skip this step and be released directly onto home video or cable. There is no reason to feel bad about this; the movie might simply be better showcased in alternative media. Film festivals, which include Cannes, The American Film Mart, Toronto, Sundance, and Telluride, are another good venue to get your films seen—and hopefully picked up for distribution. The foreign market is another good venue, and can be accessed through the film festivals.

Congratulations!

Your film is finished and has been picked up for distribution. You are now an independent filmmaker—one of the most exciting yet uncertain lifestyles on the face of the earth. This is not a career for the faint-hearted or those looking for security. You must be a gambler and have supreme confidence in your ability to win.

I wish you luck and hope your film is a big success. Keep your fingers crossed.

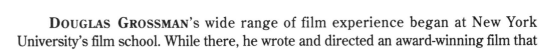

DOUGLAS GROSSMAN's wide range of film experience began at New York University's film school. While there, he wrote and directed an award-winning film that was shown on WNET, a public television station in New York City.

Producer Frank Yablans saw Douglas's film and brought him to California as his assistant on Paramount's *Silver Streak*, starring Gene Wilder and Richard Pryor. He continued working with Yablans on the Twentieth Century Fox production *The Fury*. Douglas next worked as assistant director on Paul Schraeder's film *Old Boyfriends* starring John Belushi and Talia Shire. In 1980, he was appointed assistant producer on the Paramount production *North Dallas Forty*.

In the summer of 1982, Mr. Grossman's screenplay *The Soldier* was released by Embassy Pictures as a full-length feature film. He later sold another screenplay, *Up the Creek* to Orion Pictures. The film starred Tim Matheson and was released in April, 1984.

In 1989, *Hell High*, a feature film that he produced and directed, was released domestically by Castle Hill and as a foreign film by ADN. Prism handled the home video and *Hell High* has been broadcast on both Home Box Office and Showtime cable channels.

Douglas has also produced, directed, and written a number of educational films on topics ranging from AIDS to teenage pregnancy, which have been distributed primarily in schools across the country.

Mr. Grossman has spent the past few years in New York City developing scripts for New Line Cinema. He will direct and produce his new film, *St. Blue* in Florida in the spring and summer of 1994.

CHAPTER SIX

Capturing the Real World: Making Documentaries

**Jon Wilkman, President,
International Documentary Association**

Would you like to explore the edges of the universe, search for sunken treasure at the bottom of the ocean, take an up-close look at animals in the wild, conjure up what the world was like hundreds of years ago, get to know some of the most interesting people who've ever lived, or help understand—and maybe even find solutions to—random violence and poverty?

If you're one of those people who just *needs to know* and loves sharing your discoveries with others, you've got the makings of a **documentary filmmaker.** The endless fascination of the real world and real people is what makes creating documentaries such an exciting and fulfilling profession. While it may *not* be a short cut to riches, producing documentaries can offer rewards that are personally invaluable. You'll have the chance to meet people and go places you may never have encountered on your own. You'll have the opportunity to enrich the lives of others, add to their understanding of themselves and their environment, and perhaps even help make the world a better place. If this sounds like your kind of job, stay tuned.

Docu-What?

Most movies we see in theaters and television are fiction. They are imaginary stories about imaginary characters. Even fiction films that claim to be *based on a real story* use actors reading a prepared script and are usually shot in specially constructed settings under highly controlled conditions.

Documentaries are different—very different. They are *real* stories with *real* people. Only in very rare and special circumstances are the characters in documentaries actors. The subjects of the film usually "play" themselves. Most important, the stories told by documentarians are not contrived by a script writer.

They are records of something that actually happened, sometimes while it's happening.

There's a lot of freedom in making a fiction film. You decide where the story goes and what the characters do. However, the fun and the challenge of making a documentary is keeping up with and capturing the energy, excitement, and sometimes unexpected directions of the real world. In my opinion, making documentaries is the most demanding kind of filmmaking. If you're not a detective digging for elusive clues from the past, you're struggling to stay on top of a rushing wave of reality. And through it all, your work is held up to the highest standard—the truth.

These days, most documentaries are seen on television. They are produced on both film and videotape. When I say *documentary filmmaker* I mean someone who works with either film or tape. And, to me, the documentary form is broad and varied, extending from in-depth journalistic reports to impressionistic visual essays.

Although a few documentarians work on staff as broadcast journalists for networks such as CNN, or local public television stations, most documentarians are *free-lance* or **independent filmmakers** who work alone or with their own small companies. The work of independent documentarians is sometimes seen in theaters, but more commonly on television, especially PBS, and more recently on cable television outlets such as the Discovery Channel, Arts and Entertainment Network, and Home Box Office (HBO).

Independents are sometimes hired to work on existing projects—on-going series such as PBS' *Frontline* or *Nova*—but often they come up with their own ideas and find a way to fund and distribute them. Like it or not, being a convincing and persistent *salesperson* is part of being a successful *independent documentarian*. Thriving as an independent is far from easy, and it's certainly not a regular 9-to-5, 40-hours a week profession—but it has the special satisfaction of working on what you care about. You certainly take on the risks, but also you benefit the most from the rewards.

The Truth and Nothing but the Truth

Whether you work with a production team or as an independent, there are many kinds of documentary styles to choose from. You've seen a common kind in the classroom—a film or video that primarily sets out to educate. The subject can be anything from science to history to art. Another kind of documentary is an extension of journalism—a straightforward report on some current event or issue. A third style adds an attitude to basic journalism. It carries a message, criticizing or exposing some injustice or wrong doing. Finally, there is the kind of documentary that uses the endless variety of the real world to entertain as well as inform. Such films might use fiction techniques such as dramatic re-enactments with actors playing the parts of real people. *Docudramas* teeter on the edge of fiction and nonfiction filmmaking. What makes a film more *docu* than drama is its emphasis on factual accuracy over entertainment or dramatic effect.

Many documentaries mix aspects of these and other nonfiction forms, but what ties them together is a firm and unshakable dedication to the search for the truth. As far as I'm concerned, the farther a filmmaker moves from these foundations, the weaker the documentary. Today, there are a lot of pseudo-nonfiction programs on television—tabloid news programs and sensationalized entertainment. These shows may be fun to watch, but raising ratings by playing fast and loose with the facts can be dangerous.

Making a documentary is based on an unspoken bond of trust between the filmmaker and the audience. Communicating a sense of the real world is a privilege that the best documentarians take very seriously. Unlike a fiction filmmaker, audiences should be able to trust what a documentarian says and shows. Keeping that trust means documentary filmmakers can have a real effect on people and their world. Losing it can create destructive cynicism and the kind of widespread indifference that only makes things worse.

Getting Real

If you want to make documentaries, there's nothing more important than a broad and deep sense of curiosity. The more you know, and the more you learn how to find out what you don't know, the better documentarian you will be.

After graduating from high school, many people who want to make movies go to film school. The advantages of film school are: you get to see and learn from a lot of good movies, and you have the opportunity to work with filmmaking equipment. This experience is valuable; but as a filmmaker who also teaches at a major film school, I've seen evidence that many film school graduates end up knowing a lot about making movies, and not enough of what to make movies about. For a future documentarian this could be a major weakness.

Although it's not essential, if you want to make documentaries, I highly recommend going to college. An advanced degree isn't necessary, but getting a broad liberal arts education can be very helpful. Learn as much about as many things as you can—from art and literature to basic science. One day you might find yourself with the opportunity to make a documentary about American history, the Amazon Rain Forest, or the life of a rap star. It wouldn't hurt to have a little knowledge about any of these subjects, or at least to know where to look for more information.

Admittedly with a little luck, I was able to begin my documentary career while I was still in college. During my junior year, I sent a letter of inquiry to a documentary production company. This led to a summer job as a production assistant and researcher on a documentary television series. I recommend this strategy to anyone interested in starting a career in documentaries. Keep an eye on the credits of documentaries you like and write to the producer or production company, telling them about yourself, why you liked their program, and why you want to make documentaries.

In a way, the work involved in my first job as a **documentary researcher** was a continuation of the process of writing papers in college. But this time, I searched for factual information and put it down on paper in a way that suggested possible uses in a documentary. It was important that my sense of a good visual story was keen, but most important that my evaluation of the facts could be trusted by my bosses.

As you can see from my example, getting that first job can be a matter of being in the right place at the right time, but there are ways to increase your odds of success.

Learning doesn't just take place in a classroom. The educational process should be endless, especially for a documentarian. Watching news and documentaries on television is a start. But regular and wide-range reading of newspapers, magazines, and books can help you keep up with what's going on—as well as make you a more attractive candidate for that first documentary job.

When I interview potential employees just out of school, I care less about what they know about filmmaking and more what their interests and values are. Even if you haven't made a documentary, you should have ideas about documentaries you'd *like* to make. And certainly you should have enough interest in the field to have watched documentaries on television and considered why you thought they were or were not successful. One thing's for sure—if you don't like watching documentaries, you're most likely not cut out to make them.

Who's Who on the Crew

Being a documentarian can involve more than just one kind of job. On a documentary, the person in charge is usually called the **producer.** On a fiction film, the producer is usually the person who puts together the money and engages the talent (director, writer, actors) to make the movie. But a documentary producer is often much more involved in the actual making of a nonfiction film or video. In most cases, the idea for the film is their own. They have the responsibility of managing, if not raising, the money. And it is not at all uncommon for a documentary producer to direct the filmmaking and sometimes even write the script that is used. In a few cases, the producer is actually a one-person band—directing, shooting, and editing the finished film or video.

This is not just a matter of artistic ego. Unlike fiction movies, most documentaries have limited budgets and smaller production crews. It's certainly valuable for a documentarian to be knowledgeable, if not minimally skilled, in many filmmaking crafts. Even if you don't actually shoot or edit your film, you'll be able to communicate more effectively with those that do. With this in mind, a documentarian should feel comfortable around technology—not just cameras and sound equipment, but computers as well. All this expertise might sound a little intimidating, but most technical experience can be gathered on the job. That's the way it was with me. Once you get started, never be afraid to ask *how* or *why.*

You can certainly have a career in documentary filmmaking and not be a producer. Since many documentaries, unlike fiction films, are made without detailed scripts, the role of the **camera operator,** and ultimately the **editor,** is vital. Since you are rarely working with actors, a documentarian often depends on the camera operator to respond quickly and thoughtfully to constantly changing situations. Being alert for a telling gesture or special look is the hallmark of a good documentary camera operator—that and a lot of technical ingenuity working in less than ideal conditions. If you are someone who likes a physical, *hands-on* job and has a sense of composition and a love of light, think about being a documentary camera operator.

Good photography is important, but without the blueprint of a script, most documentaries are *made in the editing room.* From the broad direction suggested by the footage, a film or video editor works with the producer to create a coherent and well-paced presentation. If you are well-organized and love the detail work of constructing coherent structures from diverse materials, you may have the makings of a **documentary editor.** And certainly, feeling comfortable with computers can be a big help in today's increasingly high-tech editing room.

Despite the critical importance of the camera person and editor, I think the most essential skill of a documentary filmmaker—of any filmmaker for that matter—is writing. Even if a documentary doesn't use a formal script, the filmmaker must communicate his or her vision to potential sponsors and collaborators. And of course, clear and forceful writing is vital for creating the narration for compelling documentary script.

In the end, even with all the technical and artistic skills that go into making a documentary, getting along with a wide range of people is essential for success. All filmmaking is collaborative. A group of people with varying experiences, temperaments, and abilities, come together to realize a project. It's the documentary producer's job to engage and focus their enthusiasm and energies. And even more important than working with the crew is working with the people who appear in your film or video. This takes sensitivity and compassion. After all, documentarians often make their livelihoods from the information and experiences of others. Without their trust and cooperation, it is almost impossible to make an effective documentary.

Women in the Hollywood Unions

Ranked by: 1993 percentage of female members.
1. Script Supervisors, with 86%
2. Studio Teachers, 78%
3. Production Office Coordinators and Accountants, 75%
4. Makeup Artists/Hairstylists, 65%
5. Costumers, 64%
6. Costume Designers, 60%
7. Publicists, 51%
8. Scenic and Title Artists, 50%
8. Studio First Aid Employees, 50%
10. Story Analysts, 46%
11. Screen Actors Guild, 43%
12. Cartoonists, 32%
13. Editors, 30%
14. Writers Guild, 25%
14. Art Directors, 25%
14. Set Designers, 25%
Source: *Premiere*

Facing the Facts

I've worked as a documentarian for almost thirty years. During this time I've had the opportunity to spend private time with an American president and his first lady. I've also shared the lives of drug addicts and homeless women. I've explored conditions in a maximum security prison and profiled a ballet dancer. My work has taken me throughout the United States and to many foreign countries. In the process, I've had the chance to learn about a wide range of subjects, from laser holography to the details of daily life in 19th century Los Angeles.

Despite all these opportunities, making documentaries can be a frustrating and uncertain profession. With increasing emphasis on pseudo-documentaries on television, satisfying jobs are rare—and as an independent producer, finding financial support can be a long and agonizing experience. Still, there are some hopeful signs for future documentarians. The explosion of new television channels on cable could mean more available airtime for quality nonfiction programming. And with new technologies like professional, low-cost Hi-8 video and desktop computers that handle moving pictures as well as text, the cost of making documentaries is coming down fast. That means more people can afford to make documentaries, and make them with high technical standards.

Even though my annual income as a documentarian looks like lunch money next to Steven Spielberg's profits from a single weekend of *Jurassic Park,* making documentaries has added to my life a richness and variety of experience that I think few other jobs could offer. And even more valuable, I've occasionally had the opportunity to do something that could really make a positive contribution to the lives of other people and the world at large. It's not a bad way to make a living, learn a lot, express yourself, and even have some fun.

▼

JON WILKMAN is the winner of three Emmys and numerous other national and international awards for his documentaries. He began his career at CBS News, working for Walter Cronkite on the *20th Century* and *21st Century* series. After founding his own production company in 1971 in New York, Mr. Wilkman produced documentaries for CBS, PBS, and ABC, as well as many major educational and corporate clients. Since moving to Los Angeles in 1978, he has been joined by his wife and partner Nancy in continuing independent work, including major specials and series for NBC and HBO. Along with his film and video work, he is a lecturer on documentary film at the University of Southern California (USC) School of Cinema-Television and president of the International Documentary Association. Mr. Wilkman was raised in Los Angeles, CA, and received a BA degree in sociology and English literature from Oberlin College in Oberlin, OH.

A Quick Take on Corporate Video Production

Timothy Sheahan, Producer/Director, Sheahan Productions, Inc.

While you're out looking for work in video, don't overlook one of the fastest growing areas of video production—corporate video. Corporate video is rapidly expanding and provides many production and management opportunities for graduates in video.

Most corporations are involved in video in some way, and are using the medium for many communication applications, including marketing and sales, training, internal employee communications, external communications to shareholders and the media, and the list goes on. They are using the latest video communication technologies, including interactive video, multimedia, and satellite teleconferencing.

The production of these programs is usually managed in one of two ways: either the corporation has an in-house fully-staffed department, or they hire independent producers or production companies.

The in-house video department can range in size depending on the volume of video produced and the size of the corporation. It can be a small, one-person operation with no equipment or facilities that relies on outside facilities and crews to help put a program together. Or, it can be a staff of 30 people, including producers, directors, writers, camera operators, editors, etc., complete with a large studio with full production capabilities.

The Role of the Corporate Video Producer

In either case, the role of the producer is essentially the same. The producer is responsible for overseeing the entire project from concept to completion. This includes getting the project produced on schedule and within budget, and the hiring of all the resources—from make-up artist to video duplication facility—to complete the project.

31

The producer's role in the pre-production stage of a video project is to consult with the client, usually another executive within the corporation, such as a marketing or training manager. Initially, a meeting will be set up to discuss the viability of the project, ideas, budget, and scheduling.

Once the video is "a go," the producer begins booking the individuals and facilities needed for the project. Set designers, graphic designers, camera crews, studios for both shooting and sound, editing facilities, and others all have to be contacted and scheduled.

In many cases, the producer is also a writer or a director. Many producers in corporate video have titles like "writer/producer" or "producer/director." Some write, produce *and* direct. Depending on the producer and the project, the producer may choose to handle all three functions, or just produce and then hire a writer or director.

The Day as a Corporate Producer

One of the reasons I love to produce video is the variety of projects, people, and new experiences I am exposed to in my work. Each day is different for me.

My last week is a good example. I was shooting physicians in Houston and Dallas for a major pharmaceutical company at the beginning of the week, and by the end of the week I was doing a sound mix in New York City for a major cookie and cracker manufacturer. Talk about diversity! Of course, there are also times when I'm in my office all day on the phone and doing paperwork.

How to Become a Corporate Producer

As with most staff positions within corporations, you'll need a college degree. I landed a job as an associate producer three months after graduating college. The reason for my success was simple—*I had hands-on experience!* Whatever you do, get some!

Be willing to work for free, *beg* if you have to. The hardest part is getting in, but once you do, you'll see how easy it is to find future work. And don't despair. If you find yourself hauling cables, typing labels, and fetching coffee, hang in there. Your opportunity will come! Remember, you could be flipping burgers and doing nothing for your video career somewhere else.

You have to be aggressive (not obnoxious!) in turning up an opportunity. Call up corporate video departments, TV stations, cable companies, production companies, advertising agencies . . . anybody that is producing video. You need *any* hands-on experience, so don't limit yourself to a corporate video department. Ask them if they offer internships. If they don't, ask them if they'd like to *start* an internship program with you. If all else fails, ask if you can work for *free*!

Yes, free! One of my most valuable work experiences while I was a student was with Nike Sports Productions. I found out they had a new video production group, so I approached one of the producers and proposed that I be their production assistant, gofer, (whatever they wanted to call me!) for the summer. All he would have to do was fill out a performance review for my advisor at the end of the term. I not only received 15 college credits, but had some of the best hands-on experience I could ever get! To top it off, after I left the full-time internship, I was hired to work freelance on other jobs.

The moral of the story is, even though a formal internship program may not be established, don't let it stop you. Show people you are enthusiastic and willing to work hard, and you will go a long way.

Eventually, you will get paid. The salary range of corporate producers can start at $20,000 a year and go to $50,000-$60,000 per year. Salaries are always dependent upon experience, the region of the country you live in, and the company itself.

▼

Top 10 Job Markets

Ranked by: Total new jobs by 1995.
1. Washington, DC, with 118,200 new jobs
2. Anaheim, CA, 108,800
3. Atlanta, GA, 104,600
4. Phoenix, AZ, 92,000
5. San Diego, CA, 77,100
6. Tampa-St. Petersburg, 76,300
7. Orlando, FL, 70,300
8. Dallas, TX, 69,300
9. Riverside, CA, 67,700
10. Minneapolis-St. Paul, 64,700
Source: *Money*

Where to Find the Jobs

Most opportunities will be found through word-of-mouth and video organizations. If you do search the newspapers, keep in mind that the job titles can vary from "producer," to "video specialist," "media production specialist," and "audiovisual producer."

One organization that is invaluable for getting contacts in corporate video, as well as for professional growth, is the International Television Association (ITVA). This organization is comprised of thousands of production executives—primarily in corporate video—and has local chapters all over the United States. I highly recommend getting involved and attending local meetings. You'll meet other professionals and stay on top of the industry with their seminars and informal meetings.

The ITVA also has a national job hotline for members that lists available positions throughout the U.S. For membership information, contact the ITVA national headquarters in Irving, Texas.

Most major cities also have local video/film organizations comprised of professionals in the business. Try to get involved with these groups and go to the meetings and seminars they offer. If they need volunteer help, by all means, sign up! This is a great way to make contacts and find opportunities.

Hang in There

Chances are you've already heard this a hundred times if you've begun your job search. Or maybe you've just been told how "competitive" the field is and that finding a job will be tough. That's true. However, if you are prepared, if you've done your homework, there's no reason you can't be just as competitive as the next person.

▼

TIMOTHY SHEAHAN has been producing and directing videos for over 10 years for a variety of major corporate clients.

Prior to starting his own company, he was a staff senior producer for Schering-Plough Corporation in New Jersey. Tim was also a staff producer for Creative Media Development, Inc., in Portland, Oregon. He has freelanced as an editor, camera operator, and photographer.

Tim has won numerous national industry awards as a producer/director. He holds a bachelor's degree in television and film and a master's degree in instructional technology from the University of Oregon. Tim currently resides in Bellevue, Washington.

Starting Your Career in Multimedia and Interactive Video Production

Kevin Gillen, President, Washington, DC Chapter, International Interactive Communications Society

America has always led the world in film and video production. Likewise, the most successful computer software is created in America. So, it should be no surprise that one of the biggest potential growth industries in this country is multimedia and interactive video production.

Film studios, television and cable networks, book publishers, phone companies, universities, and all levels of government are involved in manufacturing such innovative products as laserdiscs, compact discs, and cable and fiber-optic based programs. So how do you enter this field as a career? Stay tuned!

Traditional Media v. Multimedia

First, let me describe the two major differences between traditional media, such as television and film programs, and multimedia. Traditional media is an analog signal. An analog would be the light switch in your dining room. An analog signal would be like the dimmer switch in your dining room. This one switch controls the entire range from light to dark. Multimedia is a digital signal. If your dining room had a digital style of control, it would have a wall full of switches. Each switch would have control of one little setting, one switch would be set for 60 watts, the next one would be set for 59 or 61 watts, etc . . . Know the difference between analog and digital!

Another major difference between traditional media and multimedia is that traditional film and video programs are linear media. They have a beginning, a middle, and an end. Multimedia is nonlinear. The viewer/participant makes choices from the screen, and the multimedia program may offer a number of different stories with very different endings. The viewer/participant controls the course of the multimedia program. The multimedia program is easy for the viewer to control, otherwise they would get bored and either walk away or throw the controller across the room. In making the multimedia program easy for the viewer to use, the production staff must go through extra steps (sometimes jokingly referred to as extra hoops of fire) during the creation cycle.

Getting Started in the Industry

The multimedia production team can consist of the following roles with some people having two or more roles: interactive designer, technical director, art director, script writer/subject matter expert, media production coordinator, software programmer/engineer, audio engineer, graphic artist/animator, and image capture/video engineer.

The multimedia production process consists of:

• Designing, which includes: writing treatments; developing storyboards; designing flowcharts/navigation charts for interactivity; and writing scripts

• Prototyping

• Creating and digitally encoding image, audio, and graphic assets

• Creating custom computer programming

• Premastering and emulation

• Fixes

• Mastering and replication

So, how does one become a member of a multimedia production team? Since multimedia is being produced all over the country, you do not have to flock to either Los Angeles or New York. For example, it is possible to create multimedia products on a personal computer in your office using desktop software. However, if you wanted to get into feature film or episodic television, you would have to move to one of those media meccas.

Locating Multimedia Producers

Here are some suggestions for finding out who is doing multimedia in your area:

1. Read the business section of your local newspaper daily.

2. Contact the International Interactive Communications Society (IICS) to find out where the nearest chapter is located. This 10-year old organization has 26 chapters around the world and close to 3,000 members. If you are near a chapter, go to the meetings and introduce yourself. Become a student member, volunteer to help get out mailings, or maybe become a board member of that chapter. The national office phone number is (503)579-4427.

3. Go to the library or bookstore and check out the stories and ads about multimedia production in your area. Investigate periodicals such as *CD-ROM World*.

4. Browse computer bulletin board services via your computer and modem for multimedia producers.

Once you have located the multimedia producers in your locale, contact them by letter or fax expressing your interest in the field, and follow it up with a phone call.

Inquire about any available jobs with the company. If openings of interest do exist, request an interview to apply.

For the interview, be sure to bring your most creative efforts, such as a videotape, audiotape, artwork, photographs, and scripts—producers want creative people! You should also have several copies of your resume, describing your background and production experience. It would be most helpful if your production experience includes the types of computers and software that you have used. In addition, list the audio and video gear that you have worked with. You will be surprised to find that there is a lot of common ground in the devices and software used in creating multimedia that you may already be very familiar with.

Your Job Options

In regard to entry-level jobs in multimedia production, there are many, including:

- **The Debugger**. No, this is not a bug exterminator. The debugger is an entry-level or internship position that involves taking a copy of the multimedia project and test driving the product, viewing it as a user or purchaser of the product. By test driving, I mean going through every possible pathway on the multimedia title. If the debugger finds a mistake or "glitch", he or she will file a report or make a videotape copy of it to have the mistake corrected. Some multimedia products currently on the market, if fully used, could take over 24 hours to completely view.

- **Graphic Artist**. Being familiar with the latest paint or graphics software is essential to being a graphic artist. Most multimedia graphics and animation are created on a MacIntosh, IBM, or Amiga PC. Familiarity with both the Mac and Windows environment is also essential.

- **Asset Manager**. Just as the debugger must review every pathway on the multimedia product, the asset manager must maintain a complete numbered system of every item or "asset", i.e., every picture, page of text, animation, motion video, and audio and computer program. Remember, this is nonlinear media—it has to make sense and work no matter what path the viewer takes in the product. Asset management is usually done with a numbering system on a computer database.

- **Image Capture and Audio Capture Engineer**. Some assets used in multimedia products exist in analog form, such as photos, motion video, audio, etc., and need to be converted to a digital form and eventually exist as a computer file. It is the responsibility of the engineers to convert these assets from an analog to a digital format that is easy for the final assembly of the product.

There will be other positions available as multimedia continues to grow.

Is College Necessary?

There is no firm answer to that question. I feel that by not having a college degree, it may prevent you from climbing up the career ladder. So if you do opt for college, get your degree, because getting the degree later will cost more money and more time.

Conclusion

I would like to conclude by offering a saying I once heard from a very wise person: "If you are not learning, you are teaching. If you are not teaching, learn because you will learn something new everyday." As it relates to multimedia and interactive production, this means that in a new and constantly expanding field, the winners are going to be the people who are constantly learning and improving their skills and expertise.

▼

KEVIN GILLEN is a multimedia consultant and independent sales representative for a multimedia production and computer graphics firm, Gillen Interactive Group, Inc. (GIG). The firm represents such companies as Forsight Inc., Nibley Communications, and Hot Source Media. Mr. Gillen has been involved in interactive video and multimedia production since 1982.

Mr. Gillen also administers the International Communications Industries Association's multimedia exhibit appearing at the INFOCOMM conferences and expos through 1995. He is the president of the Washington, DC chapter of the International Interactive Communications Society and its representative for the Washington, DC Communications Council.

Toon Trade Tricks: Getting Started, and Possibly Respect, in the Animation Industry

John Cawley, Board Member, International Animated Film Association

Almost everyone loves animation, or as we used to call them, cartoons. To the trained eye, animation is almost everywhere you look. It's breaking box office records on movie screens and getting top ratings on prime time television. But it doesn't stop there. Animation pops up in television commercials, video games, computer programs, and in just about every visual media imaginable.

Animation has been around for centuries, but became more accessible with the invention of the motion picture. Originally a novelty, theatrical cartoons took on their own life and following with the help of such pioneer producers as Walt Disney, Walter Lantz, the Fleischer brothers, and many others too numerous to list.

Today, animation is a part of our lives. If being part of a cartoon character's life sounds appealing, then you may be drawn to a career in animation.

How Is Animation Done?

Everyone has no doubt seen a television special, news item, or trailer on a videocassette (of an animated film) that shows a studio busy at work creating animation. These short clips usually focus on a group of artists dividing their time between playful antics and drawing. One might get the impression that it's more like Santa's workshop than a serious job.

The actual steps involved in animation are almost as numerous as the army of artists, technicians, and production people needed to do them. Animation is a complex, tedious, and detail-oriented profession requiring a variety of skills, depending on where in the chain you work. Whether your talent is writing, drawing, acting, programming, managing, or watching, animation offers many job opportunities.

The animation industry is just that—an industry. Like most industries, there are more people than jobs available. The good news is that there is always a need for fresh talent. If for no other reason than that new talent is usually cheaper—and for some studios, money is the bottom line.

Getting Started

There are so many departments in an animation studio, the first thing for you to decide is what you want to do. Nothing is worse than receiving a resume or conducting an interview in which the newcomer states, "I love animation and can do *anything.*" The *jack of all trades, master of none* is not wanted. Anyone interested in this business must *specialize* to get in. Once you are in, there will be time to grow and diversify later.

Choose Your Specialty

If art is your forte, you may wish to think about working as an **animator** and draw the art that moves. (Keep in mind that most of the animation you see is actually done outside of the United States, so jobs here are scarce.) A **storyboard artist** turns the script into a comic strip version for the animator to follow. A **layout artist**, like a set designer, visualizes the worlds the characters live in. **Model** or **prop designers** create the characters and objects found in the script. **Background painters** paint the layouts. **Color key specialists** choose colors for characters. Additional specialties include **development** (creating ideas), **blue line** (tracing art), and **painting.**

Building Your Portfolio

Once you've chosen your specialty, try to build a portfolio of your art—make sure to have plenty of *original* work to show. Photocopies are good to leave with a prospective studio, but the person talking with you will usually want to see the originals to better gauge your technique. For **animation,** studios prefer to see a lot of quick sketch and life drawing. **Layout** and **prop artists** should show talent at rendering places or objects. **Character designer** portfolios should focus on expressions and mood. **Storyboard trainees** have the toughest time because only storyboards can show your work. **Painters** should include a variety of styles. Remember: **Only include your best work.** A portfolio of a dozen *good* pieces will be more impressive than a portfolio containing dozens of samples of varying quality.

Of course, the biggest question is one of experience. If you don't have any, that will greatly lower your chances. Today's animation industry is under continually shrinking deadlines. Only 10 years ago, studios spent an average of 2 to 3 years on feature films, and television series took around 1 year. Today, most features are done in one year or less (of actual work), while television programs are completed in a matter of months. This doesn't allow studios the time to train people. As mentioned earlier, the places to look might be studios more interested in cost than quality. Of course, no studio will come out and say that quality is less important, but watching samples of any studio's product will tell the real story.

The Other Areas

Not an artist? There are other jobs available at studios. Production work is one area to get into. **Production assistants, coordinators,** or **managers** (there are many titles, often indicating skill, responsibility, seniority, etc.) are in charge of getting the animation out. Though it is a somewhat thankless task—and in the beginning low paying, production work does offer the chance to see how animation is done and a ground-up view of the entire process. All you need to break into production is general office skills and (hopefully) some knowledge of animation. As your knowledge grows, you will find it possible to move into other areas of management.

Writing is another possibility, but a difficult one. **Animation writers** hold a very tight grip on the field. In one of the oddest catch-22's in the business, studios and networks often complain about the level of writing, yet when new talent is offered to them, the reaction is usually, "let's stick with someone we know." Feature writing in animation is even more difficult to break into than live action features (for the simple reason that for every 100 live action films made, only one animated film is done). In television, networks or studios often pick a **story editor** who will oversee the writing on a series. Frequently they will only work with writers they know.

Computer users are finding work in various areas. As technology continues to move into entertainment, animation is increasingly utilizing computers. Besides such obvious tasks as assisting in tracking production and budgets, computers are now involved in the art itself. Whether it is in the coloring of animation art (once hand painted), the creation of three-dimensional backgrounds (seen in big budget feature films), the creation of creatures for special effects, or the creation of an entire film, computers are used. Still new—and still being experimented with—a knowledge of computers and some art skills can be a powerful combination.

Actually Working in Animation

As mentioned previously, animation production time is constantly shrinking. This means that the industry is very deadline-oriented. When there is work, one can expect deadline pressure and long hours. When there is no work, one can expect layoffs. Few studios can afford to keep an idle work force for long. To prevent this problem, many studios resort to having small staffs and using free-lance artists to handle the overflow. These **free-lance artists** work piecemeal from assignment to assignment.

An average studio consists of a mixture of opposing forces. Creators wish to take their time, perfecting each element. Management is worried about deadlines and expenses. Both sides—creators and management—have their own additional pressures due to egos and politics. In years past, big egos were for the creators, and politics for management. Since the 1980s, most animation studios have gone *Hollywood* and one can find managers with big egos, and politicking in the drawing room. When proper production management is in place, these forces can be handled—and a quality product will result.

Even with all the pressures, politics, and posturing (i.e., egos), working in animation is still enjoyable. Most studios maintain a very casual atmosphere. At many studios, management frequently follows the artists' lead and dispenses with the need for ties and coats. The need to release built-up pressure leads to camaraderie and a variety of activities. Team play is essential in animation due to the large number of people involved and the multiple ways the tasks are interlocked. This creates almost a college-like atmosphere that is seldom dull.

Funny Money

Can you make money in animation? Yes. Can you make a lot of money? Possibly. Because animation is so labor-intensive, studios try to cut costs by keeping a close eye on salaries. A key art position (animator, layout, storyboard, or background painter) could expect to start at around $1,000 per week—higher at some studios, a little less at others. Other art jobs, ranging from model designer to color keyer to cel painter can pay around $800 per week. Production work starts at around $400 per week. Writers start at approximately $3,500 for a half-hour script.

As with other industries, experience and skill can bring higher wages. But since animation is also an entertainment industry, reputation can also bring higher wages. Being visibly connected to a high-profile project (a hit series or money making feature) can get you offers of better pay from competing studios. Some animation professionals (in films, they'd call them *superstars*) make three or four times the amount of the average creator.

One key factor should be considered, however. A highly paid artist at one studio who is laid off because a project has been completed may have to take a pay cut to get the next job from another studio that has work but pays less for its talent. During dry times, I've had artists call me and say that they'd be willing to work for half of their usual rate.

Top Grossing Films

Ranked by: 1991 box office gross, in millions of dollars.
1. *The Addams Family* (Paramount), with $101.7 million
2. *Hook* (TriStar), $90.7
3. *Beauty and the Beast* (Buena Vista), $88.9
4. *Cape Fear* (Universal), $68.8
5. *Star Trek VI* (Paramount), $64.6
6. *My Girl* (Columbia), $51.4
7. *Father of the Bride* (Buena Vista), $51.3
8. *The Last Boy Scout* (Warner Bros.), $49.7
9. *The Prince of Tides* (Columbia), $40.5
10. *JFK* (Warner Bros.), $37.9
Source: *Boxoffice*

Where Can You Go from Here?

If you start in the animation business and decide the stress, irregular employment, or other factors are not to your liking, your skills can lead you to other careers. As an artist, you can move to other creative opportunities. Many artists have moved on to other areas such as comic books or comic strips, advertising, and even children's books. A few have even gone on to direct live action films.

People on the production end can take their skills to other entertainment or even standard business management ventures. Some have started their *own* animation studios. Writers, of course, can write for live action productions, comics, books, etc.

How Do I Start?

Before you can decide what to do, you have to prepare to get into the business. If you are already on a career path as an artist, and have samples to show, you can begin applying to studios immediately. A number of top people joined right out of high school.

Of course, if you wish to start at a fairly high level, some skills would help. A number of colleges around the country offer animation programs. Some are better than others (or at least more famous or more expensive). As long as you receive good training, any school will do. Just be certain the school curriculum offers plenty of life drawing and at least one year of actual animation training. The animation training will help you see the various tools and techniques. The life drawing will teach you artistic skills. Any studio will tell you that it's easier to train an artist how to work in animation than to teach an animator how to be an artist!

These same rules apply to any of the other fields in animation— from production to writing. Learn the basics first . . . and learn them *well*. Then begin to focus on the specifics of an animation career.

To Union or Not to Union

There is an animation union, but not *every* studio is a union studio. Anyone wanting to work in the animation industry must be aware of this factor. One cannot judge by the quality of the finished product if a studio is a union shop. While some union studios produce excellent work, others produce films that are clearly inferior to those at nonunion studios.

If you are just starting out in the business, it will generally be easier to get a job in a non-union studio. However, once you've switched to a union studio, you will have to join. As a union member, you will be *discouraged* from working for a non-union studio. Some union workers actually request no-screen credit for their work at non-union studios so that the union will not discover they are *crossing the line*.

Take a Breath . . .

If you still feel that being a part of a mouse, a rabbit, or a super hero sounds fun, then animation could be for you. It will be hard work, but like all entertainers, you will get the chance to experience an audience enjoying your skill. Having someone come up with a big smile and ask, "You worked on *that* character?" is a thrill many jobs don't offer.

JOHN CAWLEY, a board member of the International Animated Film Association (ASIFA)-Hollywood has been in animation production for more than two decades. His projects have won an Oscar and an Emmy. On-screen credits include *An American Tail, Garfield and Friends,* and *Cro.* He is also a well-known animation authority and the author of several books, including *How to Create Animation* and *Cartoon Confidential.*

43

ASIFA-Hollywood is the southern California branch of ASIFA, an international animated film society created in the early 1960s. ASIFA is responsible for the presentation of the Annies, which are animation's Oscar. For information on ASIFA, ASIFA-Hollywood, or animation, write ASIFA, PO Box 787, Burbank, CA 91503.

Following Your Star: What It Takes to Become an Actor in Television and Film

Timothy Fall, Actor/Writer

There's a whirring camera pointed right at you. A make-up artist touches up your nose and the wardrobe assistant straightens your collar. Then, beyond a bank of blinding lights you hear someone yell, "Quiet on the set! Rolling! And . . . Action!"

Does acting in television shows and movies sound like the kind of work you'd like to do for a living? Do you think you might have what it takes for a career as a professional **actor**—and maybe even a shot at the big time? Have you ever wondered how to get there? Well, find a comfortable seat and hang on for the roller-coaster ride of your life, because, to say the least, if you choose a life as an actor, you're in for some ups and downs.

First, the Bad Stuff

The first director I ever worked with—I was a 17-year-old apprentice with a summer theatre company—gave two pieces of advice to everyone thinking of becoming an actor:

First, don't do it.

Second, if you're too thick-headed to heed the first piece of advice, then be as prepared as you possibly can be.

"Don't do it" is not *bad* advice. As you probably know, if you're thinking about a career as an actor in television and film, you are not alone. I wouldn't be honest if I didn't fill you in on some of the realities of the industry that an actor faces.

Before you get too excited about the lights and the cameras—or about stardom—you should think about this: The Screen Actors Guild (SAG), the professional union that every actor you see on television or in movies is a member, has 88,000 members (as of 1993), 10,000 more than just four years ago. That's pretty tough competition. Then, consider the fact that in any given year only 15 percent of the total membership—about 14,000 actors in 1993—will earn any money as an actor . . . and that means *any* money. Only 3 percent of that 88,000—around 2,500 actors—earn more than $10,000 in a year. And in cities like Los Angeles, New York, and Chicago, where the majority of SAG actors live, you'll definitely need another job to pay the rent on those wages.

So while all your friends are graduating from college with degrees in accounting and finance and business and going off to accept plump job offers, you'll be waiting tables, delivering pizzas, or driving a cab, all because you're holding out for your dream of being an actor. Even when you finally get a job, you may earn less in a year than most of your friends earn in a month or two.

Training: The Most Important Thing

Still want to give it a shot? Are you willing to make the sacrifices it takes? Then you need to start getting ready as soon as possible. With all that competition, *you* have to be that much better.

Actors come from a variety of educational backgrounds, but the vast majority—if not all—of the actors that repeatedly star in movies or television shows are actors with formal training and years—usually decades—of experience. Although being an actor doesn't mean that you have to do nothing but be an actor, it is nevertheless imperative that you gain experience in acting, even though you may also be on the basketball team, in business school, or working at a grocery store.

You can't begin your training as an actor too early. Chances are, if you're considering a future as an actor, you've already become involved in school plays or community theatre. Maybe you live in an area where professional actors work in theatre, film, or television and you've gotten involved. Anything you can do will help you, because only through experience will you begin to feel at ease and confident as an actor.

Does your school have a drama department or acting classes? If you haven't already given them a try, do it now. Do you have free time during summer vacations? Many communities produce *summer stock* or *summer repertory* seasons (usually a series of plays or musicals) that may bring in professional actors from around the country. Talk to the directors of these companies and see if there may be a place for you. As an intern or apprentice, you may end up acting in some of the shows.

Remember, the training you need to act in television and film is the same theatrical training you undergo for a career on the stage. Many actors, throughout their careers, continue to do both stage and on-camera acting—so start it now. Today the school play, tomorrow your own TV series!

After High School, then What?

Once you graduate from high school and enter a college or university, you face the decision of how to direct your education toward your chosen career. In your case, the natural course of study would seem to be a major in drama or theatre. I say "seem" because a major in theatre is not always the best route for everyone who is interested in acting. I was not a theatre major. (My degree is in international relations.) Although I always acted in plays and musicals, I decided to also learn about the rest of the world, too. This is not necessarily the best way, or the only way to enter the field. You have to find the mix that works for you. Don't be afraid to give acting all of your time, but also don't be afraid to take advantage of all that's available to you in college—nothing is superfluous to an actor. It will all come in handy in good time.

What a theatre degree *does* mean is that you have experience and training as an actor. You can walk and talk at the same time, and not fall off the stage—and believe it or not, that's something to be proud of! Because for all those thousands of well-qualified actors you'll be competing with, there are thousands more who haven't prepared, have less talent than you, and won't cut it. You're already ahead of the game, so don't stop now.

Okay, I'm Ready. Now What?

Once you have your college degree, find a nice frame for it and mail it to your parents, or give it a page in your scrapbook. You can forget about it because you won't be needing it. Agents and casting directors may be interested in the fact that you're a theatre major, that you starred in all the school plays—but remember, so did practically every other actor they've ever met. Even if you went to one of the prestigious undergraduate acting schools in the country, like the University of California, Los Angeles or Northwestern, or got a graduate degree from Julliard or Yale, literally thousands of other actors have the same credentials.

Now you're ready to get started. The first step, if you don't already live in a city with opportunities for actors, is to move to one. We'll start with a list of the possibilities:

1. Los Angeles.

That's right, that's the end of the list.

Forget about going to live with your eighth cousin, the actor, who's been in New York for 12 years. He's probably never worked, right? Guess what: In New York he may never. Plus, he'll probably freeze to death. The same goes for Chicago, Dallas, San Francisco, Atlanta, Vancouver, and Miami. You may hear about these cities having active film industries, but not *that* active—certainly not active enough.

If you are serious about film and television acting, there is no other place for you like Los Angeles. As you know, Los Angeles is the home of Hollywood, and Hollywood is the home of *The Industry.* Plus, Los Angeles really isn't as bad as you may have heard. After a few months of getting used to the perfect weather and the constant, obsessive talk about movies, you'll feel right at home.

Once you're in LA, your first move is to assemble the professional tools you need to impress agents and casting directors. But how do you even find them, much less impress them? Maybe the most important thing with which you'll leave your college (assuming you have been active in theatre) is a list of contacts—people in the business who may be able to help you get started. If the head of your theatre program knows an agent, or your acting teacher has an old friend who is a friend of a casting director, then you may have a contact. Have your friend or teacher get in touch with that person on your behalf, or write you a letter of introduction or recommendation. They will probably be willing to meet you, based on your relationship with the person who has recommended you. Remember, however, that you may have to be persistent with calls and postcards to get your meeting.

If you don't have a convenient contact or two, don't sweat it. It is an agent's and casting director's job to find new, talented actors. And since it is an actor's job to find agents and casting directors, you're bound to run into each other. Look for a play to be in. SAG provides a list of all agents and casting directors, so you can just go down the list knocking on doors.

After making that first contact, there are other tools an actor must have. Foremost among these is the all-important headshot and resume. A headshot is a black and white photograph, usually of just your face. The headshot is not a glamour pose or a fashion statement. It is you, relaxed, looking just as you would sitting in the agent or casting person's office. It is your calling card. Make sure that what the agent or casting person sees in your picture is what they get. The only surprises you give them should be pleasant ones. Your resume should highlight your acting credits as well as your education and training.

Another great tool to have is a videotape of your acting. This tape can be anything from on-camera work you've done (local commercials, student films, etc.) to a scene or monologue you put together yourself. Actors with no other on-camera experience often rehearse a scene and record it themselves, then send the tape to agents and directors. If you're good, chances are the tape will be good—and it could get you noticed.

Finally, it is smart to stay prepared by having a monologue or two—characters that suit you, from a published play—rehearsed and ready to perform. Occasionally, a director or casting director will ask to see a monologue, and if you've done your homework, you'll be a step ahead.

What Actors Earn

The Screen Actors Guild establishes minimums for actors' salaries, based on contracts with producers that are renegotiated every three years. For 1993, the daily minimum wage was $485. The weekly guarantee was $1,685. These are the minimums, though, and many television shows and films pay more. Typical half-hour shows pay guest cast (any actor who isn't part of the regular cast) in the neighborhood of $2,400 per week. Hour-long shows pay guest cast closer to $3,500.

Series regular cast members can earn many times these amounts, as can actors in leading roles in films. In those cases, the actor's salary is negotiated by the agent. Commercials pay actors in the form of holding fees and residuals. A holding fee (usually the daily minimums mentioned above, depending on how many days the actor worked on the commercial) is paid at the beginning of every 13-week period in which the commercial will air. In addition to this fee, the actor is paid a residual for each time the commercial actually airs.

Agents and SAG

Now it's time for the weird part. You must be a member of the Screen Actors Guild (SAG) to get a part in a film, television show, or commercial. But you have to get a part before you're allowed to join SAG. Also, you must be a member of SAG to get an agent. But you have to have an agent to get an audition for a part. Confused? Frustrated? Just wait until you're in the middle of it. The only hope any new actor has for getting an agent and getting in the union is that every rule has an exception, and sometimes it's possible to get in through the back door.

All legitimate casting in Hollywood is done through agents. Casting directors are not interested in actors without agents, reasoning that if they were any good, they'd have an agent. So *you* must have one. The only formula for getting one is by using your contacts and resources, and by trusting that your talent will eventually bring you and an agent together.

SAG is the legitimizing credential all actors must have. The Catch-22 membership requirements, however, keep thousands of actors from ever joining. The exception to the rule comes thanks to the Taft-Hartley act, which provides that a union production may hire a nonunion actor under a union contract, which then qualifies the actor to join the union. What that means in practical terms is that if a casting director or producer likes you enough, they'll give you a part even though you're not in SAG. Then you'll have to join SAG, which in 1993, cost $1,012.50 for initiation and $85 per year in dues, which may be more than you've earned on the job—yet another Catch-22!

When I was in college in Tennessee, I was cast in a SAG movie by answering a casting call. So when I moved to LA, all I had to do was pay the membership fee, and I was an official member.

Who Does What?

Being acquainted with who's who in the television and film industry saves you a lot of time and confusion. Here are a few of the people who make things happen—people you need to know about:

Casting director: the person who conducts auditions with actors. A casting director must know an actor's credits and talents, and after an audition can be very influential in making the final decision to cast an actor.

Agent: the actor's representative. It is an agent's job to know what films, television shows, or commercials are being cast, and to try to get auditions for the actors he/she represents. When you get a job, your agent negotiates how much you are to be paid.

Director: the creative force behind a film, television show, or commercial. The director often has the final say in hiring actors for his projects, along with the producer.

Producer: the financial (and sometimes creative) force behind a film, television show, or commercial. The producer and director can sometimes be one and the same. The producer usually has the final say in hiring actors.

Screen Actors Guild Average Earnings in 1992

1992 yearly income in dollars.

Age	Men	Women
0-9	$12,896	$12,158
10-19	14,918	12,619
20-29	12,521	13,559
30-39	15,287	11,831
40-49	15,834	10,844
50-59	15,840	6,768
60-69	12,864	7,226
70-79	9,060	5,181
80-89	7,020	5,656
90-99	1,616	1,414

Source: *Premiere*

SAG: Screen Actors Guild. This is the union that works for actors, guaranteeing certain standard working conditions and wages, as well as pension and health benefits.

A Typical Day

You may wait years for an agent, or you may be lucky and get the ball rolling sooner. I was waiting tables in a restaurant for four months after moving to LA when a casting director approached me about auditioning for a movie. I got it, a tiny part in a Clint Eastwood film. After that, I met some agents and started going out on auditions.

What to Expect Next

So once all that happens to you, what should you expect? Here's the way things typically work:

Your agent calls but you're working a lunch shift at the restaurant, so he leaves a message on your answering machine. After work, you dash home, check your messages, and call your agent back. Now he's busy, so he has to call you back. Finally, you hook up. He has an audition for you the next day at two o'clock with the casting director of a movie at Warner Brothers. Your agent reads you a description of the character, and you think it sounds perfect for you. You drive to Warner Brothers to pick up a copy of the scene you'll be auditioning from. In five o'clock traffic (round trip), this takes you an hour and a half. You then remember that you're supposed to work the next day at two o'clock, so you panic to cover your shift. In the meantime, you begin to rehearse the scene, saying your lines over and over to yourself in your car—and people think you're crazy.

The next day, you show up 15 minutes early at Warner Brothers. In a long row of chairs sit 13 guys or girls who look just like you. You sign in and wait 30 minutes until the casting director calls you into her office. You chat about some of the credits on your resume, then she asks if you're ready. You do the audition, she thanks you, and you leave. In your car, you're still saying the lines, wishing you'd done them differently.

Sometimes you get a call back, which means that the casting director liked you and wants the director and the producer to meet you. If they all like you, then you get the job.

If not, then there's always another audition.

The secret is to stick it out, and always have confidence that something good is on the way. Some actors give themselves time limits—I never did. I just stayed tuned up, enjoyed whatever was happening in my life—acting or not—and waited for things to happen. If this is what you really want, then you owe yourself the time to let it happen.

Be prepared, wait for the right doors to open, then walk through them . . . and good luck!

TIMOTHY FALL is an actor and writer living in Los Angeles, CA. Most recently, he was a series regular on *Bob* (starring Bob Newhart), playing the role of Chad, a far-out comic book artist. Over the past seven years, he has had numerous roles in television shows, television movies, and in two films, *Heartbreak Ridge* and *Making the Grade.*

In addition to acting, he has worked as an office manager, an agent's assistant, a waiter, and a limousine driver. He has traveled in Europe, Australia, New Zealand, and Southeast Asia.

Mr. Fall grew up in Missouri and Arkansas and has a BA in international relations from Memphis State University.

Falling Down on the Job: Working as a Stunt Player/Stunt Coordinator in Film and Television

Danny Aiello III, Stunt Coordinator and Unit Director

L ights, camera . . . mayhem?

If you've turned on your television or been to the movies recently, you've seen it: action, action, and more action. Of course, action and adventure have always been popular commodities at the box office, but our growing appetite for authenticity on both the large and small screens has contributed to increasingly incredible depictions of danger and excitement. Behind the scenes, creating and executing everything from pratfalls to skydiving to the horrors of war, are **stunt players** and **stunt coordinators.** These men and women, contrary to popular opinion, are anything but daredevils; they are, in fact, masters of illusion, combining physical ability, skill, ingenuity, and extensive preparation to keep their audiences on the edge of their seats while keeping themselves—as well as the actors they double—out of the hospital. In other words, there's a method to *this* mayhem.

Life on the Set

On the set, the stunt coordinator is the department head responsible for the interpretation and administration of action sequences. The coordinator first works with the director to identify and choreograph stunts presented by the script, which may include anything from simple pushing and shoving between actors, to more elaborate sequences such as those involving fights, vehicles, heights, fire, or athletics. This person communicates with other members of the production team, such as the special effects coordinator and propmaster, to ensure that related issues—firearms, for example—are addressed appropriately. The coordinator then prepares a budget, reflecting the estimated manpower required, and proceeds with the hiring of stunt players to satisfy the particular needs of the project. Stunt players are generally hired in one of two capacities:

1. As doubles for principal actors, who are either incapable of, or prohibited from (usually for insurance reasons) performing certain difficult and/or dangerous scenes; or

2. To fulfill small roles, with little or no dialogue, consisting primarily of action.

Stunt players also assist the coordinator and other members of the crew with equipment and safety-related matters.

During shooting, the stunt coordinator once again collaborates with the director to determine how best to achieve favorable camera angles in the ongoing search for the safest, most effective way to capture the action. It's worth repeating: Stunt personnel are no more interested in risking their lives than most professionals, and consider it their primary objective to *fool* the camera. Wherever possible, danger is taken out of the equation.

Raw Materials

There are so many different skills and abilities called for in this branch of the film and television industry that it is virtually impossible to describe the attributes of the ideal stunt person. There are, however, certain general qualities common to most successful stunt players:

Athletic ability—This is probably the most significant common denominator, especially among entry-level stunt people. Expertise in a particular athletic discipline may help (gymnastics and boxing are among those that are particularly useful), but the advantage clearly belongs to those who *cross-train,* who possess a comfortable knowledge of their bodies' capabilities, and are able to move easily in response to various physical demands.

Good physical condition—As a corollary to the above, it is worth emphasizing that a career performing stunts is not the place to test your health. The hours are long, the conditions unpredictable, and the work itself can be physically punishing.

Temperament—Harder to define, there is nonetheless a certain combination of personality traits that surface in most successful stunt players. A realistic knowledge of your capabilities is vital, as is the ability to understand the authority structure on the set, and to be ready and willing to take direction from the appropriate person—almost always the stunt coordinator. Stunt players who perform as doubles must be capable of establishing diplomatic and protective relationships with the actors who are their counterparts. Most important is what might be called good old-fashioned nerve, the capacity to remain calm and focused in the face of tremendous pressure. Employing every known trick and safeguard doesn't change the fact that action sequences are always expensive, frequently dangerous, and physically grueling. In other words, it's important—if not imperative—*to get the shot in one take.* In this respect, the production of stunts for film and television most closely approximates live performance, with all of its accompanying anxiety. However, when you channel your adrenaline into a great high fall, or shoot-out, you'll probably be rewarded with a burst of applause from cast and crew members, which is an infrequent happening in film and television studios!

Stunt coordinators (who will almost always have spent several years as stunt players) must also be able to draw upon fairly extensive creative resources in order to successfully transform a few sentences of description into an exciting, believable action sequence. Coordinators must be capable of sustaining the added administrative pressure of deadlines, changeable schedules, and, of course, responsibility for the safety of the stunt personnel, actors, and crew members under their supervision.

Action University

Q: How do you learn to fall down a flight of stairs?

The answer to the above might well vary from one stunt person to another, but it is likely to include a football helmet, a substantial number of body pads, a few well-chosen words of advice from an established stunt performer, and a Hail Mary or two. As you may have suspected, this is not a profession pursued via traditional channels of formal education. It is, in many cases, an education provided by mentors, by observation, and by on-the-job training. Most would-be stunt players actually complete much of their training subsequent to their first professional experience in the business by *apprenticing* themselves to a willing stunt player, coordinator, or professional association thereof. Aspiring stunt players generally seek out any opportunity to gain access to sets where stunts are being performed. Their observations serve as a base of instruction, not only in the mechanics of performing stunts, but in the general protocol of the set. Stunt players may then hone their skills, as is practical, on their own, or in the company of a more experienced performer.

Soooo . . . the $10,000 question begins to emerge: How and where can you hope to connect with the important person (or persons) willing and able to provide you with that all important first break?

Top 10 Box Office Performers

Ranked by: 1993 Box office gross (through August 15), in millions of dollars.
1. *Jurassic Park* (Universal), with $299.5 million
2. *The Firm* (Paramount), $139.2
3. *Indecent Proposal* (Paramount), $104.8
4. *Sleepless in Seattle* (Universal), $101.5
5. *Aladdin* (Buena Vista), $98.6
6. *In the Line of Fire* (Columbia), $84.2
7. *Cliffhanger* (TriStar), $80.5
8. *Groundhog Day* (Columbia), $70.8
9. *A Few Good Men* (Columbia), $64.1
10. *Dave* (Warner Bros.), $62.6
Source: *Boxoffice*

Getting Started

First, it obviously helps to seek out the appropriate geography. Los Angeles and New York have the largest concentration of movie and television studio activity in the United States, and are also heavily trafficked remote locations. These are places where the opportunities are most plentiful; unfortunately, so is the competition. Studios are also operating in a number of other cities, among them: Chicago, IL; Wilmington, NC; and Orlando, FL. In many cases, stunt personnel are still routinely *imported* to these venues from New York and Los Angeles, as there are not yet sufficient numbers of local stunt personnel to satisfy demand.

However and wherever you are best able to do it, you have to find a way to begin networking with people in the industry. These need not be stunt personnel. The door was opened for me by an actor who had encouraged me to audition for a part in a film. This led to the introduction that made the difference, to the stunt coordinator whose interest in me launched my career. Occasionally, being hired to work as an extra can offer the opportunity to be noticed by the stunt coordinator.

I wish there were a more orderly process to suggest, but—as with most of the performing arts—the ugly fact remains that luck and connections are major factors, at least as far as your initial contact goes. Many stunt people try to obtain the names and addresses of as many stunt coordinators as possible (the Screen Actors' Guild, to which all stunt players belong, is one resource), then proceed to send photos, resumes, and postcards in the hope of catching someone's attention. (I have also had people mount persistent phone campaigns, which is *not* the best idea.) I don't usually consider hiring someone I've only "met" through a resume, but it can happen if I find myself desperate for a physically appropriate double.

The bottom line is that this is a highly competitive specialization, which can be still more insular than most because of inherent risk factors. Stunt people want to work with colleagues they know and trust, so cultivate your *people* skills, as well as the more obviously marketable ones, and be patient.

So Where Do I Land?

One of the great things about working as a stunt person is that once the long-awaited lucky break arrives, you will probably find yourself working right alongside established stunt players, doing whatever it is that your talents allow, and for the same basic compensation. Technically speaking, all stunt personnel working in television and/or film must belong to the appropriate union: The Screen Actors' Guild (SAG). SAG governs any production using film; the American Federation of Television & Radio Artists (AFTRA) governs productions using tape. What usually happens is that whoever hires you for your first job will certify to the union that you, and *only* you, (as opposed to someone who's already a union member) were available and capable of performing the job function in question. You are then obligated to join the union (by paying dues) and are, from that point forward, guaranteed a standard daily (or weekly) wage, the informal term for which is *scale*. Current SAG daily contracts are issued at $489; weekly contracts at $1,808. You may be paid an additional fee, called an adjustment, at the discretion of the coordinator, depending upon such variables as the difficulty or danger of a particular stunt, and the number of times you are called upon to repeat it. Adjustments generally range from $50 to $1,000—accomplished specialists may earn considerably more for certain high-risk jobs.

If you aspire to work as a coordinator, you will have to negotiate your own contracts, also on a daily or weekly basis. Successful coordinators can eventually expect to reach a mid-six-figure income.

All in a Day's Work . . .

It would be unfair to close without the reminder that although exciting, working in film and/or television is relatively short on glamour and long on discomfort. As a stunt person, you can expect to spend 8 to 10 hours a day on the job, day and/or night, often in extreme temperatures, uncomfortable wardrobe, etc., etc., etc. You can expect extensive travel obligations, and all kinds of strain on your personal life. And you can expect to do all of this with a smile, because as you'll soon discover, this branch of the entertainment business requires close quarters and an unfailing spirit of cooperation.

I can only say that the joy of being hit by a speeding vehicle makes it all worthwhile.

▼

DANNY AIELLO III took drastic measures to get his first film job: He shaved his head. Originally from the Bronx, Aiello was a natural for his role as a member of the Fordham Baldies, the real-life gang profiled in Phil Kaufman's 1979 movie, *The Wanderers*. During filming, it was Aiello's athletic ability that caught the attention of stunt coordinator Vic Magnotta. He has since appeared in over 125 films (*The Last Boy Scout, Ricochet, The Hard Way, Miller's Crossing, State of Grace, Do the Right Thing, Last Exit to Brooklyn*) and episodic television shows (*Law and Order, The Equalizer, Beauty and the Beast*), doubling such actors as his father, Danny Aiello, John Lithgow, Tim Robbins, and Ron Perlman. Aiello has also become a successful stunt coordinator and second-unit director in his own right, equally at home on a film set (recent projects have included *Whispers in the Dark,* and actor John Turturro's directorial debut, *Mac*) in the studios of such ABC daytime dramas as *One Life to Live, Loving,* and *All My Children,* and in the re-created mean streets of prohibition-era Chicago, where he has for the past 14 months juggled coordinating and second-unit directing responsibilities for the hit Paramount series, *The Untouchables*.

Giving Art a Direction: How to Become a TV/Motion Picture Art Director/Production Designer

Roy Christopher, Art Director/Production Designer

Does designing the sets for the Academy Awards or creating Murphy Brown's townhouse sound like a great way to make a living? Well, it is, and here's what you have to do to land a job like that.

First of all, let's get to know what the correct job title is for the person doing this work. Generally, in television and motion picture production, the person designing the scenery is called the **art director** or, on more prestigious productions, the **production designer**. If there is a **production designer**, his or her assistant is called the **art director**. If there is no **production designer,** then the art director is assisted by the **assistant art director.** The person who drafts the blueprints of the sets for the shops to build from is called the **set designer,** even though the production designer or art director does the actual designing. The set designer should be called the draftsperson, but isn't. Confusing? Try this on for size.

In the theater, the person who designs the scenery is called the **scenic designer,** which makes perfect sense to me. The person who dresses the sets, that is, who selects the furnishings, drapes, accessories, etc., for the production, is called the **set decorator.** Sometimes the art director does everything: designs the sets, draws them up for the shops, and decorates. In any case, anyone desiring to enter this field must be able to *design, draft,* and *decorate*—the three Ds.

Career Preparation

People enter this profession with various backgrounds, but they all share one overriding characteristic: a strong *visual* sense. From as far back as you can remember, has how things *look* been the most important thing to you? Have you always been creating things: drawing, painting, building, making models, playing make believe? This inner desire to *create* is essential. You don't have to be a Picasso to succeed, but you *must* have a very strong need to create visually. If the written word is more important to you than the visual image, I would suggest you seek another career.

Let's say that you have this desire to create visually. No one is going to hire you at the entry level, if that's all you have. You must also have education and experience. Sorry. At the very least, you will need a BA degree in a field closely related, such as: theater arts (my personal favorite—in fact, I have never hired an assistant who didn't have his or her degree in theater arts); architecture (especially good for motion picture work); communications (a bit too general for my tastes); or the fine and applied arts, such as graphics or illustration. A splendid combination is a BA in art or architecture and a MFA in theater arts.

I like to hire people with theater arts degrees because it teaches us the most important thing we have to learn: how to interpret the written word visually. That *is* the job: *interpreting the written word visually.* The most successful art director/production designers are those who do this best. When Dean Tavoularis read the script for *The Godfather,* you can bet your T-square that he *saw* those scenes very vividly and was able to convey that to the director, Francis Ford Coppola. When you read something, do you *see* it? If you do, that is half the battle.

Getting the proper training will teach you how to put on paper the image you see. How to make the sketches, build the scale models, draft the blueprints, and select the colors, the wallpapers, the carpets, drapes, etc. A million decisions based on the *vision* you had when you read the script. Fun, huh?

Getting Started

OK, you've come to Los Angeles armed with your MFA in theater arts from Prestige U. ready to design your first feature. Where do you begin? If your drafting, model-making skills are excellent, and if you have a really professional portfolio of your work (samples of your drafting and sketches, plus photos of any theatrical production you have designed in school or elsewhere), you can immediately begin contacting established art directors, hoping to get an interview and landing a job as a runner, gofer, or an assistant.

A tip on landing the interview—know who you are trying to get the interview with. Do *not* send a hundred letters to every art director from some list. Go after a few people whose work you know and, hopefully, admire. Watch television and motion pictures and make note of the names of the art directors and production designers whose work you like. Write or call them at the studios that produce their shows or films. This is *very important:* Tell them that you saw their work and were impressed. Discuss some aspect of their work that you admire. Be *very* specific. Make the person you are trying to see feel as though he or she is the most terrific person in the business. You *will* get the interview. *Never* tell someone that you got his or her name from some list. These successful designers like a little ego massage as much as anyone. Keep it sincere and don't gush!

While you are contacting the designers who you would like to work with, it is very important that you stay creatively alive by offering your services (usually for

Creative Executives at Film Studios

1990-91 percentage of women creative executives (vice-presidents and above) employed.
1. MGM, with 56%
2. 20th Century Fox, 50%
3. Universal, 43%
3. Tri-Star, 43%
5. Warner Bros., 42%
6. Touchstone/Disney, 35%
7. Paramount, 27%
8. Columbia, 25%
9. Hollywood Pictures, 20%
Source: *Premiere*

free) to one or more of the hundreds of little theaters in Los Angeles as scenic designer, set painter, prop person, or whatever. Get involved with production and with people in production—there is no better way to begin your "networking." Also, this can lead to working on nonunion films, such as those done at the American Film Institute. There are many places looking for volunteer scenic people. Do *not* expect to make money at this point. If you do, fine, but you probably won't. Give your talent away! There's a lot more where that came from. Nothing ever happens by staying home waiting for the phone to ring. Get out there and create something for someone, somewhere. It will all come back to you in spades . . . eventually.

Waiting for Your Big Break

Yes, eventually you will probably land the job, and with enough talent and perseverance, you will probably succeed. The problem usually is that it all takes so much longer than you think it will. In my case, I was almost 30 years old before I got my first job painting scenery at NBC. But once that happened, I was in the door and, within a year, had my own show at NBC as art director. The point is that, in such a highly competitive industry, the only ones who succeed are the ones who do not put a time limit on their success. They simply decide that this is the field for them, and they will stick to it until it happens.

In the meantime, unless you are independently wealthy, you will have to find a way to support yourself. Don't you hate that? It is a reality which we have all had to face. The best type of job to look for is something you don't hate, and one that isn't so demanding that you don't have time to pursue your art directing career. When I came to Los Angeles, I landed a job as assistant to the vice president of a major retail chain, and after a year, I had to give up this interesting position because it was in a career field that I did not want to remain in. This was a tough decision, since I had nothing to go to, but I had to do it or give up my goal.

Entry-Level Responsibilities

Once you do land that entry-level job as someone's assistant at some production company or studio (Don't forget there are many different venues to try for: the networks, the major film studios, nonunion television and film, commercial studios, music video production companies, etc.), what can you expect in the way of responsibilities? As indicated, earlier responsibilities are generally in the drafting and model-making areas. In addition, you might be expected to make the coffee, run the blueprint machine, pick up research or scripts, take drawings to the production office, etc.

As you work up the ladder you, hopefully, will become the production designer's art director and participate more fully in many of the creative decisions. This is a terrific position to be in, since you get to enjoy much of the creative process without having the ultimate responsibility. Eventually, of course, you will welcome the ultimate responsibility and the sleepless nights that come with it. Don't say that I didn't warn you!

What You'll Earn

By now, I'm sure you're curious about how much money you will make doing this fascinating work. That is very hard to say. I imagine the entry-level jobs which we discussed above probably begin somewhere in the neighborhood of $250 to $300 per week. A full assistant (nonunion) should make somewhere between $600 and $1,200 per week. Union assistants on a major feature film can make up to $2,000 per week. Once you've hit the big-time, a free-lance production designer with proper agent representation can reach a mid six-figure income. Less than Madonna, perhaps, but not bad.

On Unions and Agents

I have not mentioned unions, so far, because it would take another article of at least this length to explain it, and then you still wouldn't understand it any better than I do, and I *don't*. Suffice to say that at some point, you will probably want union affiliation, and, at some point, someone in power will want your services badly enough to see that you join the appropriate union or guild. The one you will want to affiliate with is The Society of Motion Picture/Television Art Directors. They are in no position to help someone just starting their career, but don't concern yourself with this. When the time is right, they will be happy to accept you as a member. The same can be said for agent representation. When the time is right, someone will want to represent you. Do not concern yourself with this. It is much more important to perfect your skills, build your resume, and broaden your contacts than to bug the unions and agents who have nothing to offer beginning talent.

Things They Never Tell Us

You are entering the entertainment industry. It is competitive and stressful. To survive and succeed, you must stay healthy and have unlimited energy. In addition, you must develop a personality that other people enjoy being around. The business is just too stressful for anyone to put up with a negative art director. Collaboration is the name of our game. Unless you enjoy working with others and can be stimulated by other peoples' talents and energy, you should choose a more solitary field.

Hollywood doesn't need another art director. It probably has enough at this moment to last a good 15 or 20 years without ever having to hire anyone new. But what Hollywood does need is talent and fresh ideas. If you have that, you will be able to beat the odds and make a place for yourself in the most interesting business there is. Good luck!

▼

ROY CHRISTOPHER is the recipient of five Emmy Awards and twenty-one Emmy nominations.

Mr. Christopher is currently art director/production designer on Murphy Brown, Love and War, and Wings. He designed The Carol Burnett 25th Anniversary Show, which was broadcast in January, 1993. In addition, he was production designer for the 1992 Academy Awards Show, the seventh time he has served in that capacity.

Mr. Christopher was born and raised in Fresno, California, and received his MA degree in theater arts from Cal State, Fresno.

Always in the Spotlight!

Richard Tilley, President, Circuit Lighting Inc.

A lighting technician is someone who is trained to illuminate a person or object to achieve a specific visual effect. In what is quickly becoming a 24-hour-a-day culture, the need for lighting has rapidly expanded the possibilities for those who wish to pursue a career in this field. Considering that Thomas Edison invented the incandescent bulb only 110 years ago, the growth in this industry has been phenomenal.

What Is the Purpose of Lighting?

There are many reasons why we use lighting. Generally, it is an attempt to enhance a subject and make it stand out. Lighting for commercials is commonly used to make a product more appealing. Special effects can be created for a rock concert or disco. The movie industry depends on lighting to bring out colors or create a natural effect. Decorative lighting is being increasingly used on a number of major buildings, hotels, and monuments throughout the world. Used correctly, it can attract attention to a building or, in some cases, only highlight the attractive parts of a structure.

We're Not Just Talking Light Bulbs Here . . .

Professional lights are known as *fixtures* or *instruments,* of which there are numerous types. Light bulbs are known as *lamps,* such as incandescent, fluorescent, quartz, and gas filled.

Lamps are contained in *fixtures,* which may be positioned in various configurations and controlled by people working with today's advanced technology. State-of-the-art technology offers computerized movement and positioning of fixtures. *Control consoles*—also known as *lighting boards* or *lighting switchboards*—may be either manual or automated.

There are many types of fixtures on the market, from the basic lamp holders that are commonly found in homes to high powered search lights. HMI, quartz, and incandescent fixtures are commonly used in theater and television. Commercial fixtures such as ellipsoidals, fresnels, moles, and pars have a wide range of uses from theatrical events to concert lighting.

What Requires Artistic Lighting?

Many objects and people require artistic lighting. Here are a few examples:

1. *Background scenery* such as a building in the distance, a stage set, a group of people, or almost anything behind the object or person to be illuminated can be dramatically changed by the use of colored gel and dimmed lighting.

   If you had to light a group of people in a garden, for example, it would be possible—with the right lighting and gel—to just highlight certain areas or to completely change the color of the trees and flowers.

2. The *setting* must also be lit. Using the same group of people and the same garden, the setting—a park bench, a lamp post, or the group itself—would be lit from at least two sides to avoid shadows and ensure good coverage.

3. Now that the trees in our background have been lit and their colors highlighted, and the group bench and lamp post illuminated, we have to decide how to light our *subject*—a specific member of the group.

4. In some instances, like a rock concert, it may also be necessary to light the *audience*.

What Affects Lighting Choices?

Economics

Many variables can affect the choices in lighting, but the most common is money. When a director or producer calls up a lighting company, what he or she wants invariably costs far more than he or she has budgeted for lighting. So the very first questions will concern how to do the job the producer wants with the money in the budget, and where "creative solutions" can save money without significantly decreasing the desired lighting effects.

Space

The amount of space available will limit how much equipment can be brought into a room and, therefore, how complex the lighting effects can be.

Equipment Available

Not all lighting companies or studios have state-of-the-art equipment. Even the ones who do, may not have enough (or the right) equipment available at the time it is needed.

The Type of Production

The type of production can dramatically change the kinds and amount of lights—video, for example, requires a different type of lighting than film.

Electricity Available

Without the use of generators, the average building only has a certain amount of electricity available—this alone can significantly affect the size and quantity of lights used.

The Market and the Consumers

The most abundant use of creative lighting is found in major metropolitan and large urban centers. New York, San Francisco, Los Angeles, Chicago, Boston, Miami, Orlando, Dallas, Fort Worth, and Houston are all cities where job opportunities are promising, but the market is not limited to these places. The following is just a partial list of typical end-users of a lighting technicians' services:

- Theater performances (plays, musicals, opera, and dance)
- Musical performances (concerts)
- Television production
- Filmmaking
- Video production
- Entertainment centers (hotels, nightclubs, restaurants, museums, and theme parks)
- Religious organizations
- Sports arenas
- Educational centers (schools, colleges, universities, and training facilities)
- Retail operations (malls, stores, and fashion events)
- Corporate functions
- Security systems (architectural, landscaping, residential, commercial, and municipal)
- Government property (bridges, monuments, and buildings)

Entering the Field

There is no hard-and-fast route to becoming a lighting technician. Pathways for entering the field are as numerous as the personalities it attracts. Some key requirements, however, are an interest in math, electrical circuitry, and electronics. Proficiency in math facilitates both power usage computations and cost estimates, both key components of any lighting job. Since much of the equipment used is not always state-of-the-art, the ability to repair, substitute, or just "make do" with what is on hand is enhanced by a sound understanding of electrical principles. Courses in math and science offered in high school and vocational technical programs provide a good foundation for work in the lighting field.

Successful lighting technicians possess not only an artistic flair, but the motivation to keep pace with a constantly changing marketplace—the need to stay abreast of the fast-paced technological improvements in lighting products, supplies, and equipment is an essential component of the job.

Getting Valuable Experience

A variety of apprenticeships are available. Time spent as an electrician's helper or as a participant in a theater group is valuable in determining latent ability and depth of interest in the field. Almost all schools and colleges stage annual theater productions, and many communities support active theater groups. The latter, however, are almost always understaffed and underbudgeted. As a result, they frequently welcome volunteers to share the work and are glad to share their knowledge in return.

Theater production is generally divided into four segments: acting, costume and makeup, set building, and lighting. Of these, set building and lighting offer opportunities for hands-on learning that has served many technicians well.

Top Employee Motivators

Ranked by: Conclusions in article by Frederick Hertzbert as published in the *Harvard Business Review.*
1. On-the-job achievement
2. Recognition
3. Type of work done
4. Responsibility assigned
5. Advancement and growth opportunities
6. Salary
7. Relationships with other employees
8. Type of supervision received
9. Working conditions
10. Company policies and administration

Source: *Homecare*

What You Can Earn

Income is largely dependent upon the experience gained and parlayed into more complex lighting challenges that a designer will have to overcome. Earning potential is limited only by the experience and learning ability of the individual. Many apprentices earn between $30 and $75 a day, depending on prevailing economic conditions and the size and policies of the firm or organization they are working for. You will not get rich on these wages, but you should always include the value of the learning and experience as part of the pay.

While serving an average apprenticeship (usually lasting from three to five years), you will learn many different ways to light up a set, as well as a variety of "tricks of the trade." Although you may think that there's nothing left to learn after five years, it's good to remember that new products and ideas are common in this industry, and the equipment you have so patiently mastered could be obsolete . . . next week.

Once qualified and accepted into the lighting profession, it becomes easier to find work and to earn more when you do work. A freelance lighting technician on a tour or in the theater can expect to earn up to $300 per day. Top-of-the-profession lighting directors collect fees in excess of several *thousand* dollars per day overseeing projects with million-dollar lighting budgets.

Most lighting technicians negotiate their income on an hourly, weekly, or per job basis. In addition, expense accounts and travel allowances are often available to cover cash outlays for food and housing while on the road.

Advancement Within the Industry

If you are creatively oriented, then your technical ability will be a sound foundation for fast advancement and job placement within the lighting design and fixture design industry. If you are a college graduate, then you could soon find yourself teaching others.

Free-lance technicians usually work in the television and concert sides of the industry, since these usually don't require a full-time commitment and allow for greater flexibility.

What Some People Have Accomplished

Howard: Obtained a college degree and started 15 years ago in a show promotion/booking agency. He is now a tour production manager for a national entertainment act and earns more than $250,000 a year with excellent benefits.

Mark: Was a college activities student, then a lighting technician, moved into theater promotion, and is now making $60,000 a year working for a major promotion agency.

George: Left school in England at 15 and worked in various discos and nightclubs as a disc jockey. Took up an interest in lighting, went back to college, and studied electrical engineering. Moved to Rome and soon became head lighting director for a large concert touring company, working with U2, Peter Gabriel, Ray Charles, B.B. King, and many other stars. He is now vice president of marketing for one of New Jersey's leading lighting companies.

And, last but not least . . .

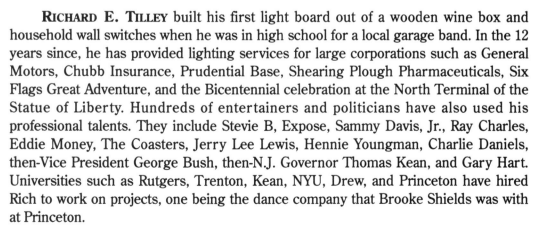

RICHARD E. TILLEY built his first light board out of a wooden wine box and household wall switches when he was in high school for a local garage band. In the 12 years since, he has provided lighting services for large corporations such as General Motors, Chubb Insurance, Prudential Base, Shearing Plough Pharmaceuticals, Six Flags Great Adventure, and the Bicentennial celebration at the North Terminal of the Statue of Liberty. Hundreds of entertainers and politicians have also used his professional talents. They include Stevie B, Expose, Sammy Davis, Jr., Ray Charles, Eddie Money, The Coasters, Jerry Lee Lewis, Hennie Youngman, Charlie Daniels, then-Vice President George Bush, then-N.J. Governor Thomas Kean, and Gary Hart. Universities such as Rutgers, Trenton, Kean, NYU, Drew, and Princeton have hired Rich to work on projects, one being the dance company that Brooke Shields was with at Princeton.

When Rich first entered the market, club shows were a major source of work, until stricter alcohol laws caused many of the clubs to close. While on the club circuit, he traveled extensively throughout the United States and overseas.

Rich is the president of Circuit Lighting Inc. in New Jersey, which designs, rents, and sells lighting systems all over the world. His current emphasis is on small to mid-sized musical productions, corporate video lighting, and educational facility lighting systems.

THE JOB
SEARCH
PROCESS

Getting Started: Self-Evaluation and Career Objectives

etting a job may be a relatively simple one-step or couple of weeks process or a complex, months-long operation.

Starting, nurturing, and developing a career (or even a series of careers) is a lifelong process.

What we'll be talking about in the five chapters that together form our **Job Search Process** are those basic steps to take, assumptions to make, things to think about if you want a job—especially a first job in some area of the film and video industry. But when these steps—this process—are applied and expanded over a lifetime, most if not all of them are the same procedures, carried out over and over again, that are necessary to develop a successful, lifelong, professional career.

What does all this have to do with putting together a resume and portfolio, writing a cover letter, heading off for interviews, and the other "traditional" steps necessary to get a job? Whether your college graduation is just around the corner or a far distant memory, you will continuously need to focus, evaluate, and re-evaluate your response to the ever-changing challenge of your future: Just what do you want to do with the rest of your life? Whether you like it or not, you're all looking for that "entry-level opportunity."

You're already one or two steps ahead of the competition—you're sure you want to pursue a career in the film and video industry. By heeding the advice of the many professionals who have written chapters for this *Career Directory*—and utilizing the extensive entry-level job, organization, and career resource listings we've included—you're well on your way to fulfilling that dream. But there are some key decisions and time-consuming preparations to make if you want to transform that hopeful dream into a real, live job.

The actual process of finding the right company, right career path, and most importantly, the right first job, begins long before you start mailing out resumes and auditioning for potential employers. The choices and decisions you make now are not irrevocable, but this first job will have a definite impact on the career options you leave yourself. To help you make some of the right decisions and choices along the way (and avoid some of the most notable traps and pitfalls), the following chapters will lead you through a series of organized steps. If the entire job search process we are recommending here is properly executed, it will undoubtedly help you land exactly the job you want.

If you're currently in high school and hope, after college, to land a job in the film and video industry, then getting the right education and training, choosing the right major, and getting the summer work experience many companies look for are all important steps. Read the section of this *Career Directory* that covers the particular field and/or job specialty in which you're interested—many of the contributors have recommended colleges or specific training programs they favor.

If you're hoping to jump right into any of these fields without professional training or education, our best and only advice is—don't do it. As you'll soon see in the detailed information included in the **Job Opportunities Databank,** there are not that many job openings for students without training or a college degree. Those that do exist are generally clerical and will only rarely lead to promising careers.

The Concept of a Job Search Process

As we've explained, a job search is not a series of random events. Rather, it is a series of connected events that together form the job search process. It is important to know the eight steps that go into that process:

1. Evaluating yourself

Know thyself. What skills and abilities can you offer a prospective employer? What do you enjoy doing? What are your strengths and weaknesses? What do you want to do?

2. Establishing your career objectives

Where do you want to be next year, three years, five years from now? What do you ultimately want to accomplish in your career and your life?

3. Creating a company target list

How to prepare a "Hit List" of potential employers—researching them, matching their needs with your skills, and starting your job search assault. Preparing company information sheets and evaluating your chances.

4. Networking for success

Learning how to utilize every contact, every friend, every relative, and anyone else you can think of to break down the barriers facing any would-be film and video professional. How to organize your home office to keep track of your communications and stay on top of your job campaign.

5. Preparing your resume

How to encapsulate years of school and little actual work experience into a professional, selling resume. Learning when and how to use it.

6. Preparing cover letters

The many ordinary and the all-too-few extraordinary cover letters, the kind that land interviews and jobs.

7. Interviewing

How to make the interview process work for you—from the first "hello" to the first day on the job.

8. Following up

Often overlooked, it's perhaps the most important part of the job search process.

We won't try to kid you—it is a lot of work. To do it right, you have to get started early, probably quite a bit earlier than you'd planned. Frankly, we recommend beginning this process one full year prior to the day you plan to start work.

So if you're in college, the end of your junior year is the right time to begin your research and preparations. That should give you enough time during summer vacation to set up your files and begin your library research.

Whether you're in college, a specific training program, or graduate school, one item may need to be planned even earlier—allowing enough time in your schedule of classes for interview preparations and appointments. Waiting until your senior year to "make some time" is already too late. Searching for a full-time job is itself a full-time job! Though you're naturally restricted by your schedule, it's not difficult to plan ahead and prepare for your upcoming job search. Try to leave at least a couple of free mornings or afternoons a week. A day or even two without classes is even better.

Otherwise, you'll find yourself crazed and distracted, trying to prepare for an interview in the 10-minute period between classes. Not the best way to make a first impression and certainly not the way you want to approach an important meeting.

The Self-Evaluation Process

Learning about who you are, what you want to be, and what you can be are critical first steps in the job search process and, unfortunately, the ones most often ignored by job seekers everywhere, especially students eager to leave the ivy behind and plunge into the "real world." But avoiding this crucial self-evaluation can hinder your progress and even damage some decent prospects.

Why? Because in order to land a job with a company at which you'll actually be happy, you need to be able to identify those employers and/or job descriptions that best match your own skills, likes, and strengths. The more you know about yourself, the more you'll bring to this process, and the more accurate the "match-ups." You'll be able to structure your presentation (resume, cover letter, interviews, follow up) to stress your most marketable skills and talents (and, dare we say it, conveniently avoid your weaknesses?). Later, you'll be able to evaluate potential employers and job offers on the basis of your own needs and desires. This spells the difference between waking up in the morning ready to enthusiastically tackle a new day of challenges or shutting off the alarm in the hopes the day (and your job) will just disappear.

Creating Your Self-Evaluation Form

If your self-evaluation is to have any meaning, you must first be honest with yourself. This self-evaluation form should help you achieve that goal by providing a structured environment to answer these tough questions.

Take a sheet of lined notebook paper. Set up eight columns across the top—Strengths, Weaknesses, Skills, Hobbies, Courses, Experience, Likes, Dislikes.

Now, fill in each of these columns according to these guidelines:

Strengths: Describe personality traits you consider your strengths (and try to look at them as an employer would)—e.g., persistence, organization, ambition, intelligence, logic, assertiveness, aggression, leadership, etc.

Weaknesses: The traits you consider glaring weaknesses—e.g., impatience, conceit, etc. Remember: Look at these as a potential employer would. Don't assume that the personal traits you consider weaknesses will necessarily be considered negatives in the business world. You may be "easily bored," a trait that led to lousy grades early on because teachers couldn't keep you interested in the subjects they were teaching. Well, many entrepreneurs need ever-changing challenges. Strength or weakness?

Skills: Any skill you have, whether you think it's marketable or not. Everything from basic business skills—like typing and word processing—to computer or teaching experience and foreign language literacy. Don't forget possibly obscure but marketable skills like "good telephone voice."

Hobbies: The things you enjoy doing that, more than likely, have no overt connection to career objectives. These should be distinct from the skills listed above, and may include activities such as reading, games, travel, sports, and the like. While these may not be marketable in any general sense, they may well be useful in specific circumstances.

Courses: All the general subject areas (history, literature, etc.) and/or specific courses you've taken that may be marketable, enjoyable, or both.

Experience: Just the specific functions you performed at any part-time (school year) or full-time (summer) jobs. Entries may include "General Office" (typing, filing, answering phones, etc.), "Office Assistant," "Retail Clerk" etc.

Likes: List all your "likes," those important considerations that you haven't listed anywhere else yet. These might include the types of people you like to be with, the kind of environment you prefer (city, country, large places, small places, quiet, loud, fast-paced, slow-paced) and anything else that hasn't shown up somewhere on this form. Try to think of "likes" that you have that are related to the job you are applying for. For example, if you're applying for a job at a major film studio, mention that you enjoy reading *Premiere* magazine. However, try not to include entries that refer to specific jobs or companies. We'll list those on another form.

Dislikes: All the people, places, and things you can easily live without.

Now assess the "marketability" of each item you've listed. (In other words, are some of your likes, skills, or courses easier to match to a film and video job description, or do they have little to do with a specific job or company?) Mark highly marketable skills with an "H." Use "M" to characterize those skills that may be marketable in a particular set of circumstances, "L" for those with minimal potential application to any job.

Referring back to the same list, decide if you'd enjoy using your marketable skills or talents as part of your everyday job—"Y" for yes, "N" for no. You may type 80 words a minute but truly despise typing or worry that stressing it too much will land you on the permanent clerical staff. If so, mark typing with an "N". (Keep one thing in mind—just because you dislike typing shouldn't mean you absolutely won't accept a job that requires it. Almost every professional job today requires computer-based work that makes typing a plus.)

Now, go over the entire form carefully and look for inconsistencies.

To help you with your own form, there's a sample one on the following page that a job-hunter might have completed.

The Value of a Second Opinion

There is a familiar misconception about the self-evaluation process that gets in the way of many new job applicants—the belief that it is a process that must be accomplished in isolation. Nothing could be further from the truth. Just because the family doctor tells you that you need an operation doesn't mean you run right off to the hospital. Prudence dictates that you check out the opinion with another physician. Getting such a "second opinion"—someone else's, not just your own—is a valuable practice throughout the job search process, as well.

So after you've completed the various exercises in this chapter, review them with a friend, relative, or parent—just be sure it's someone who knows you well and cares about you. These second opinions may reveal some aspects of your self-description on which you and the rest of the world differ. If so, discuss them, learn from them and, if necessary, change some conclusions. Should everyone concur with your self-evaluation, you will be reassured that your choices are on target.

Establishing Your Career Objective(s)

For better or worse, you now know something more of who and what you are. But we've yet to establish and evaluate another important area—your overall needs, desires, and goals. Where are you going? What do you want to accomplish?

If you're getting ready to graduate from college, a specific training program, or graduate school, the next five years are the most critical period of your whole career. You need to make the initial transition from college to the workplace, establish yourself in a new and completely unfamiliar work environment, and begin to build the professional credentials necessary to achieve your career goals.

If that strikes you as a pretty tall order, well, it is. Unless you've narrowly prepared yourself for a specific profession, you're probably most ill-prepared for any

	Strength	Weakness	Skill	Hobby	Course	Experience	Like	Dislike
Marketable?								
Enjoy?								
Marketable?								
Enjoy?								
Marketable?								
Enjoy?								

real job. Instead, you've (hopefully) learned some basic principles—research and analytical skills that are necessary for success at almost any level—and, more or less, how to think.

It's tough to face, but face it you must: No matter what your college, major, or degree, all you represent right now is potential. How you package that potential and what you eventually make of it is completely up to you. It's an unfortunate fact that many employers will take a professional with barely a year or two experience over any newcomer, no matter how promising. Smaller companies, especially, can rarely afford to hire someone who can't begin contributing immediately.

So you have to be prepared to take your comparatively modest skills and experience and package them in a way that will get you interviewed and hired. Quite a challenge.

There are a number of different ways to approach such a task. If you find yourself confused or unable to list such goals, you might want to check a few books in your local library that have more time to spend on the topic of "goal-oriented planning."

But Is the Film and Video Industry Right for You?

Presuming you now have a much better idea of yourself and where you'd like to be, let's make sure some of your basic assumptions are right. We presume you purchased this *Career Directory* because you're considering a career in some area of film and video production. Are you sure? Do you know enough about the industry as a whole and the particular part you're heading for to decide whether it's right for you? Probably not. So start your research now—learn as much about your potential career field as you now know about yourself.

Start with the essays in the **Advice for the Pro's** section—these will give you an excellent overview of the film and video industry, some very specialized (and growing) areas, and some things to keep in mind as you start on your career search. They will also give you a relatively simplified, though very necessary, understanding of just what people who work in all these areas of film and video actually do.

Other sources you should consider consulting to learn more about this business are listed in the **Career Resources** section of this book.

In that section, we've listed trade associations and publications associated with film and video professions together with many other resources that will help your job search. (Consult the front of this directory for a complete description of the **Career Resources** section.) Where possible in the association entries, we've included details on educational information they make available, but you should certainly consider writing each of the pertinent associations, letting them know you're interested in a career in their area of specialization and would appreciate whatever help and advice they're willing to impart. You'll find many sponsor seminars and conferences throughout the country, some of which you may be able to attend.

The trade publications are dedicated to the highly specific interests of film and video professionals. These magazines are generally not available at newsstands, but you may be able to obtain back issues at your local library (most major libraries have extensive collections of such journals) or by writing to the magazines' circulation/subscription departments. We've also included regional and local magazines.

You may also try writing to the publishers and/or editors of these publications. State in your cover letter what area of film and video you're considering and ask them for whatever help and advice they can offer. But be specific. These are busy professionals and they do not have the time or the inclination to simply "tell me everything you can about working in the film and video business."

If you can afford it now, we strongly suggest subscribing to whichever trade magazines are applicable to the specialty you're considering. If you can't subscribe to all of them, make it a point to regularly read the copies that arrive at your local public or college library.

These publications may well provide the most imaginative and far-reaching information for your job search. Even a quick perusal of an issue or two will give you an excellent feel for the industry. After reading only a few articles, you'll already get a handle on what's happening in the field and some of the industry's peculiar and particular jargon. Later, more detailed study will aid you in your search for a specific job.

Authors of the articles themselves may well turn out to be important resources. If an article is directly related to your chosen specialty, why not call the author and ask some questions? You'd be amazed how willing many of these professionals will be to talk to you and answer your questions, and the worst they can do is say no. (But *do* use common sense—authors will not *always* respond graciously to your invitation to "chat about the business." And don't be *too* aggressive here.)

You'll find such research to be a double-edged sword. In addition to helping you get a handle on whether the area you've chosen is really right for you, you'll slowly learn enough about particular specialties, companies, the industry, etc., to actually sound like you know what you're talking about when you hit the pavement looking for your first job. And nothing is better than sounding like a pro—except being one.

Film and Video Is It. Now What?

After all this research, we're going to assume you've reached that final decision—you really do want a career in the film and video industry. It is with this vague certainty that all too many of you will race off, hunting for any employer willing to give you a job. You'll manage to get interviews at a couple and, smiling brightly, tell everyone you meet, "I want a career in film and video." The interviewers, unfortunately, will all ask the same awkward question—"What *exactly* do you want to do at our company?"—and that will be the end of that.

It is simply not enough to narrow your job search to a specific industry. And so far, that's all you've done. You must now establish a specific career objective—the job you want to start, the specialty you want to pursue. Just knowing that you "want to get into film and video" doesn't mean anything to anybody. If that's all you can tell an interviewer, it demonstrates a lack of research into the industry itself and your failure to think ahead.

Interviewers will *not* welcome you with open arms if you're still vague about your career goals. If you've managed to get an "informational interview" with a professional whose company currently has no job openings, what is he or she supposed to do with your resume after you leave? Who should he or she send it to for future consideration? Since *you* don't seem to know exactly what you want to do, how's he or she going to figure it out? Worse, that person will probably resent your asking him or her to function as your personal career counselor.

Remember, the more specific your career objective, the better your chances of finding a job. It's that simple and that important. Naturally, before you declare your objective to the world, check once again to make sure your specific job target matches the skills and interests you defined in your self-evaluation. Eventually, you may want to state such an objective on your resume, and "To obtain an entry-level position as a production assistant at a major film studio," is quite a bit better than "I want a career in film and video." Do not consider this step final until you can summarize your job/career objective in a single, short, accurate sentence.

CHAPTER FIFTEEN

Targeting Prospective Employers and Networking for Success

As you move along the job search path, one fact will quickly become crystal clear—it is primarily a process of **elimination**: your task is to consider and research as many options as possible, then—for good reasons—**eliminate** as many as possible, attempting to continually narrow your focus.

Your Ideal Company Profile

Let's establish some criteria to evaluate potential employers. This will enable you to identify your target companies, the places you'd really like to work. (This process, as we've pointed out, is not specific to any industry or field; the same steps, with perhaps some research resource variations, are applicable to any job, any company, any industry.)

Take a sheet of blank paper and divide it into three vertical columns. Title it "Target Company—Ideal Profile." Call the lefthand column "Musts," the middle column "Preferences," and the righthand column "Nevers".

We've listed a series of questions below. After considering each question, decide whether a particular criteria *must* be met, whether you would simply *prefer* it or *never* would consider it at all. If there are other criteria you consider important, feel free to add them to the list below and mark them accordingly on your Profile.

1. What are your geographical preferences? (Possible answers: U.S., Canada, International, Anywhere). If you only want to work in the U.S., then "Work in United States" would be the entry in the "Must" column. "Work in Canada or Foreign Country" might be the first entry in your "Never" column. There would be no applicable entry for this question in the "Preference" column. If, however, you will consider working in two of the three, then your "Must" column entry might read "Work in U.S. or Canada," your "Preference" entry—if you preferred one over the other—could read "Work in U.S.," and the "Never" column, "Work Overseas."

2. If you prefer to work in the U.S. or Canada, what area, state(s) or province(s)? If overseas, what area or countries?

3. Do you prefer a large city, small city, town, or somewhere as far away from civilization as possible?

4. In regard to question three, any specific preferences?

5. Do you prefer a warm or cold climate?

6. Do you prefer a large or small company? Define your terms (by sales, income, employees, offices, etc.).

7. Do you mind relocating right now? Do you want to work for a company or studio with a reputation for *frequently* relocating top people?

8. Do you mind travelling frequently? What percent do you consider reasonable? (Make sure this matches the normal requirements of the job specialization you're considering.)

9. What salary would you *like* to receive (put in the "Preference" column)? What's the *lowest* salary you'll accept (in the "Must" column)?

10. Are there any benefits (such as an expense account, medical and/or dental insurance, company car, etc.) you must or would like to have?

11. Are you planning to attend graduate school at some point in the future and, if so, is a tuition reimbursement plan important to you?

12. Do you feel that a formal training program is necessary?

13. If applicable, what kinds of specific products or services would you prefer to work with?

It's important to keep revising this new form, just as you should continue to update your Self-Evaluation Form. After all, it contains the criteria by which you will judge every potential employer. Armed with a complete list of such criteria, you're now ready to find all the companies that match them.

Targeting Individual Companies

To begin creating your initial list of targeted companies, start with the **Job Opportunities Databank** in this directory. We've listed many major film and video studios and production companies that offer the most potential for those seeking a career in the film and video industry; most of these companies were contacted by telephone for this edition. These listings provide a plethora of data concerning the companies' overall operations, hiring practices, and other important information on entry-level job opportunities. This latter information includes key contacts (names), the average number of entry-level people they hire each year, along with complete job descriptions and requirements.

One word of advice. You'll notice that some of the companies list "0" under average entry-level hiring. This is more a reflection of the current economic times than a long-range projection. In the past, these companies probably did list an average number of new hires, and they will again in the future. We have listed these companies for three reasons: 1) to present you with the overall view of prospective employers; 2) because even companies that don't plan to do any hiring will experience unexpected job openings; and 3) things change, so as soon as the economy begins to pick up, expect entry-level hiring to increase again.

We have attempted to include information on those major companies that represent many of the entry-level jobs out there. But there are, of course, many other companies of all sizes and shapes that you may also wish to research. In the **Career Resources** section, we have listed other reference tools you can use to obtain more information on the companies we've listed, as well as those we haven't.

The Other Side of the Iceberg

You are now better prepared to choose those companies that meet your own list of criteria. But a word of caution about these now-"obvious" requirements—they are not the only ones you need to take into consideration. And you probably won't be able to find all or many of the answers to this second set of questions in any reference book—they are known, however, by those persons already at work in the industry. Here is the list you will want to follow:

Promotion

If you are aggressive about your career plans, you'll want to know if you have a shot at the top. Look for companies that traditionally promote from within.

Training

Look for companies in which your early tenure will actually be a period of on-the-job training, hopefully ones in which training remains part of the long-term process. As new techniques and technologies enter the workplace, you must make sure you are updated on these skills. Most importantly, look for training that is craft- or function-oriented—these are the so-called **transferable skills**, ones you can easily bring along with you from job-to-job, company-to-company, sometimes industry-to-industry.

Ask the Person Who Owns One

Some years ago, this advice was used as the theme for a highly successful automobile advertising campaign. The prospective car buyer was encouraged to find out about the product by asking the (supposedly) most trustworthy judge of all—someone who was already an owner.

You can use the same approach in your job search. You all have relatives or friends already out in the workplace—these are your best sources of information about those industries. Cast your net in as wide a circle as possible. Contact these valuable resources. You'll be amazed at how readily they will answer your questions. I suggest you check the criteria list at the beginning of this chapter to formulate your own list of pertinent questions. Ideally and minimally you will want to learn: how the industry is doing, what its long-term prospects are, the kinds of personalities they favor (aggressive, low key), rate of employee turnover, and the availability of training.

Salary

Some industries are generally high paying, some are not. But even an industry with a tradition of paying abnormally low salaries may have particular companies or job functions (like sales) within companies that command high remuneration. But it's important you know what the industry standard is.

Benefits

Look for companies in which health insurance, vacation pay, retirement plans, 401(k) accounts, stock purchase opportunities, and other important employee benefits are extensive—and company paid. If you have to pay for basic benefits like medical coverage yourself, you'll be surprised at how expensive they are. An exceptional benefit package may even lead you to accept a lower-than-usual salary.

Unions

Early in your career in film and video, you'll find yourself contemplating unionization. What are the prominent unions in the film and video industry? Why is there a union? Will I be compelled to join a union?

All unions in the film and video industry are chartered by the American Federation of Labor and Congress of Industrial Organizations (AFL-CIO). There are several separate unions that represent those working in the film and video industry:

- **Screen Actors Guild (SAG)**—represents performers working in any type of production work on film, including actors, stunt players, singers, dancers, extras, and voice-over artists.

- **American Federation of Television and Radio Artists (AFTRA)**—represents performers working on live television, radio programs, radio commercials, and musical recordings (includes educational and industrial films).

- **National Association of Broadcast Employees and Technicians (NABET)**—represents technical personnel working behind the scenes.

- **Screen Extras Guild (SEG)**—represents background players for film and television.

- **Society of Motion Picture/Television Art Directors (SMP/TAD)**—represents supervisors of the design, construction, and decor of motion pictures and settings.

- **Society of Motion Picture and Television Engineers (SMPTE)**—represents professional engineers and technicians in motion pictures, television, and allied arts and sciences.

Each union has a different set of eligibility requirements, membership fees, and annual dues. As labor organizations, they negotiate wages, working conditions, and benefits (such as medical, dental, pension plans, and casting information) for their members. Therefore, union affiliation is something that you will eventually want. However, joining one is not as easy as you may think.

Union membership is a catch-22 situation. You generally need to have union affiliation to get a job in film and video, but you cannot join a union until you have worked in the industry. Luckily, there is an exception to this rule. Thanks to the Taft-Hartley Act of 1947, no one can legally be refused a job in the industry just because he or she is not affiliated with a particular union. It is recommended, then, that you take work as you can get it. You can be hired by a union company so that you can meet the requirements for union benefits, or you can work in a nonunion setting with no benefits and then build up the necessary credentials to eventually join a union.

In short, if you seek wide recognition, high position, and maximum income, it is unlikely that joining a film and/or video-related union or professional organization can be avoided for very long.

Agents

Agents serve to represent those in the film and video industry, such as performers, directors, writers, cinematographers, etc. They work with studios and producers to try obtain employment for clients. All legitimate casting in Hollywood is handled by agents. To be granted an audition for an acting part, for example, you must have an agent. In addition, you must belong to a union to get an agent. Therefore, once union membership is established, use your contacts to find one. If you are good enough in the business, however, chances are an agent will find you first.

Making Friends and Influencing People

Networking is a term you have probably heard; it is definitely a key aspect of any successful job search and a process you must master.

Informational interviews and **job interviews** are the two primary outgrowths of successful networking.

Referrals, an aspect of the networking process, entail using someone else's name, credentials, and recommendation to set up a receptive environment when seeking a job interview.

All of these terms have one thing in common: Each depends on the actions of other people to put them in motion. Don't let this idea of "dependency" slow you down, however. A job search *must* be a very pro-active process—*you* have to initiate the action. When networking, this means contacting as many people as you can. The more you contact, the better the chances of getting one of those people you are "depending" on to take action and help you out.

So what *is* networking? How do you build your own network? And why do you need one in the first place? The balance of this chapter answers all of those questions and more.

Get your telephone ready. It's time to make some friends.

Not the World's Oldest Profession, but . . .

Networking is the process of creating your own group of relatives, friends, and acquaintances who can feed you the information you need to find a job—identifying where the jobs are and giving you the personal introductions and background data necessary to pursue them.

If the job market were so well-organized that details on all employment opportunities were immediately available to all applicants, there would be no need for such a process. Rest assured the job market is *not* such a smooth-running machine—most applicants are left very much to their own devices. Build and use your own network wisely and you'll be amazed at the amount of useful job intelligence you will turn up.

It is a well-known fact that getting started in the film and video business is very difficult—that you need to know someone to get a job in the field. Well, this is true . . . to an extent. Your friend's uncle might work as a motion picture director and get you a job on the set, but can he help you keep it? Doubtful. Everyone knows someone who would love to break into the business, and if you can't work up to the standards, they'll find someone who can. Therefore, just as important as *who* you know is *what* you know.

Even if you currently have no connections to the industry, there are options. One is by getting into an industry training program, such as the Assistant Director's Training program sponsored by the Directors Guild of America. This is a formal training program for assistant directors—albeit, a fierce one—only about one percent of the applicants actually pass the tough oral and written exams required. Another option is to simply **find** the contacts you need . . . by networking.

While the term networking didn't gain prominence until the 1970s, it is by no means a new phenomenon. A selection process that connects people of similar skills, backgrounds, and/or attitudes—in other words, networking—has been in existence in a variety of forms for centuries. Attend any Ivy League school and you're automatically part of its very special centuries-old network.

And it works. Remember your own reaction when you were asked to recommend someone for a job, club, or school office? You certainly didn't want to look foolish, so you gave it some thought and tried to recommend the best-qualified person that you thought would "fit in" with the rest of the group. It's a built-in screening process.

Creating the Ideal Network

As in most endeavors, there's a wrong way and a right way to network. The following tips will help you construct your own wide-ranging, information-gathering, interview-generating group—*your* network.

Diversify

Unlike the Harvard or Princeton network—confined to former graduates of each school—your network should be as diversified and wide-ranging as possible. You never know who might be in a position to help, so don't limit your group of friends. The more diverse they are, the greater the variety of information they may supply you with.

Don't Forget . . .

. . . to include everyone you know in your initial networking list: friends, relatives, social acquaintances, classmates, college alumni, professors, teachers, your dentist, doctor, family lawyer, insurance agent, banker, travel agent, elected officials in your community, ministers, fellow church members, local tradesmen, and local business or social club officers. And everybody they know!

Be Specific

Make a list of the kinds of assistance you will require from those in your network, then make specific requests of each. Do they know of jobs at their company? Can they introduce you to the proper executives? Have they heard something about or know someone at the company you're planning to interview with next week?

The more organized you are, the easier it will be to target the information you need and figure out who might have it. Begin to keep a business card file or case so you can keep track of all your contacts. A small plastic case for file cards that is available at any discount store will do nicely. One system you can use is to staple the card to a 3 x 5 index card. On the card, write down any information about that contact that you might need later—when you talked to them, job leads they provided, specific job search advice, etc. You will then have all the information you need about each company or contact in one easily accessible location.

Learn the Difference . . .

. . . between an **informational** interview and a **job** interview. The former requires you to cast yourself in the role of information gatherer; *you* are the interviewer and knowledge is your goal—about an industry, company, job function, key executive, etc. Such a meeting with someone already doing what you soon hope to be doing is by far the best way to find out everything you need to know—before you walk through the door and sit down for a formal job interview, at which time your purpose is more sharply defined: to get the job you're interviewing for.

If you learn of a specific job opening during an informational interview, you are in a position to find out details about the job, identify the interviewer and, possibly, even learn some things about him or her. In addition, presuming you get your contact's permission, you may be able to use his or her name as a referral. Calling up the interviewer and saying, "Joan Smith in your human resources department suggested I contact you regarding openings for production assistants," is far superior to "Hello. Do you have any job openings at your film studio?"

(In such a case, be careful about referring to a specific job opening, even if your contact told you about it. It may not be something you're supposed to know about. By presenting your query as an open-ended question, you give your prospective employer the option of exploring your background without further commitment. If there is a job there and you're qualified for it, you'll find out soon enough.)

Don't Waste a Contact

Not everyone you call on your highly-diversified networking list will know about a job opening. It would be surprising if each one did. But what about *their* friends and colleagues? It's amazing how everyone knows someone who knows someone. Ask—you'll find that someone.

Value Your Contacts

If someone has provided you with helpful information or an introduction to a friend or colleague, keep him or her informed about how it all turns out. A referral that's panned out should be reported to the person who opened the door for you in the first place. Such courtesy will be appreciated—and may lead to more contacts. If someone has nothing to offer today, a call back in the future is still appropriate and may pay off.

The lesson is clear: Keep your options open, your contact list alive. Detailed records of your network—whom you spoke with, when, what transpired, etc.—will help you keep track of your overall progress and organize what can be a complicated and involved process.

Informational Interviews

So now you've done your homework, built your network, and begun using your contacts. It's time to go on your first informational interview.

A Typical Interview

You were, of course, smart enough to include John Fredericks, the bank officer who handled your dad's mortgage, on your original contact list. He knew you as a bright and conscientious college senior; in fact, your perfect three-year repayment record on the loan you took out to buy that '67 Plymouth impressed him. When you called him, he was happy to refer you to his friend, Carol Jones, a human resources manager at XYZ Video Production, Inc. Armed with permission to use Fredericks' name and recommendation, you wrote a letter to Carol Jones, the gist of which went something like this:

I am writing at the suggestion of Mr. John Fredericks at Fidelity National Bank. He knows of my interest in a career in video production, and given your position at XYZ Video Production, Inc., thought you might be able to help me gain a better understanding of this specialized field and the career opportunities it presents.

While I am majoring in communications, I know I need to speak with professionals such as yourself to learn how to apply my studies to a work environment. If you could spare a half hour to meet with me, I'm certain I would be able to get enough information about this specialty to give me the direction I need.

I'll call your office next week in the hope that we can schedule a meeting.

Send a copy of this letter to Mr. Fredericks at the bank—it will refresh his memory should Ms. Jones call to inquire about you. Next step: the follow-up phone call. After you get Ms. Jones' secretary on the line, it will, with luck, go something like this:

"Hello, I'm Paul Smith. I'm calling in reference to a letter I wrote to Ms. Jones requesting an appointment."

"Oh, yes. Ms. Jones can see you on June 23rd. Will 10 A.M. be satisfactory?"

"That's fine. I'll be there."

Well, the appointed day arrives. Well-scrubbed and dressed in your best (and most conservative) suit, you are ushered into Ms. Jones' office. She offers you coffee (you decline) and says that it is okay to light up if you wish to smoke (you decline). The conversation might go something like this:

You: "Thank you for seeing me, Ms. Jones. I know you are busy and appreciate your taking the time to talk with me."

You: "As I stated in my letter, my interest in video production is very real, but I'm having trouble seeing how all of my studies will adapt to the work environment. I think I'll be much better prepared to evaluate future job offers if I can learn more about your experiences. May I ask you a few questions about XYZ?"

Jones: "Well it's my pleasure since you come so highly recommended. I'm always pleased to meet someone interested in this field."

Jones: "Fire away, Paul".

Ms. Jones relaxes. She realizes this is a knowledge hunt you are on, not a thinly-veiled job interview. Your approach has kept her off the spot—she doesn't have to be concerned with making a hiring decision. You've already gotten high marks for not putting her on the defensive.

You: "I have a few specific questions I'd like to ask. First, at a company such as yours, where does an entry-level person start?"

Jones: "In this company, you would be assigned to an experienced video producer to work as that person's assistant for the first month of your employment. This gives you a chance to see the way we work and to become comfortable with our facilities and equipment. After that, if you had progressed well, you may receive your own projects to work on."

You: "Where and how fast does someone progress after that?"

Jones: "Obviously, that depends on the person, but given the proper aptitude and ability, that person would simply get more responsibilities to handle. How well you do all along the way will determine how far and how fast you progress."

You: "What is the work environment like—is it pretty hectic?"

Jones: "We try to keep the work load at an even keel. The comfort of our workers is of prime importance to us. Excessive turnover is costly, you know. But this is an exciting business, and things change sometimes minute-to-minute. It's not a profession for the faint-hearted!"

You: "If I may shift to another area, I'd be interested in your opinion about film and video careers in general and what you see as the most likely areas of opportunity in the foreseeable future. Do you think this is a growth career area?"

Jones: "Well, judging by the hiring record of our company, I think you'll find it's an area worth making a commitment to. At the entry level, we've hired a number of new people in the past three or four years. There always seems to be opportunities, though it's gotten far more competitive."

You: "Do you think someone with my qualifications and background could get started in video production? Perhaps a look at my resume would be helpful to you." *(Give it to Ms. Jones.)*

Jones: "Your course work looks appropriate. I especially like the internships you've held every summer. I think you have a real chance to break into this field. I don't think we're hiring right now, but I know a couple of companies that are looking for bright young people with qualifications like yours. Let me give you a couple of phone numbers." *(Write down names and phone numbers.)*

You: "You have been very generous with your time, but I can see from those flashing buttons on your phone that you have other things to do. Thank you again for taking the time to talk with me."

Jones: "You're welcome."

After the Interview

The next step should be obvious: **Two** thank-you letters are required, one to Ms. Jones, the second to Mr. Fredericks. Get them both out immediately. (And see the chapter on writing letters if you need help writing them.)

Keeping Track of the Interview Trail

Let's talk about record keeping again. If your networking works the way it's supposed to, this was only the first of many such interviews. Experts have estimated that the average person could develop a contact list of 250 people. Even if we limit your initial list to only 100, if each of them gave you one referral, your list would suddenly have 200 names. Presuming that it will not be necessary or helpful to see all of them, it's certainly possible that such a list could lead to 100 informational and/or job interviews! Unless you keep accurate records, by the time you're on No. 50, you won't even remember the first dozen!

So get the results of each interview down on paper. Use whatever format with which you're comfortable. You should create some kind of file, folder, or note card that is an "Interview Recap Record." If you have access to a personal computer, take advantage of it. It will be much easier to keep your information stored in one place and well-organized. Your record should be set up and contain something like the following:

> *Name: XYZ Video Production, Inc.*
> *Address: 333 E. 54th St., Rochester, NY 10000*
> *Phone: (212) 555-4000*
> *Contact: Carol Jones*
> *Type of Business: Video production*
> *Referral Contact: Mr. Fredericks, Fidelity National Bank*
> *Date: April 23, 1994*

At this point, you should add a one- or two-paragraph summary of what you found out at the meeting. Since these comments are for your eyes only, you should be both objective and subjective. State the facts—what you found out in response to your specific questions—but include your impressions—your estimate of the opportunities for further discussions, your chances for future consideration for employment.

"I Was Just Calling to . . ."

Find any logical opportunity to stay in touch with Ms. Jones. You may, for example, let her know when you graduate and tell her your grade point average, carbon her in on any letters you write to Mr. Fredericks, even send a congratulatory note if her company's year-end financial results are positive or if you read something in the local paper about her company. This type of follow up has the all-important effect of keeping you and your name in the forefront of others' minds. Out of sight *is* out of mind. No matter how talented you may be or how good an impression you made, you'll have to work hard to "stay visible."

There Are Rules, Just Like Any Game

It should already be obvious that the networking process is not only effective, but also quite deliberate in its objectives. There are two specific groups of people you must attempt to target: those who can give you information about an industry or career area and those who are potential employers. The line between these groups may often blur. Don't be concerned—you'll soon learn when (and how) to shift the focus from interviewer to interviewee.

To simplify this process, follow a single rule: Show interest in the field or job area under discussion, but wait to be asked about actually working for that company. During your informational interviews, you will be surprised at the number of times the person you're interviewing turns to you and asks, "Would you be interested in . . . ?" Consider carefully what's being asked and, if you *would* be interested in the position under discussion, make your feelings known.

If the Process Scares You

Some of you will undoubtedly be hesitant about, even fear, the networking process. It is not an unusual response—it is very human to want to accomplish things "on your own," without anyone's help. Understandable and commendable as such independence might seem, it is, in reality, an impediment if it limits your involvement in this important process. Networking has such universal application because **there is no other effective way to bridge the gap between job applicant and job.** Employers are grateful for its existence. You should be, too.

Whether you are a first-time applicant or reentering the work force now that the children are grown, the networking process will more than likely be your point of entry. Sending out mass mailings of your resume and answering the help wanted ads

Why Should You Network?

- To unearth current information about the industry, company, and pertinent job functions. Remember: Your knowledge and understanding of broad industry trends, financial health, hiring opportunities, and the competitive picture are key.
- To investigate each company's hiring policies—who makes the decisions, who the key players are (personnel, staff managers), whether there's a hiring season, whether they prefer applicants going direct or through recruiters, etc.
- To sell yourself—discuss your interests and research activities—and leave your calling card, your resume.
- To seek out advice on refining your job search process.
- To obtain the names of other persons (referrals) who can give you additional information on where the jobs are and what the market conditions are like.
- To develop a list of follow-up activities that will keep you visible to key contacts.

may well be less personal (and, therefore, "easier") approaches, but they will also be far less effective. The natural selection process of the networking phenomenon is your assurance that water does indeed seek its own level—you will be matched up with companies and job opportunities in which there is a mutual fit.

Six Good Reasons to Network

Many people fear the networking process because they think they are "bothering" others with their own selfish demands. Nonsense! There are good reasons—six of them, at least—why the people on your networking list will be happy to help you:

1. **Some day you will get to return the favor.** An ace insurance salesman built a successful business by offering low-cost coverage to first-year medical students. Ten years later, these now-successful practitioners remembered the company (and person) that helped them when they were just getting started. He gets new referrals every day.

2. **They, too, are seeking information.** An employer who has been out of school for several years might be interested in what the latest developments in the classroom are. He or she may be hoping to learn as much from you as you are from them, so be forthcoming in offering information. This desire for new information may be the reason he or she agreed to see you in the first place.

3. **Internal politics.** Some people will see you simply to make themselves appear powerful, implying to others in their organization that they have the authority to hire (they may or may not), an envied prerogative.

4. **They're "saving for a rainy day".** Executives know that it never hurts to look and that maintaining a backlog of qualified candidates is a big asset when the floodgates open and supervisors are forced to hire quickly.

5. **They're just plain nice.** Some people will see you simply because they feel it's the decent thing to do or because they just can't say "no."

6. **They are looking themselves.** Some people will see you because they are anxious to do a friend (whoever referred you) a favor. Or because they have another friend seeking new talent, in which case you represent a referral they can make (part of their own continuing network process). You see, networking never does stop—it helps them and it helps you.

Before you proceed to the next chapter, begin making your contact list. You may wish to keep a separate sheet of paper or note card on each person (especially the dozen or so you think are most important), even a separate telephone list to make your communications easier and more efficient. However you set up your list, be sure to keep it up to date—it won't be long before you'll be calling each and every name on the list.

Preparing Your Resume

Your resume is a one-page summary of you—your education, skills, employment experience, and career objective(s). It is not a biography, but a "quick and dirty" way to identify and describe you to potential employers. Most importantly, its real purpose is to sell you to the company you want to work for. It must set you apart from all the other applicants (those competitors) out there.

So, as you sit down to formulate your resume, remember you're trying to present the pertinent information in a format and manner that will convince an executive to grant you an interview, the prelude to any job offer. All resumes must follow two basic rules—excellent visual presentation and honesty—but it's important to realize that different career markets require different resumes. The resume you are compiling for your career in film and video is different than one you would prepare for a finance career. As more and more resume "training" services become available, employers are becoming increasingly choosy about the resumes they receive. They expect to view a professional presentation, one that sets a candidate apart from the crowd. Your resume has to be perfect and it has to be specialized—clearly demonstrating the relationship between your qualifications and the job you are applying for.

An Overview of Resume Preparation

- **Know what you're doing**—your resume is a personal billboard of accomplishments. It must communicate your worth to a prospective employer in specific terms.
- **Your language should be action-oriented,** full of "doing"-type words. And less is better than more—be concise and direct. Don't worry about using complete sentences.

- **Be persuasive.** In those sections that allow you the freedom to do so, don't hesitate to communicate your worth in the strongest language. This does not mean a numbing list of self-congratulatory superlatives; it does mean truthful claims about your abilities and the evidence (educational, experiential) that supports them.

- **Don't be cheap or gaudy.** Don't hesitate to spend the few extra dollars necessary to present a professional-looking resume. Do avoid outlandish (and generally ineffective) gimmicks like oversized or brightly-colored paper.

- **Find an editor.** Every good writer needs one, and you are writing your resume. At the very least, it will offer you a second set of eyes proofreading for embarrassing typos. But if you are fortunate enough to have a professional in the field—a recruiter or personnel executive—critique a draft, grab the opportunity and be immensely grateful.

- **If you're the next Michelangelo,** so multitalented that you can easily qualify for jobs in different career areas, don't hesitate to prepare two or more completely different resumes. This will enable you to change the emphasis on your education and skills according to the specific career objective on each resume, a necessary alteration that will correctly target each one.

- **Choose the proper format.** There are only three we recommend—chronological, functional, and targeted format—and it's important you use the one that's right for you.

Considerations in the Electronic Age

Like most other areas of everyday life, computers have left their mark in the resume business. There are the obvious changes—the increased number of personal computers has made it easier to produce a professional-looking resume at home—and the not so obvious changes, such as the development of resume databases.

There are two kinds of resume databases: 1) An internal file maintained by a large corporation to keep track of the flood of resumes it gets each day (*U.S. News and World Report* stated that Fortune 50 companies receive more than 1,000 unsolicited resumes a day and that four out of every five are thrown away after a quick review); 2) Commercial databases that solicit resumes from job-seekers around the United States and make them available to corporations, who pay a fee to search the database.

Internal Databases Mean Some of the Old Rules Don't Apply

The internal databases maintained by large companies are changing some of the time-honored traditions of resume preparation. In the past, it was acceptable, even desirable, to use italic type and other eye-catching formats to make a resume more visually appealing. Not so today. Most of the companies that have a database enter resumes into it by using an optical scanner that reads the resume character by character and automatically enters it into the database. While these scanners are becoming more and more sophisticated, there are still significant limits as to what they can recognize and interpret.

What does this mean to you? It means that in addition to the normal screening process that all resumes go through, there is now one more screening step that determines if the scanner will be able to read your resume. If it can't, chances are your resume is going to be one of the four that is thrown away, instead of the one that is kept. To enhance the chances of your resume making it past this scanner test, here are some simple guidelines you can follow:

- Use larger typefaces (nothing smaller than 12 point), and avoid all but the most basic typefaces. Among the most common are Times Roman and Helvetica.

- No italics or underlining, and definitely no graphic images or boxes.

- Do not send copies. Either print a fresh copy out on your own printer, or take the resume to a print shop and have it professionally copied onto high-quality paper. Avoid dot matrix printers.

- Use 8 1/2 x 11 paper, unfolded. Any words that end up in a crease will not be scannable.

- Use only white or beige paper. Any other color will lessen the contrast between the paper and the letters and make it harder for the scanner to read.

- Use only a single column format. Scanners read from right to left on a page, so two- or three-column formats lead to nonsensical information when the document is scanned.

- While it is still appropriate to use action words to detail your accomplishments (initiated, planned, implemented, etc.), it is also important to include precise technical terms whenever possible as well. That's because databases are searched by key words, and only resumes that match those key words will be looked at. For example, if a publishing company was seeking someone who was experienced in a desktop publishing, they might search the database for all occurrences of "PageMaker" or "Ventura," two common desktop publishing software packages. If your resume only said "Successfully implemented and oversaw in-house desktop publishing program," it would be overlooked, and you wouldn't get the job!

National Databases: Spreading Your Good Name Around

Commercial resume databases are also having an impact on the job search process in the 1990s, so much so that anyone about to enter the job market should seriously consider utilizing one of these services.

Most of these new services work this way: Job-seekers send the database company a copy of their resume, or they fill out a lengthy application provided by the company. The information is then loaded into the company's computer, along with hundreds of other resumes from other job-seekers. The cost of this listing is usually nominal—$20 to $50 for a six- to 12-month listing. Some colleges operate systems for their graduates that are free of charge, so check with your placement office before utilizing a commercial service.

Once in the system, the resumes are available for viewing by corporate clients who have openings to fill. This is where the database companies really make their money—depending on the skill-level of the listees and the professions covered, companies can pay thousands of dollars for annual subscriptions to the service or for custom searches of the database.

Worried that your current employer might just pull up *your* resume when it goes searching for new employees? No need to be—most services allow listees to designate companies that their resume should not be released to, thus allowing you to conduct a job search with the peace of mind that your boss won't find out!

One warning about these services—most of them are new, so do as much research as you can before paying to have your resume listed. If you hear about a database you think you might want to be listed in, call the company and ask some questions:

- How long have they been in business?
- What has their placement rate been?
- What fields do they specialize in? (In other words, will the right people even *see* your resume?)
- Can you block certain companies from seeing your resume?
- How many other resumes are listed in the database? How many in your specialty?
- Is your experience level similar to that of other listees in the database?

The right answers to these questions should let you know if you have found the right database for you.

To help you locate these resume databases, we have listed many of them in the **Career Resources** chapter of this book.

Headshots—The Performer's Business Card

To have a legitimate chance at success, a performer needs some sort of calling card—a way to introduce oneself to casting directors, agents, and directors. Headshots are the essential tool of the trade to accomplish this. A headshot is an 8 x 10 black and white photograph that shows you looking your best, but more importantly, like yourself. It must reflect what you will actually look like when walking through an agent's door. Headshots are considered to be an actor's business card—they can be mailed out with resumes or given out at auditions. For an inexperienced performer, a headshot is sometimes the only way into an agent's door. A good headshot may not make your career, but the wrong one can surely break it. Before paying the costly price of getting headshots taken, there are several steps you should take.

1. Find a *good* photographer. Photographers charge hundreds of dollars for a session and it costs hundreds of dollars for reproductions. You need to shop around, ask others in the industry, and make appointments with photographers to see their work.

2. Find a photographer you feel comfortable with. In order to get a headshot that represents the *real* you, a good rapport with the photographer is crucial.

3. Bring your favorite clothing—something you feel confident in. This will show in your face. Never wear pale clothing or anything too gaudy, and make sure to bring three or four different outfits.

4. Don't wear too much make-up. For an additional charge, some photographers can do the make-up for you or bring in a make-up artist.

5. Wear your hair just as you do every day. If you have problem hair, bring in a hairdresser.

6. Do the shoot at the time of day at which you normally look your best. You should look fresh and awake. You should consider eating before the shoot to energize yourself.

7. Know the personality you want the pictures to convey. Match your clothing, your expression, and your hairstyle to the appropriate image or role you are after. At first glance, the viewer should know if you are going for a glamorous look, a comical look, or a commercial look.

8. Practice, practice, practice. Get to know your mirror—and show your mirror your best expressions.

The Records You Need

Well, now that you've heard all the do's and don't's and rules about preparing a resume, it's time to put those rules to work. The resume-writing process begins with the assembly and organization of all the personal, educational, and employment data from which you will choose the pieces that actually end up on paper. If this information is properly organized, writing your resume will be a relatively easy task, essentially a simple process of just shifting data from a set of the worksheets to another, to your actual resume. At the end of this chapter, you'll find all the forms you need to prepare your resume, including worksheets, fill-in-the-blanks resume forms, and sample resumes.

As you will soon see, there is a great deal of information you'll need to keep track of. In order to avoid a fevered search for important information, take the time right now to designate a single location in which to store all your records. My recommendation is either a filing cabinet or an expandable pocket portfolio. The latter is less expensive, yet it will still enable you to sort your records into an unlimited number of more-manageable categories.

Losing important report cards, citations, letters, etc., is easy to do if your life's history is scattered throughout your room or, even worse, your house! While copies of many of these items may be obtainable, why put yourself through all that extra work? Making good organization a habit will ensure that all the records you need to prepare your resume will be right where you need them when you need them.

For each of the categories summarized below, designate a separate file folder in which pertinent records can be kept. Your own notes are important, but keeping actual report cards, award citations, letters, etc. is even more so. Here's what your record-keeping system should include:

Transcripts (Including GPA and Class Rank Information)

Transcripts are your school's official record of your academic history, usually available, on request, from your high school's guidance office or college registrar's office. Your college may charge you for copies and "on request" doesn't mean "whenever you want"—you may have to wait some time for your request to be processed (so **don't** wait until the last minute!).

Your school-calculated GPA (Grade Point Average) is on the transcript. Most schools calculate this by multiplying the credit hours assigned to each course times a numerical grade equivalent (e.g., "A" = 4.0, "B" = 3.0, etc.), then dividing by total credits/courses taken. Class rank is simply a listing of GPAs, from highest to lowest.

Employment Records

Details on every part-time or full-time job you've held, including:
- Each employer's name, address, and telephone number
- Name of supervisor
- Exact dates worked
- Approximate numbers of hours worked per week
- Specific duties and responsibilities
- Specific skills utilized and developed
- Accomplishments and honors
- Copies of awards and letters of recommendation

Volunteer Activities

Just because you weren't paid for a specific job—stuffing envelopes for the local Democratic candidate, running a car wash to raise money for the homeless, manning a drug hotline—doesn't mean that it wasn't significant or that you shouldn't include it on your resume.

So keep the same detailed notes on these volunteer activities as you have on the jobs you've held:
- Each organization's name, address, and telephone number
- Name of supervisor
- Exact dates worked
- Approximate numbers of hours worked per week
- Specific duties and responsibilities
- Specific skills utilized
- Accomplishments and honors
- Copies of awards and letters of recommendation

Extracurricular Activities

List all sports, clubs, or other activities in which you've participated, either inside or outside school. For each, you should include:
- Name of activity/club/group
- Office(s) held
- Purpose of club/activity
- Specific duties/responsibilities

• Achievements, accomplishments, and awards

If you were a long-standing member of a group or club, also include the dates that you were a member. This could demonstrate a high-level of commitment that could be used as a selling point.

Honors and Awards

Even if some of these honors are previously listed, specific data on every honor or award you receive should be kept, including, of course, the award itself! Keep the following information in your awards folder:

• Award name

• Date and from whom received

• What it was for

• Any pertinent details

Military Records

Complete military history, if pertinent, including:

• Dates of service

• Final rank awarded

• Duties and responsibilities

• All citations and awards

• Details on specific training and/or special schooling

• Skills developed

• Specific accomplishments

At the end of this chapter are seven **Data Input Sheets**. The first five cover employment, volunteer work, education, activities, and awards and are essential to any resume. The last two—covering military service and language skills—are important if, of course, they apply to you. I've only included one copy of each but, if you need to, you can copy the forms you need or simply write up your own using these as models.

Here are some pointers on how to fill out these all-important Data Sheets:

Employment Data Input Sheet: You will need to record the basic information—employer's name, address, and phone number; dates of employment; and supervisor's name—for your own files anyway. It may be an important addition to your networking list and will be necessary should you be asked to supply a reference list.

Duties should be a series of brief action statements describing what you did on this job. For example, if you worked as a hostess in a restaurant, this section might read: "Responsible for the delivery of 250 meals at dinner time and the supervision of 20 waiters and busboys. Coordinated reservations. Responsible for check and payment verification."

Skills should enumerate specific capabilities either necessary for the job or developed through it.

If you achieved *specific results*—e.g., "developed new filing system," "collected over $5,000 in previously-assumed bad debt," "instituted award-winning art program," etc.—or *received any award, citation, or other honor*—"named Employee of the Month three times," "received Mayor's Citation for Innovation," etc.—make sure you list these.

Prepare one employment data sheet for each of the last three positions you have held; this is a basic guideline, but you can include more if relevant. Do not include sheets for short-term jobs (i.e., those that lasted one month or less).

Volunteer Work Data Input Sheet: Treat any volunteer work, no matter how basic or short (one day counts!), as if it were a job and record the same information. In both cases, it is especially important to note specific duties and responsibilities, skills required or developed and any accomplishments or achievements you can point to as evidence of your success.

Educational Data Input Sheet: If you're in college, omit details on high school. If you're a graduate student, list details on both graduate and undergraduate course work. If you have not yet graduated, list your anticipated date of graduation. If more than a year away, indicate the numbers of credits earned through the most recent semester to be completed.

Activities Data Input Sheet: List your participation in the Student Government, Winter Carnival Committee, Math Club, Ski Patrol, etc., plus sports teams and/or any participation in community or church groups. Make sure you indicate if you were elected to any positions in clubs, groups, or on teams.

Awards and Honors Data Input Sheet: List awards and honors from your school (prestigious high school awards can still be included here, even if you're in graduate school), community groups, church groups, clubs, etc.

Military Service Data Input Sheet: Many useful skills are learned in the armed forces. A military stint often hastens the maturation process, making you a more attractive candidate. So if you have served in the military, make sure you include details in your resume. Again, include any computer skills you gained while in the service.

Language Data Input Sheet: An extremely important section for those of you with a real proficiency in a second language. And do make sure you have at least conversational fluency in the language(s) you list. One year of college French doesn't count, but if you've studied abroad, you probably are fluent or proficient. Such a talent could be invaluable, especially in today's increasingly international business climate.

While you should use the Data Input Sheets to summarize all of the data you have collected, do not throw away any of the specific information—report cards, transcripts, citations, etc.—just because it is recorded on these sheets. Keep all records in your files; you'll never know when you'll need them again!

Creating Your First Resume

There are many options that you can include or leave out. In general, we suggest you always include the following data:

1. Your name, address, and telephone number
2. Pertinent educational history (grades, class rank, activities, etc.) Follow the grade point "rule of thumb"—mention it only if it is above 3.0.

3. Pertinent work history

4. Academic honors

5. Memberships in organizations

6. Military service history (if applicable)

You have the option of including the following:

1. Your career objective

2. Personal data

3. Hobbies

4. Summary of qualifications

5. Feelings about travel and relocation (Include this if you know in advance that the job you are applying for requires it. Oftentimes, for future promotion, job seekers **must** be willing to relocate.

6. Photographs or illustrations (see the section on headshots)

And you should never include the following:

1. Why you left past jobs

2. References

3. Salary history or present salary objectives/requirements (if salary history is specifically requested in an ad, it may be included in your cover letter)

Special note: There is definitely a school of thought that discourages any mention of personal data—marital status, health, etc.—on a resume. While I am not vehemently opposed to including such information, I am not convinced it is particularly necessary, either.

As far as hobbies go, I would only include such information if it were in some way pertinent to the job/career you're targeting, or if it shows how well-rounded you are. Your love of reading is pertinent if, for example, you are applying for a part-time job at a library. But including details on the joys of "hiking, long walks with my dog, and Isaac Asimov short stories" is nothing but filler and should be left out.

Maximizing Form and Substance

Your resume should be limited to a single page if possible. A two-page resume should be used **only** if you have an extensive work background related to a future goal. When you're laying out the resume, try to leave a reasonable amount of "white space"—generous margins all around and spacing between entries. It should be typed or printed (not Xeroxed) on 8 1/2" x 11" white, cream, or ivory stock. The ink should be black. Don't scrimp on the paper quality—use the best bond you can afford. And since printing 100 or even 200 copies will cost only a little more than 50, if you do decide to print your resume, *over*estimate your needs and opt for the highest quantity you think you may need. Prices at various "quick print" shops are not exorbitant and the quality look printing affords will leave the impression you want.

Use Power Words for Impact

Be brief. Use phrases rather than complete sentences. Your resume is a summary of your talents, not a term paper. Choose your words carefully and use "power words" whenever possible. "Organized" is more powerful than "put together;" "supervised" better than "oversaw;" "formulated" better than "thought up." Strong words like these can make the most mundane clerical work sound like a series of responsible, professional positions. And, of course, they will tend to make your resume stand out. Here's a starter list of words that you may want to use in your resume:

accomplished	contributed	instructed	recruited
achieved	coordinated	introduced	regulated
acted	critiqued	invented	remodeled
adapted	defined	issued	renovated
addressed	delegated	launched	reorganized
administered	delivered	learned	researched
advised	demonstrated	lectured	restored
allocated	designed	led	reviewed
analyzed	determined	litigated	revised
applied	developed	lobbied	rewrote
approved	devised	made	saved
arranged	directed	managed	scheduled
assembled	discovered	marketed	selected
assessed	drafted	mediated	served
assigned	edited	negotiated	sold
assisted	established	obtained	solved
attained	estimated	operated	started
budgeted	evaluated	organized	streamlined
built	executed	overhauled	studied
calculated	expanded	oversaw	suggested
chaired	fixed	participated	supervised
changed	forecast	planned	systematized
classified	formulated	prepared	taught
collected	gathered	presented	tested
communicated	gave	presided	trained
compiled	generated	produced	updated
completed	guided	programmed	upgraded
composed	implemented	promoted	utilized
computed	improved	proposed	won
conceptualized	initiated	publicized	wrote
conducted	installed	ran	
consolidated	instituted	recommended	

Choose the Right Format

There is not much mystery here—your background will generally lead you to the right format. For an entry-level job applicant with limited work experience, the chronological format, which organizes your educational and employment history by date (most recent first) is the obvious choice. For older or more experienced applicants, the functional—which emphasizes the duties and responsibilities of all your jobs over the course of your career, may be more suitable. If you are applying for a specific position in one field, the targeted format is for you. While I have tended to emphasize the chronological format in this chapter, one of the other two may well be the right one for you.

A List of Do's and Don't's

In case we didn't stress them enough, here are some rules to follow:

- **Do** be brief and to the point—two pages if absolutely necessary, one page if at all possible. Never longer!
- **Don't** be fancy. Multicolored paper and all-italic type won't impress employers, just make your resume harder to read (and easier to discard). Use plain white or ivory paper, black ink, and an easy-to-read standard typeface.
- **Do** forget rules about sentences. Say what you need to say in the fewest words possible; use phrases, not drawn-out sentences.
- **Do** stick to the facts. Don't talk about your dog, vacation, etc.
- **Don't** ever send a resume blind. A cover letter should always accompany a resume and that letter should always be directed to a specific person.
- **Don't** have any typos. Your resume must be perfect—proofread everything as many times as necessary to catch any misspellings, grammatical errors, strange hyphenations, or typos.
- **Do** use the spell check feature on your personal computer to find errors, and also try reading the resume backwards—you'll be surprised at how errors jump out at you when you do this. Finally, have a friend proof your resume.
- **Do** use your resume as your sales tool. It is, in many cases, as close to you as an employer will ever get. Make sure it includes the information necessary to sell yourself the way you want to be sold!
- **Do** spend the money for good printing. Soiled, tattered, or poorly reproduced copies speak poorly of your own self-image. Spend the money and take the time to make sure your resume is the best presentation you've ever made.
- **Do** help the reader, by organizing your resume in a clear-cut manner so key points are easily gleaned.
- **Don't** have a cluttered resume. Leave plenty of white space, especially around headings and all four margins.
- **Do** use bullets, asterisks, or other symbols as "stop signs" that the reader's eye will be naturally drawn to.

On the following pages, I've included a "fill-in-the-blanks" resume form so you can construct your own resume right away, plus one example each of a chronological, functional, and targeted resume.

EMPLOYMENT DATA INPUT SHEET

Employer name: _____

Address: _____

Phone: _____ Dates of employment: _____

Hours per week: _____ Salary/Pay: _____

Supervisor's name and title: _____

Duties: _____

_____

_____

Skills utilized: _____

_____

_____

_____

Accomplishments/Honors/Awards: _____

_____

_____

_____

Other important information: _____

_____

_____

_____

VOLUNTEER WORK DATA INPUT SHEET

Organization name:_____

Address: _____

Phone: _____ Dates of activity: _____

Hours per week: _____

Supervisor's name and title: _____

Duties: _____

_____

_____

Skills utilized: _____

_____

_____

_____

Accomplishments/Honors/Awards: _____

_____

_____

_____

Other important information: _____

_____

_____

_____

_____

HIGH SCHOOL DATA INPUT SHEET

School name: _____

Address: _____

Phone: _____ Years attended: _____

Major studies: _____

GPA/Class rank: _____

Honors: _____

Important courses: _____

_____

_____

_____

OTHER SCHOOL DATA INPUT SHEET

School name: _____

Address: _____

Phone: _____ Years attended: _____

Major studies: _____

GPA/Class rank: _____

Honors: _____

Important courses _____

_____

_____

_____

_____

COLLEGE DATA INPUT SHEET

College: _____

Address: _____

Phone: _____ Years attended: _____

Degrees earned: _____ Major: _____ Minor: _____

Honors: _____

Important courses: _____

_____

_____

_____

_____

GRADUATE SCHOOL DATA INPUT SHEET

College: _____

Address: _____

Phone: _____ Years attended: _____

Degrees earned: _____ Major: _____ Minor: _____

Honors: _____

Important courses: _____

_____

_____

_____

_____

MILITARY SERVICE DATA INPUT SHEET

Branch: _____

Rank (at discharge): _____

Dates of service: _____

Duties and responsibilities: _____

_____

_____

_____

Special training and/or school attended: _____

_____

_____

_____

Citations or awards: _____

_____

_____

_____

Specific accomplishments: _____

_____

_____

_____

_____

_____

ACTIVITIES DATA INPUT SHEET

Club/activity: _____Office(s) held: _____

Description of participation: _____

_____

_____

Duties/responsibilities: _____

_____

Club/activity: _____Office(s) held: _____

Description of participation: _____

_____

_____

Duties/responsibilities: _____

_____

Club/activity: _____Office(s) held: _____

Description of participation: _____

_____

_____

Duties/responsibilities: _____

_____

_____

_____

AWARDS AND HONORS DATA INPUT SHEET

Name of Award or Citation: _____

From Whom Received: _____ Date: _____

Significance: _____

_____

Other pertinent information: _____

_____

Name of Award or Citation: _____

From Whom Received: _____ Date: _____

Significance: _____

_____

Other pertinent information: _____

_____

Name of Award or Citation: _____

From Whom Received: _____ Date: _____

Significance: _____

_____

Other pertinent information: _____

_____

LANGUAGE DATA INPUT SHEET

Language: _____

___Read   ___Write   ___Converse

Background (number of years studied, travel, etc.) _____

_____

_____

_____

Language: _____

___Read   ___Write   ___Converse

Background (number of years studied, travel, etc.) _____

_____

_____

_____

Language: _____

___Read   ___Write   ___Converse

Background (number of years studied, travel, etc.) _____

_____

_____

_____

FILL-IN-THE-BLANKS RESUME OUTLINE

Name: _____

Address: _____

City, state, ZIP Code: _____

Telephone number: _____

OBJECTIVE: _____

_____

_____

_____

_____

SUMMARY OF QUALIFICATIONS: _____

_____

_____

_____

EDUCATION

GRADUATE SCHOOL: _____

Address: _____

City, state, ZIP Code: _____

Expected graduation date:_____Grade Point Average: _____

Degree earned (expected):_____Class Rank: _____

Important classes, especially those related to your career: _____

_____

_____

_____

_____

_____

_____

_____

_____

COLLEGE: _____

Address: _____

City, state, ZIP Code: _____

Expected graduation date:_____Grade Point Average: _____

Class rank:_____Major:_____Minor:_____

Important classes, especially those related to your career: _____

_____

_____

_____

_____

_____

_____

_____

_____

_____

_____

HIGH SCHOOL: _____

Address: _____

City, state, ZIP Code: _____

Expected graduation date: _____ Grade Point Average: _____

Class rank: _____

Important classes, especially those related to your career: _____

_____

_____

_____

_____

_____

_____

_____

_____

HOBBIES AND OTHER INTERESTS (OPTIONAL) _____

_____

_____

_____

_____

_____

_____

_____

_____

_____

EXTRACURRICULAR ACTIVITIES (Activity name, dates participated, duties and responsibilities, offices held, accomplishments): _____

_____

_____

_____

_____

_____

_____

_____

_____

AWARDS AND HONORS (Award name, from whom and date received, significance of the award and any other pertinent details): _____

_____

_____

_____

_____

_____

_____

_____

_____

_____

_____

_____

WORK EXPERIENCE. Include job title, name of business, address and telephone number, dates of employment, supervisor's name and title, your major responsibilities, accomplishments, and any awards won. Include volunteer experience in this category. List your experiences with the most recent dates first, even if you later decide not to use a chronological format.

_____

_____

_____

_____

_____

_____

_____

_____

_____

_____

_____

_____

_____

_____

_____

_____

_____

REFERENCES. Though you should *not* include references in your resume, you do need to prepare a separate list of at least three people who know you fairly well and will recommend you highly to prospective employers. For each, include job title, company name, address, and telephone number. Before you include anyone on this list, make sure you have their permission to use their name as a reference and confirm what they intend to say about you to a potential employer.

1. _____

_____

_____

2. _____

_____

_____

3. _____

_____

_____

4. _____

_____

_____

5. _____

_____

_____

JASON MACOMBS

Local
457 Oak Drive
Chicago, Il 60018
(708) 453-8794

Permanent
483 Abbott Lane
Kansas City, MO
(712) 947-2957

EDUCATION

Bachelor of Arts
Concentration: **Illustration/Animation**
School of Art   Chicago, Il
May, 1995   GPA: 3.9   Summa Cum Laude

Associate Degree in Art
Pallotine Community College   Kansas City, MO
June, 1993   GPA: 3.6   Cum Laude

INTERNSHIPS
6/94 - 8/94

Kansas City Workshop   Kansas City, MO
Created films for local community public access channel.

6/93 - 8/93

Allied Film and Video   Rockhurst, MO
Learned techniques of animation and video production.

EMPLOYMENT
9/94 - Present
9/93 - 5/94
9/92 - 5/93

School of Art Admissions Department   Chicago, Il
Assist staff with clerical work and computer input.
Represent college during Admissions outreach events and
on-campus tours. Create and layout design for high school
outreach newsletter.

HONORS

• Dean's List
• Insignis Scholarship
• National Honor Society

AWARDS

• Scholastic Art Award Scholarship
• Kansas City Power and Light Cartooning Contest,
  1st Place

ACTIVITIES

• Free-lance Artist
• Water Aerobics, YWCA Instructor
• Intramural Soccer Team

PORTFOLIO

Furnished Upon Request

SHERINE SARATOGA

17354 Herman Drive   Albuquerque, NM 87105   (415) 002-3496

OBJECTIVE   Entry-level position in Video.
Special Area of Interest: **Corporate Training Area**

EDUCATION   University of New Mexico   Albuquerque, NM
Bachelor of Arts
Major: Film Production
May, 1995   GPA: 3.5
Honors: Cum Laude   Dean's List

Film Background
Orchestrated complete cable "spot" entitled: *How Do You Handle Stress?*
Filmed random shots of public reaction to questions/situations.
Edited film into thirty minute cable program.

Communications Ability
Interfaced with video, sound, editing departments.
Wrote effective script for video program.

Technical Expertise
Exposed to various facets of corporate video department.
Scheduler for cable programming.

**PROFESSIONAL
EXPERIENCE**

5/94 - 9/94	Oakland Cable Intern	Albuquerque, NM
9/93 - 12/93	Parke Davis Video Co-op	Albuquerque, NM
6/92 - 8/93	F & M Distributors Counter/Sales	Las Cruces, NM

HONORS/ACTIVITIES
Dean's List
Film Club, Secretary
Classic Film Enthusiast

VIDEO PORTFOLIO/REFERENCES
Furnished Upon Request

SAMPLE RESUME - TARGETED

ANDREW LEE
562 Luke Rd.
Ferndale, MI 48220
(313) 539-0021

ACTOR - VOICE OVER

Hair - Brown
Eyes - Hazel
Height - 5'7"

THEATRICAL EXPERIENCE

Agamenon	Chorus	The Athens Centre
Play It Again Sam	Allan	Holly Festival
Jack and the Beanstalk	Giant	Huron Valley Commun. Theatre
Snow White	Hunter	Children's Comedy Playhouse
One for the Road	Victor	University of Detroit Mercy
Murder Among Friends	Dewey	Flint Public Library
South Pacific	Billis	University of Detroit Mercy

COMMERCIAL VOICE OVER

WXYZ - TV	TV V.O.	Able Carpeting
Oakland County Cable	Spokesperson	PSA
MetroCable	Spokesperson	PSA

EDUCATION AND TRAINING

Bachelor of Arts in Theatre		University of Detroit Mercy
Classic Theatre Study Abroad	Arthur J. Willis	University of Detroit Mercy
Maria Yost Workshop (audit)	Maria Yost	The Actors Studio
On-Camera Training	Sandra Rogge	Performance Workshops
Voice Over	John Macon	Macon Productions

HOBBIES/SPECIAL INTERESTS
Singing, dancing, skiing, tennis, bicycling, hiking, rollerblading, and carpentry.

PORTFOLIO/REFERENCES
Available Upon Request

CHAPTER SEVENTEEN

Writing Better Letters

Stop for a moment and review your resume draft. It is undoubtedly (by now) a near-perfect document that instantly tells the reader the kind of job you want and why you are qualified. But does it say anything personal about you? Any amplification of your talents? Any words that are ideally "you?" Any hint of the kind of person who stands behind that resume?

If you've prepared it properly, the answers should be a series of ringing "no's"—your resume should be a mere sketch of your life, a bare-bones summary of your skills, education, and experience.

To the general we must add the specific. That's what your letters must accomplish—adding the lines, colors, and shading that will help fill out your self-portrait. This chapter will cover the kinds of letters you will most often be called upon to prepare in your job search. There are essentially nine different types you will utilize again and again, based primarily on what each is trying to accomplish. One well-written example of each is included at the end of this chapter.

Answer these Questions

Before you put pencil to paper to compose any letter, there are five key questions you must ask yourself:

- **Why** are you writing it?
- To **Whom**?
- **What** are you trying to accomplish?
- **Which** lead will get the reader's attention?
- **How** do you organize the letter to best accomplish your objectives?

Why?

There should be a single, easily definable reason you are writing any letter. This reason will often dictate what and how you write—the tone and flavor of the letter—as well as what you include or leave out.

Have you been asked in an ad to amplify your qualifications for a job and provide a salary history and college transcripts? Then that (minimally) is your objective in writing. Limit yourself to following instructions and do a little personal selling—but very little. Including everything asked for and a simple, adequate cover letter is better than writing a "knock 'em, sock 'em" letter and omitting the one piece of information the ad specifically asked for.

If, however, you are on a networking search, the objective of your letter is to seek out contacts who will refer you for possible informational or job interviews. In this case, getting a name and address—a referral—is your stated purpose for writing. You have to be specific and ask for this action.

You will no doubt follow up with a phone call, but be certain the letter conveys what you are after. Being vague or oblique won't help you. You are after a definite yes or no when it comes to contact assistance. The recipient of your letter should know this. As they say in the world of selling, at some point you have to ask for the order.

Who?

Using the proper "tone" in a letter is as important as the content—you wouldn't write to the owner of the local meat market using the same words and style as you would employ in a letter to the director of personnel of a major company. Properly addressing the person or persons you are writing to is as important as what you say to them.

Always utilize the recipient's job title and level (correct title and spelling are a **must**). If you know what kind of person he or she is (based on your knowledge of the area of involvement) use that knowledge to your advantage as well. It also helps if you know his or her hiring clout, but even if you know the letter is going through a screening stage instead of to the actual person you need to contact, don't take the easy way out. You have to sell the person doing the screening just as convincingly as you would the actual contact, or else you might get passed over instead of passed along! Don't underestimate the power of the person doing the screening.

For example, it pays to sound technical with technical people—in other words, use the kinds of words and language which they use on the job. If you have had the opportunity to speak with them, it will be easy for you. If not, and you have formed some opinions as to their types then use these as the basis of the language you employ. The cardinal rule is to say it in words you think the recipient will be comfortable hearing, not in the words you might otherwise personally choose.

What?

What do you have to offer that company? What do you have to contribute to the job, process, or work situation that is unique and/or of particular benefit to the recipient of your letter.

For example, if you were applying for a sales position and recently ranked number one in a summer sales job, then conveying this benefit is logical and desirable. It is a factor you may have left off your resume. Even if it was listed in the skills/accomplishment section of the resume, you can underscore and call attention to it in your letter. Repetition, when it is properly focused, can be a good thing.

Which?

Of all the opening sentences you can compose, which will immediately get the reader's attention? If your opening sentence is dynamic, you are already 50 percent of the way to your end objective—having your entire letter read. Don't slide into it. Know the point you are trying to make and come right to it. One word of caution: your first sentence **must** make mention of what led you to write—was it an ad, someone at the company, a story you saw on television? Be sure to give this point of reference.

How?

While a good opening is essential, how do you organize your letter so that it is easy for the recipient to read in its entirety? This is a question of *flow*—the way the words and sentences naturally lead one to another, holding the reader's interest until he or she reaches your signature.

If you have your objective clearly in mind, this task is easier than it sounds: Simply convey your message(s) in a logical sequence. End your letter by stating what the next steps are—yours and/or the reader's.

One More Time

Pay attention to the small things. Neatness still counts. Have your letters typed. Spend a few extra dollars and have some personal stationery printed.

And most important, make certain that your correspondence goes out quickly. The general rule is to get a letter in the mail during the week in which the project comes to your attention or in which you have had some contact with the organization. I personally attempt to mail follow-up letters the same day as the contact; at worst, within 24 hours.

When to Write

- To answer an ad
- To prospect (many companies)
- To inquire about specific openings (single company)
- To obtain a referral
- To obtain an informational interview
- To obtain a job interview
- To say "thank you"
- To accept or reject a job offer
- To withdraw from consideration for a job

In some cases, the letter will accompany your resume; in others, it will need to stand alone. All of the above circumstances are described in the pages that follow. I have included at least one sample of each type of letter at the end of this chapter.

Answering an Ad

Your eye catches an ad in the Positions Available section of the Sunday paper for a production assistant. It tells you that the position is with a major film studio and that, though some experience would be desirable, it is not required. Well, you possess *those* skills. The ad asks that you send a letter and resume to a Post Office Box. No salary is indicated, no phone number given. You decide to reply.

Your purpose in writing—the objective (why?)—is to secure a job interview. Since no person is singled out for receipt of the ad, and since it is a large company, you assume it will be screened by Human Resources.

Adopt a professional, formal tone. You are answering a "blind" ad, so you have to play it safe. In your first sentence, refer to the ad, including the place and date of publication and the position outlined. (There is a chance that the company is running more than one ad on the same date and in the same paper, so you need to identify the one to which you are replying.) Tell the reader what (specifically) you have to offer that company. Include your resume, phone number, and the times it is easiest to reach you. Ask for the order—tell them you'd like to have an appointment.

Blanket Prospecting Letter

In June of this year you will graduate from a four-year college with a degree in television and film. You seek a position (internship or full-time employment) at a motion picture production company. You have decided to write to 20 top companies, sending each a copy of your resume. You don't know which, if any, have job openings.

Such blanket mailings are effective given two circumstances: 1) You must have an exemplary record and a resume that reflects it; and 2) You must send out a goodly number of packages, since the response rate to such mailings is very low.

A blanket mailing doesn't mean an impersonal one—you should always be writing to a specific executive. If you have a referral, send a personalized letter to that person. If not, do not simply mail a package to the Human Resources department; identify the department head and *then* send a personalized letter. And make sure you get on the phone and follow up each letter within about 10 days. Don't just sit back and wait for everyone to call you. They won't.

Just Inquiring

The inquiry letter is a step above the blanket prospecting letter; it's a "cold-calling" device with a twist. You have earmarked a company (and a person) as a possibility in your job search based on something you have read about them. Your general research tells you that it is a good place to work. Although you are not aware of any specific openings, you know that they employ entry-level personnel with your credentials.

While ostensibly inquiring about any openings, you are really just "referring yourself" to them in order to place your resume in front of the right person. This is what I would call a "why not?" attempt at securing a job interview. Its effectiveness depends on their actually having been in the news. This, after all, is your "excuse" for writing.

Networking

It's time to get out that folder marked "Contacts" and prepare a draft networking letter. The lead sentence should be very specific, referring immediately to the friend, colleague, etc. "who suggested I write you about..." Remember: Your objective is to secure an informational interview, pave the way for a job interview, and/or get referred to still other contacts.

This type of letter should not place the recipient in a position where a decision is necessary; rather, the request should be couched in terms of "career advice." The second paragraph can then inform the reader of your level of experience. Finally, be specific about seeking an appointment.

Unless you have been specifically asked by the referring person to do so, you will probably not be including a resume with such letters. So the letter itself must highlight your credentials, enabling the reader to gauge your relative level of experience. For entry-level personnel, education, of course, will be most important.

For an Informational Interview

Though the objectives of this letter are similar to those of the networking letter, they are not as personal. These are "knowledge quests" on your part and the recipient will most likely not be someone you have been referred to. The idea is to convince the reader of the sincerity of your research effort. Whatever selling you do, if you do any at all, will arise as a consequence of the meeting, not beforehand. A positive response to this type of request is in itself a good step forward. It is, after all, exposure, and amazing things can develop when people in authority agree to see you.

Thank-You Letters

Although it may not always seem so, manners do count in the job world. But what counts even more are the simple gestures that show you actually care—like writing a thank-you letter. A well-executed, timely thank-you note tells more about your personality than anything else you may have sent, and it also demonstrates excellent follow-through skills. It says something about the way you were brought up—whatever else your resume tells them, you are, at least, polite, courteous and thoughtful.

Thank-you letters may well become the beginning of an all-important dialogue that leads directly to a job. So be extra careful in composing them, and make certain that they are custom made for each occasion and person.

The following are the primary situations in which you will be called upon to write some variation of a thank-you letter:

1. After a job interview
2. After an informational interview
3. Accepting a job offer
4. Responding to rejection: While optional, such a letter is appropriate if you

have been among the finalists in a job search or were rejected due to limited experience. Remember: Some day you'll *have* enough experience; make the interviewer want to stay in touch.

5. Withdrawing from consideration: Used when you decide you are no longer interested in a particular position. (A variation is usable for declining an actual job offer.) Whatever the reason for writing such a letter, it's wise to do so and thus keep future lines of communication open.

10 E. 89th Street
New York, NY 10028
April 4, 1994

The *New York Times*
PO Box 7520
New York, NY 10128

Dear Sir or Madam:

This letter is in response to your advertisement for a production assistant that appeared in the March 24th issue of the *New York Times*.

I have the qualifications you are seeking. I graduated from American University with a BS in mass communications with a minor in film and video production.

I worked as a production intern for two summers at Raleigh Communications, Inc. and as a volunteer for the International Film Festival of America throughout North America. For the past year, I have been working in a production capacity at my local cable company. I am also a member of the National Film Production Association.

My resume is enclosed. I would like to have the opportunity to meet with you personally to discuss your requirements for the position. I can be reached at (212) 785-1225 between 8:00 a.m. and 5:00 p.m. and at (212) 785-4221 after 5:00 p.m. I look forward to hearing from you.

Sincerely,

Karen Weber

Kim Kerr
8 Robutuck Hwy.
Hammond, IN 54054
555-875-2392

April 4, 1994

Mr. Fred Jones
Personnel Director
Universal Pictures Corp.
Chicago, Illinois 91221

Dear Mr. Jones:

The name of Universal continually pops up in our classroom discussions of superb motion picture companies. Given my interest in motion picture production as a career, I've taken the liberty of enclosing my resume.

As you can see, I have just completed a very comprehensive educational program at Warren University, majoring in mass communications with a double minor in film production and broadcasting. Though my resume does not indicate it, I will be graduating in the top 10 percent of my class, with honors.

I will be in the Chicago area on April 20th and will call your office to see when it is convenient to arrange an appointment.

Sincerely yours,

Kim Kerr

42 7th Street
Ski City, VT 85722
April 4, 1994

Mr. Michael Maniaci
Personnel Director
Pinnacle Productions, Inc.
521 West Elm Street
Indianapolis, IN 83230

Dear Mr. Maniaci:

I just completed reading the article in the March issue of *Corporate Video World* on your company's record-breaking quarter. Congratulations!

Your innovative approach to recruiting minorities is of particular interest to me because of my background in video production and minority recruitment.

I am interested in learning more about your work as well as the possibilities of joining your company. My qualifications include:

- BS in broadcasting
- Research on minority recruitment
- Corporate Video Production Seminar participation (Univ. of Virginia)
- Reports preparation on corporate videos, job satisfaction, and minority recruitment

I will be in Connecticut during the week of April 18th and hope your schedule will permit us to meet briefly to discuss our mutual interests. I will call your office next week to see if such a meeting can be arranged.

I appreciate your consideration.

Sincerely yours,

Ronald W. Sommerville

Rochelle A. Starky
42 Bach St.,
Musical City, MO 20202
317-555-1515

April 4, 1994

Ms. Michelle Fleming
Personnel Director
Heights Productions, Inc.
42 Jenkins Avenue
Fulton, MO 23232

Dear Ms. Fleming:

Sam Kinney suggested I write you. I am interested in an editing position at a large film production company. Sam felt it would be mutually beneficial for us to meet and talk.

I have a BS from Musical City University in mass communications and an MFA in film and television production from the University of Kettering. While working on my postgraduate degree, I worked as a production intern with an independent film company making documentaries on the homeless in New York City.

I know from Sam how similar our backgrounds are—the same training, the same interests. And, of course, I am aware of how successful you have managed your career—three awards in four years!

As I begin my job search during the next few months, I am certain your advice would help me. Would it be possible for us to meet briefly? My resume is enclosed.

I will call your office next week to see when your schedule would permit such a meeting.

Sincerely,

Rochelle A. Starky

TO OBTAIN AN INFORMATIONAL INTERVIEW

16 NW 128th Street
Raleigh, NC 57755
April 4, 1994

Ms. Jackie B. McClure
Personnel Director
Golden Entertainment
484 Smithers Road
Awkmont, CA 76857

Dear Ms. McClure:

I'm sure a good deal of the credit for your facility's success last year is attributable to the highly-motivated and knowledgeable production staff you have recruited during the last three years. I hope to obtain a film and video production position with a facility just as committed to growth.

I have two years of film and video experience, which I acquired while working as a production assistant at Gullway Productions, Inc. in New York City. I graduated from Gresham University with a BFA in communications and a minor in film and television production. I believe that my experience and education have properly prepared me for a career in film and video production.

As I begin my job search, I am trying to gather as much information and advice as possible before applying for positions. Could I take a few minutes of your time next week to discuss my career plans? I will call your office on Monday, April 11th to see if such a meeting can be arranged.

I appreciate your consideration and look forward to meeting you.

Sincerely,

Karen R. Burns

**FILM AND
VIDEO
CAREER
DIRECTORY**

Lazelle Wright
921 West Fourth Street
Steamboat, Colorado 72105
303-310-3303

April 4, 1994

Mr. James R. Payne
Casting Director
Finch Entertainment, Inc.
241 Snowridge
Ogden, Utah 72108

Dear Mr. Payne:

Jinny Bastienelli was right when she said you would be most helpful in advising me on a motion picture acting career.

I appreciated your taking the time from your busy schedule to meet with me. Your advice was most helpful and I have incorporated your suggestions into my resume. I will send you a copy next week.

Again, thanks so much for your assistance. As you suggested, I will contact Joe Simmons at Cregskill Productions next week in regard to a possible position.

Sincerely,

Lazelle Wright

AFTER A JOB INTERVIEW

1497 Lilac Street
Old Adams, MA 01281
April 4, 1994

Mr. Rudy Delacort
Director of Personnel
Grace Productions Corp.
175 Boylston Avenue
Ribbit, MA 02857

Dear Mr. Delacort:

Thank you for the opportunity to interview yesterday for the lighting technician position. I enjoyed meeting with you and Mr. Cliff Stoudt and learning more about Grace.

Your facility appears to be growing in a direction that parallels my interests and goals. The interview with you and your staff confirmed my initial positive impressions of Grace, and I want to reiterate my strong interest in working for you.

I am convinced that my prior experience as a production intern with Fellowes Communications, Inc., bachelor's degree in theater design and technology and master's in instructional technology from the University of Adams would enable me to progress steadily through your training program and become a productive member of your staff.

Again, thank you for your consideration. If you need any additional information from me, please feel free to call.

Yours truly,

Harold Beaumont

cc: Mr. Cliff Stoudt

ACCEPTING A JOB OFFER

1497 Lilac Street
Old Adams, MA 01281
April 4, 1994

Mr. Rudy Delacort
Director of Personnel
Grace Productions Corp.
175 Boylston Avenue
Ribbit, MA 01281

Dear Mr. Delacort:

I want to thank you and Mr. Stoudt for giving me the opportunity to work for Grace. I am very pleased to accept the position as a lighting technician. The position entails exactly the kind of work I want to do, and I know that I will do a good job for you.

As we discussed, I shall begin work on May 23, 1994. In the interim, I shall complete all the necessary employment forms, obtain the required physical examination and locate housing.

I plan to be in Ribbit within the next two weeks and would like to deliver the paperwork to you personally. At that time, we could handle any remaining items pertaining to my employment. I'll call next week to schedule an appointment with you.

Sincerely yours,

Harold Beaumont

cc: Mr. Cliff Stoudt

WITHDRAWING FROM CONSIDERATION

1497 Lilac Street
Old Adams, MA 01281
April 4, 1994

Mr. Rudy Delacort
Director of Personnel
Grace Productions Corp.
175 Boylston Avenue
Ribbit, MA 01281

Dear Mr. Delacort:

It was indeed a pleasure meeting with you and Mr. Stoudt last week to discuss your needs for a lighting technician. Our time together was most enjoyable and informative.

As I discussed with you during our meeting, I believe one purpose of preliminary interviews is to explore areas of mutual interest and to assess the fit between the individual and the position. After careful consideration, I have decided to withdraw from consideration for the position.

I want to thank you for interviewing me and giving me the opportunity to learn about your needs. You have a fine staff and I would have enjoyed working with them.

Yours truly,

Harold Beaumont

cc: Mr. Cliff Stoudt

IN RESPONSE TO REJECTION

1497 Lilac Street
Old Adams, MA 01281
April 4, 1994

Mr. Rudy Delacort
Director of Personnel
Grace Productions Corp.
175 Boylston Avenue
Ribbit, MA 01281

Dear Mr. Delacort:

Thank you for giving me the opportunity to interview for the lighting technician position. I appreciate your consideration and interest in me.

Although I am disappointed in not being selected for your current vacancy, I want to you to know that I appreciated the courtesy and professionalism shown to me during the entire selection process. I enjoyed meeting you, Mr. Cliff Stoudt, and the other members of your staff. My meetings confirmed that Grace would be an exciting place to work and build a career.

I want to reiterate my strong interest in working for you. Please keep me in mind if a similar position becomes available in the near future.

Again, thank you for the opportunity to interview and best wishes to you and your staff.

Sincerely yours,

Harold Beaumont

cc: Mr. Cliff Stoudt

CHAPTER EIGHTEEN

Questions for You, Questions for Them

You've finished your exhaustive research, contacted everyone you've known since kindergarten, compiled a professional-looking and sounding resume, and written brilliant letters to the dozens of companies your research has revealed are perfect matches for your own strengths, interests, and abilities. Unfortunately, all of this preparatory work will be meaningless if you are unable to successfully convince one of those firms to hire you.

If you were able set up an initial meeting at one of these companies, your resume and cover letter obviously piqued someone's interest. Now you have to traverse the last minefield—the job interview itself. It's time to make all that preparation pay off.

This chapter will attempt to put the interview process in perspective, giving you the "inside story" on what to expect and how to handle the questions and circumstances that arise during the course of a normal interview—and even many of those that surface in the bizarre interview situations we have all experienced at some point.

Why Interviews Shouldn't Scare You

Interviews shouldn't scare you. The concept of two (or more) persons meeting to determine if they are right for each other is a relatively logical idea. As important as research, resumes, letters, and phone calls are, they are inherently impersonal. The interview is your chance to really see and feel the company firsthand, so think of it as a positive opportunity, your chance to succeed.

That said, many of you will still be put off by the inherently inquisitive nature of the process. Though many questions *will* be asked, interviews are essentially experiments in chemistry. Are you right for the company? Is the company right for you? Not just on paper—*in the flesh.*

If you decide the company is right for you, your purpose is simple and clear-cut—to convince the interviewer that you are the right person for the job, that you will fit in, and that you will be an asset to the company now and in the future. The interviewer's purpose is equally simple—to decide whether he or she should buy what you're selling.

This chapter will focus on the kinds of questions you are likely to be asked, how to answer them, and the questions you should be ready to ask of the interviewer. By removing the workings of the interview process from the "unknown" category, you will reduce the fear it engenders.

But all the preparation in the world won't completely eliminate your sweaty palms, unless you can convince yourself that the interview is an important, positive life experience from which you will benefit—even if you don't get the job. Approach it with enthusiasm, calm yourself, and let your personality do the rest. You will undoubtedly spend an interesting hour, one that will teach you more about yourself. It's just another step in the learning process you've undertaken.

What to Do First

Start by setting up a calendar on which you can enter and track all your scheduled appointments. When you schedule an interview with a company, ask them how much time you should allow for the appointment. Some require all new applicants to fill out numerous forms and/or complete a battery of intelligence or psychological tests—all before the first interview. If you've only allowed an hour for the interview—and scheduled another at a nearby firm 10 minutes later—the first time you confront a three-hour test series will effectively destroy any schedule.

Some companies, especially if the first interview is very positive, like to keep applicants around to talk to other executives. This process may be planned or, in a lot of cases, a spontaneous decision by an interviewer who likes you and wants you to meet some other key decision makers. Other companies will tend to schedule such a series of second interviews on a separate day. Find out, if you can, how the company you're planning to visit generally operates. Otherwise, a schedule that's too tight will fall apart in no time at all, especially if you've traveled to another city to interview with a number of firms in a short period of time.

If you need to travel out-of-state to interview with a company, be sure to ask if they will be paying some or all of your travel expenses. (It's generally expected that you'll be paying your own way to firms within your home state.) If they don't offer—and you don't ask—presume you're paying the freight.

Even if the company agrees to reimburse you, make sure you have enough money to pay all the expenses yourself. While some may reimburse you immediately, the majority of firms may take from a week to a month to send you an expense check.

Research, Research, and More Research

The research you did to find these companies is nothing compared to the research you need to do now that you're beginning to narrow your search. If you followed our detailed suggestions when you started targeting these companies in the first place, you've already amassed a great deal of information about them. If you didn't do the research *then,* you sure better decide to do it *now.* Study each company as if you were going to be tested on your detailed knowledge of their organization and operations. Here's a complete checklist of the facts you should try to know about each company you plan to visit for a job interview:

The Basics

1. The address of (and directions to) the office you're visiting
2. Headquarters location (if different)
3. Some idea of domestic and international branches
4. Relative size (compared to other similar companies)
5. Annual billings, sales, and/or income (last two years)
6. Subsidiary companies and/or specialized divisions
7. Departments (overall structure)
8. Major accounts, products, or services

The Subtleties

1. History of the firm (specialties, honors, awards, famous names)
2. Names, titles, and backgrounds of top management
3. Existence (and type) of training program
4. Relocation policy
5. Relative salaries (compared to other companies in field or by size)
6. Recent developments concerning the company and its products or services (from your trade magazine and newspaper reading)
7. Everything you can learn about the career, likes, and dislikes of the person(s) interviewing you

The amount of time and work necessary to be this well prepared for an interview is considerable. It will not be accomplished the day before the interview. You may even find some of the information you need is unavailable on short notice.

Is it really so important to do all this? Well, somebody out there is going to. And if you happen to be interviewing for the same job as that other, well-prepared, knowledgeable candidate, who do you think will impress the interviewer more?

As we've already discussed, if you give yourself enough time, most of this information is surprisingly easy to obtain. In addition to the reference sources covered in the **Career Resources** chapter, the company itself can probably supply you with a great deal of data. A firm's annual report—which all publicly-owned companies must publish yearly for their stockholders—is a virtual treasure trove of information. Write each company and request copies of their last two annual reports. A comparison of sales, income, and other data over this period may enable you to discover some interesting things about their overall financial health and growth potential. Many libraries also have collections of annual reports from major corporations.

Attempting to learn about your interviewer is hard work, the importance of which is underestimated by most applicants (who then, of course, don't bother to do it). Being one of the exceptions may get you a job. Find out if he or she has written any articles that have appeared in the trade press or, even better, books on his or her area(s) of expertise. Referring to these writings during the course of an interview, without making it too obvious a compliment, can be very effective. We all have egos and we all like people to talk about us. The interviewer is no different from the rest of us. You might also check to see if any of your networking contacts worked with him or her at his current (or a previous) company and can help fill you in.

Selection vs. Screening Interviews

The process to which the majority of this chapter is devoted is the actual **selection interview,** usually conducted by the person to whom the new hire will be reporting. But there is another process—the **screening interview**—which many of you may have to survive first.

Screening interviews are usually conducted by a member of the human resources department. Though they may not be empowered to hire, they are in a position to screen out or eliminate those candidates they feel (based on the facts) are not qualified to handle the job. These decisions are not usually made on the basis of personality, appearance, eloquence, persuasiveness, or any other subjective criteria, but rather by clicking off yes or no answers against a checklist of skills. If you don't have the requisite number, you will be eliminated from further consideration. This may seem arbitrary, but it is a realistic and often necessary way for corporations to minimize the time and dollars involved in filling even the lowest jobs on the corporate ladder.

Remember, screening personnel are not looking for reasons to *hire* you; they're trying to find ways to *eliminate* you from the job search pack. Resumes sent blindly to the personnel department will usually be subjected to such screening; you will be eliminated without any personal contact (an excellent reason to construct a superior resume and not send out blind mailings).

If you are contacted, it will most likely be by telephone. When you are responding to such a call, keep these four things in mind: 1) It is an interview, be on your guard; 2) Answer all questions honestly; 3) Be enthusiastic; and 4) Don't offer any more information than you are asked for. Remember, this is another screening step, so don't say anything that will get you screened out before you even get in. You will get the standard questions from the interviewer—his or her attempts to "flesh out" the information included on your resume and/or cover letter. Strictly speaking, they are seeking out any negatives that may exist. If your resume is honest and factual (and it should be), you have no reason to be anxious, because you have nothing to hide.

Don't be nervous—be glad you were called and remember your objective: to get past this screening phase so you can get on to the real interview.

The Day of the Interview

On the day of the interview, wear a conservative (not funereal) business suit—*not* a sports coat, *not* a "nice" blouse and skirt. Shoes should be shined, nails cleaned, hair cut and in place. And no low-cut or tight-fitting clothes.

It's not unusual for resumes and cover letters to head in different directions when a company starts passing them around to a number of executives. If you sent them, both may even be long gone. So bring along extra copies of your resume and your own copy of the cover letter that originally accompanied it.

Whether or not you make them available, we suggest you prepare a neatly-typed list of references (including the name, title, company, address, and phone number of each person). You may want to bring along a copy of your high school or college transcript, especially if it's something to brag about. (Once you get your first job, you'll probably never use it—or be asked for it—again, so enjoy it while you can!)

On Time Means 15 Minutes Early

Plan to arrive 15 minutes before your scheduled appointment. If you're in an unfamiliar city or have a long drive to their offices, allow extra time for the unexpected delays that seem to occur with mind-numbing regularity on important days.

Arriving early will give you some time to check your appearance, catch your breath, check in with the receptionist, learn how to correctly pronounce the interviewer's name, and get yourself organized and battle ready.

Arriving late does not make a sterling first impression. If you are only a few minutes late, it's probably best not to mention it or even excuse yourself. With a little luck, everybody else is behind schedule and no one will notice. However, if you're more than 15 minutes late, have an honest (or at least serviceable) explanation ready and offer it at your first opportunity. Then drop the subject as quickly as possible and move on to the interview.

The Eyes Have It

When you meet the interviewer, shake hands firmly. People notice handshakes and often form a first impression based solely on them.

Try to maintain eye contact with the interviewer as you talk. This will indicate you're interested in what he or she has to say. Eye contact is important for another reason—it demonstrates to the interviewer that you are confident about yourself and your job skills. That's an important message to send.

Sit straight. Body language is also another important means of conveying confidence.

Should coffee or a soft drink be offered, you may accept (but should do so only if the interviewer is joining you).

You Don't Have to Say a Word

"Eighty percent of the initial impression you make is nonverbal," asserts Jennifer Maxwell Morris, a New York-based image consultant, quoting a University of Minnesota study. Some tips: walk tall, enter the room briskly while making eye contact with the person you're going to speak to, keep your head up, square your shoulders, and keep your hand ready for a firm handshake that involves the whole hand but does not pump.

Source: *Working Woman*

Keep your voice at a comfortable level, and try to sound enthusiastic (without imitating Charleen Cheerleader). Be confident and poised and provide direct, accurate, and honest answers to the trickiest questions.

And, as you try to remember all this, just be yourself, and try to act like you're comfortable and almost enjoying this whole process!

Don't Name Drop . . . Conspicuously

A friendly relationship with other company employees may have provided you with valuable information prior to the interview, but don't flaunt such relationships. The interviewer is interested only in how you will relate to him or her and how well he or she surmises you will fit in with the rest of the staff. Name dropping may smack of favoritism. And you are in no position to know who the interviewer's favorite (or least favorite) people are.

On the other hand, if you have established a complex network of professionals through informational interviews, attending trade shows, reading trade magazines, etc., it is perfectly permissible to refer to these people, their companies, conversations you've had, whatever. It may even impress the interviewer with the extensiveness of your preparation.

Fork on the Left, Knife on the Right

Interviews are sometimes conducted over lunch, though this is not usually the case with entry-level people. If it does happen to you, though, try to order something in the middle price range, neither filet mignon nor a cheeseburger.

Do not order alcohol—ever! If your interviewer orders a carafe of wine, politely decline. You may meet another interviewer later who smells the alcohol on your breath, or your interviewer may have a drinking problem. It's just too big a risk to take after you've come so far. Just do your best to maintain your poise, and you'll do fine.

The Importance of Last Impressions

There are some things interviewers will always view with displeasure: street language, complete lack of eye contact, insufficient or vague explanations or answers, a noticeable lack of energy, poor interpersonal skills (i.e., not listening or the basic inability to carry on an intelligent conversation), and a demonstrable lack of motivation.

Every impression may count. And the very *last* impression an interviewer has may outweigh everything else. So, before you allow an interview to end, summarize why you want the job, why you are qualified, and what, in particular, you can offer their company.

Then, take some action. If the interviewer hasn't told you about the rest of the interview process and/or where you stand, ask him or her. Will you be seeing other people that day? If so, ask for some background on anyone else with whom you'll be interviewing. If there are no other meetings that day, what's the next step? When can you expect to hear from them about coming back?

Ask for a business card. This will make sure you get the person's name and title right when you write your follow-up letter. You can staple it to the company file for easy reference as you continue networking. When you return home, file all the business cards, copies of correspondence, and notes from the interview(s) with each company in the appropriate files. Finally, but most importantly, ask yourself which firms you really want to work for and which you are no longer interested in. This will quickly determine how far you want the process at each to develop before you politely tell them to stop considering you for the job.

Immediately send a thank-you letter to each executive you met. These should, of course, be neatly typed business letters, not handwritten notes (unless you are most friendly, indeed, with the interviewer and want to stress the "informal" nature of your note). If you are still interested in pursuing a position at their company, tell them in no uncertain terms. Reiterate why you feel you're the best candidate and tell each of the executives when you hope (expect?) to hear from them.

On the Eighth Day God Created Interviewers

Though most interviews will follow a relatively standard format, there will undoubtedly be a wide disparity in the skills of the interviewers you meet. Many of these executives (with the exception of the human resources staff) will most likely not have extensive interviewing experience, have limited knowledge of interviewing techniques, use them infrequently, be hurried by the other duties, or not even view your interview as critically important.

Rather than studying standardized test results or utilizing professional evaluation skills developed over many years of practice, these nonprofessionals react intuitively—their initial (first five minutes) impressions are often the lasting and over-riding factors they remember. So you must sell yourself—fast.

The best way to do this is to try to achieve a comfort level with your interviewer. Isn't establishing rapport—through words, gestures, appearance common interests, etc.—what you try to do in *any* social situation? It's just trying to know one another better. Against this backdrop, the questions and answers will flow in a more natural way.

A new style of interview called the "situational interview," or low-fidelity simulation, asks prospective employees what they would do in hypothetical situations, presenting illustrations that are important in the job opening. Recent research is encouraging employers to use this type of interview approach, because studies show that what people say they would do is pretty much what they will do when the real-life situation arises.

Source: *Working Woman*

The Set Sequence

Irrespective of the competence levels of the interviewer, you can anticipate an interview sequence roughly as follows:

- Greetings
- Social niceties (small talk)
- Purpose of meeting (let's get down to business)
- Broad questions/answers
- Specific questions/answers

• In-depth discussion of company, job, and opportunity

• Summarizing information given and received

• Possible salary probe (this should only be brought up at a second interview)

• Summary/indication as to next steps

When you look at this sequence closely, it is obvious that once you have gotten past the greeting, social niceties, and some explanation of the job (in the "getting down to business" section), the bulk of the interview will be questions—yours and the interviewer's. In this question and answer session, there are not necessarily any right or wrong answers, only good and bad ones.

Be forewarned, however. This sequence is not written in stone, and some interviewers will deliberately **not** follow it. Some interviewers will try to fluster you by asking off-the-wall questions, while others are just eccentric by nature. Be prepared for anything once the interview has started.

It's Time to Play Q & A

You can't control the "chemistry" between you and the interviewer—do you seem to "hit it off" right from the start or never connect at all? Since you can't control such a subjective problem, it pays to focus on what you *can* control—the questions you will be asked, your answers, and the questions you had better be prepared to ask.

Not surprisingly, many of the same questions pop up in interview after interview, regardless of company size, type, or location. I have chosen the 14 most common—along with appropriate hints and answers for each—for inclusion in this chapter. Remember: There are no right or wrong answers to these questions, only good and bad ones.

Substance counts more than speed when answering questions. Take your time and make sure that you listen to each question—there is nothing quite as disquieting as a lengthy, intelligent answer that is completely irrelevant to the question asked. You wind up looking like a programmed clone with stock answers to dozens of questions who has, unfortunately, pulled the wrong one out of the grab bag.

Once you have adequately answered a specific question, it is permissible to go beyond it and add more information if doing so adds something to the discussion and/or highlights a particular strength, skill, course, etc. But avoid making lengthy speeches just for the sake of sounding off. Even if the interviewer asks a question that is right up your "power alley", one you could talk about for weeks, keep your answers short. Under two minutes for any answer is a good rule of thumb.

Study the list of questions (and hints) that follow, and prepare at least one solid, concise answer for each. Practice with a friend until your answers to these most-asked questions sound intelligent, professional and, most importantly, unmemorized and unrehearsed.

"Why do you want to be in this field?"

Using your knowledge and understanding of the particular field, explain why you find the business exciting and where and what role you see yourself playing in it.

"Why do you think you will be successful in this business?"

Using the information from your self-evaluation and the research you did on that particular company, formulate an answer that marries your strengths to their's and to the characteristics of the position for which you're applying.

"Why did you choose our company?"

This is an excellent opportunity to explain the extensive process of training and research you've undertaken. Tell them about your strengths and how you match up with their company. Emphasize specific things about their company that led you to seek an interview. Be a salesperson—be convincing.

"What can you do for us?"

Construct an answer that essentially lists your strengths, the experience you have which will contribute to your job performance, and any other unique qualifications that will place you at the head of the applicant pack. Use action-oriented words to tell exactly what you think you can do for the company—all your skills mean nothing if you can't use them to benefit the company you are interviewing with. Be careful: This is a question specifically designed to *eliminate* some of that pack. Sell yourself. Be one of the few called back for a second interview.

"What position here interests you?"

If you're interviewing for a specific position, answer accordingly. If you want to make sure you don't close the door on other opportunities of which you might be unaware, you can follow up with your own question: "I'm here to apply for your production assistant opening. Is there another position open for which you feel I'm qualified?"

If you've arranged an interview with a company without knowing of any specific openings, use the answer to this question to describe the kind of work you'd like to do and why you're qualified to do it.

If you're on a first interview with the human resources department, just answer the question. They only want to figure out where to send you.

"What jobs have you held and why did you leave them?"

Or the direct approach: "Have you ever been fired?" Take this opportunity to expand on your resume, rather than precisely answering the question by merely recapping your job experiences. In discussing each job, point out what you liked about it, what factors led to your leaving, and how the next job added to your continuing professional education. If you have been fired, say so. It's very easy to check.

"What are your strengths and weaknesses?"

Or **"What are your hobbies (or outside interests)?"** Both questions can be easily answered using the data you gathered to complete the self-evaluation process. Be wary of being too forthcoming about your glaring faults (nobody expects you to volunteer every weakness and mistake), but do not reply, "I don't have any." They won't believe you and, what's worse, you won't believe you. After all, you did the evaluation—you know it's a lie!

Good answers to these questions are those in which the interviewer can identify benefits for him or herself. For example: "I consider myself to be an excellent planner. I am seldom caught by surprise and I prize myself on being able to anticipate problems and schedule my time to be ahead of the game. I devote a prescribed number of hours each week to this activity. I've noticed that many people just react. If you plan ahead, you should be able to cut off most problems before they arise."

You may consider disarming the interviewer by admitting a weakness, but doing it in such a way as to make it relatively unimportant to the job function. For example: "Mathematics has never been my strong suit. In this industry, though, I haven't found this to be a liability."

"Do you think your extracurricular activities were worth the time you devoted to them?"

This is a question often asked of entry-level candidates. One possible answer: "Very definitely. As you see from my resume, I have been quite active in the Student Government and French Club. My language fluency allowed me to spend my junior year abroad as an exchange student, and working in a functioning government gave me firsthand knowledge of what can be accomplished with people in the real world. I suspect my marks would have been somewhat higher had I not taken on so many activities outside of school, but I feel the balance they gave me contributed significantly to my overall growth as a person."

"What are your career goals?"

Interviewers are always seeking to probe the motivations of prospective employees. Nowhere is this more apparent than when the area of ambition is discussed. The key answer to this question might be: "Given hard work, company growth, and personal initiative, I'd look forward to being in a top production position by the time I'm 35. I believe in effort and the risk/reward system—my research on this company has shown me that it operates on the same principles. I would hope it would select its future leaders from those people who displaying such characteristics."

"At some future date would you be willing to relocate?"

Pulling up one's roots is not the easiest thing in the world to do, but it is often a fact of life in the corporate world. If you're serious about your career (and such a move often represents a step up the career ladder), you will probably not mind such a move. Tell the interviewer. If you really *don't* want to move, you may want to say so, too—though I would find out how probable or frequent such relocations would be before closing the door while still in the interview stage.

Keep in mind that as you get older, establish ties in a particular community, marry, have children, etc., you will inevitably feel less jubilation at the thought of moving once a year or even "being out on the road." So take the opportunity to experience new places and experiences while you're young. If you don't, you may never get the chance.

"How did you get along with your last supervisor?"

This question is designed to understand your relationship with (and reaction to) authority. Remember: Companies look for team players, people who will fit in with their hierarchy, their rules, their ways of doing things. An answer might be: "I prefer to work with smart, strong people who know what they want and can express themselves. I learned in the military that in order to accomplish the mission, someone has to be the leader and that person has to be given the authority to lead. Someday I aim to be that leader. I hope then my subordinates will follow me as much and as competently as I'm ready to follow now."

"What are your salary requirements?"

If they are at all interested in you, this question will probably come up, though it is more likely at a second interview. The danger, of course, is that you may price yourself too low or, even worse, right out of a job you want. Since you will have a general idea of industry figures for that position (and may even have an idea of what that company tends to pay new people for the position), why not refer to a range of salaries, such as $25,000 - $30,000?

If the interviewer doesn't bring up salary at all, it's doubtful you're being seriously considered, so you probably don't need to even bring the subject up. (If you know you aren't getting the job or aren't interested in it if offered, you may try to nail down a salary figure in order to be better prepared for the next interview.)

"Tell me about yourself"

Watch out for this one! It's often one of the first questions asked. If you falter here, the rest of the interview could quickly become a downward slide to nowhere. Be prepared, and consider it an opportunity to combine your answers to many of the previous questions into one concise description of who you are, what you want to be, and why that company should take a chance on you. Summarize your resume—briefly—and expand on particular courses or experiences relevant to the company or position. Do not go on about your hobbies or personal life, where you spent your summer vacation, or anything that is not relevant to securing that job. You may explain how that particular job fits in with your long-range career goals and talk specifically about what attracted you to their company in the first place.

"Do you have any questions?"

It's the last fatal question on our list, often the last one an interviewer throws at you after an hour or two of grilling. Even if the interview has been very long and unusually thorough, you *should* have questions—about the job, the company, even the industry. Unfortunately, by the time this question off-handedly hits the floor, you are already looking forward to leaving and may have absolutely nothing to say.

Preparing yourself for an interview means more than having answers for some of the questions an interviewer may ask. It means having your own set of questions—at least five or six—for the interviewer. The interviewer is trying to find the right person for the job. You're trying to find the right job. So you should be just as curious about him or her and the company as he or she is about you. Be careful with any list of questions prepared ahead of time. Some of them were probably answered during the course of the interview, so to ask that same question at this stage would demonstrate poor listening skills. Listening well is becoming a lost art, and its importance cannot be stressed enough. (See the box on this page for a short list of questions you may consider asking on any interview).

The Not-So-Obvious Questions

Every interviewer is different and, unfortunately, there are no rules saying he or she has to use all or any of the "basic" questions covered above. But we think the odds are against his or her avoiding all of them. Whichever of these he or she includes, be assured most interviewers do like to come up with questions that are "uniquely theirs." It may be just one or a whole series—questions developed over the years that he or she feels help separate the wheat from the chaff.

You can't exactly prepare yourself for questions like, "What would you do if . . . (fill in the blank with some obscure occurrence)?," "What do you remember about kindergarten?," or "What's your favorite ice cream flavor?" Every interviewer we know has his or her favorites and all of these questions seem to come out of left field. Just stay relaxed, grit your teeth (quietly), and take a few seconds to frame a reasonably intelligent reply.

Your Turn to Ask the Questions

1. What will my typical day be like?
2. What happened to the last person who had this job?
3. Given my attitude and qualifications, how would you estimate my chances for career advancement at your company?
4. Why did you come to work here? What keeps you here?
5. If you were I, would you start here again?
6. How would you characterize the management philosophy of your company?
7. What characteristics do the successful employees at your company have in common?
8. What's the best (and worst) thing about working here?

The Downright Illegal Questions

Some questions are more than inappropriate—they are illegal. The Civil Rights Act of 1964 makes it illegal for a company to discriminate in its hiring on the basis of race, color, religion, sex, or national origin. It also means that any interview questions covering these topics are strictly off-limits. In addition to questions about race and color, what other types of questions can't be asked? Some might surprise you:

- Any questions about marital status, number and ages of dependents, or marriage or child-bearing plans.

- Any questions about your relatives, their addresses, or their place of origin.

- Any questions about your arrest record. If security clearance is required, it can be done after hiring but before you start the job.

A Quick Quiz to Test Your Instincts

After reading the above paragraphs, read through the 10 questions below. Which ones do you think would be legal to ask at a job interview? Answers provided below.

1. Confidentially, what is your race?
2. What kind of work does your spouse do?
3. Are you single, married, or divorced?

4. What is your native language?

5. Who should we notify in case of an emergency?

6. What clubs, societies, or organizations do you belong to?

7. Do you plan to have a family?

8. Do you have any disability?

9. Do you have a good credit record?

10. What is your height and weight?

The answer? Not a single question out of the 10 is legal at a job interview, because all could lead to a discrimination suit. Some of the questions would become legal once you were hired (obviously a company would need to know who to notify in an emergency), but none belong at an interview.

Now that you know what an interviewer can't ask you, what if he or she does? Well, don't lose your cool, and don't point out that the question may be outside the law—the nonprofessional interviewer may not realize such questions are illegal, and such a response might confuse, even anger, him or her.

Instead, whenever any questions are raised that you feel are outside legal boundaries, politely state that you don't understand how the question has bearing on the job opening and ask the interviewer to clarify his or herself. If the interviewer persists, you may be forced to state that you do not feel comfortable answering questions of that nature. Bring up the legal issue as a last resort, but if things reach that stage, you probably don't want to work for that company after all. Also, performers should be aware that physical type is often a factor when roles are cast.

Testing and Applications

Though not part of the selection interview itself, job applications and skill and psychological tests are often part of the pre-interview process. You should know something about them.

The job application is essentially a record-keeping exercise—simply the transfer of work experience and educational data from your resume to a printed application forms. Though taking the time to recopy data may seem like a waste of time, some companies simply want the information in a particular order on a standard form. One difference: Applications often require the listing of references and salary levels achieved. Be sure to bring your list of references with you to any interview (so you can transfer the pertinent information), and don't lie about salary history; it's easily checked.

Many companies now use a variety of psychological tests as additional mechanisms to screen out undesirable candidates. Although their accuracy is subject to question, the companies that use them obviously believe they are effective at identifying applicants whose personality makeups would preclude their participating positively in a given work situation, especially those at the extreme ends of the behavior spectrum.

Their usefulness in predicting job accomplishment is considered limited. If you are normal (like the rest of us), you'll have no trouble with these tests and may even find them amusing. Just don't try to outsmart them—you'll just wind up outsmarting yourself.

Stand Up and Be Counted

Your interview is over. Breathe a sigh of relief. Make your notes—you'll want to keep a file on the important things covered for use in your next interview. Some people consider one out of 10 (one job offer for every 10 interviews) a good score—if you're keeping score. We suggest you don't. It's virtually impossible to judge how others are judging you. Just go on to the next interview. Sooner than you think, you'll be hired. For the right job.

Auditions

Auditioning is an unavoidable process in landing a performing role in a film or video production. However, it is important to enter an audition in the right frame of mind—you should not feel desperate or needy. Your ego should not be wrapped up in one job.

Upon entering the reception area, sign in. The casting director will call performers into the studio based on the sign-up sheet, and those who don't sign in risk being passed over. After signing in, if you are an actor, take a script and begin going over the lines. Become familiar with it, but don't over-rehearse—try to maintain spontaneity and freshness. For other types of work, simply take a seat and be prepared when the casting director calls, "Next!"

Once called into the auditioning room, the audition begins. A team of about eight people decide on which performer gets the job. If you are selected among the finalists for the role, you will receive a **callback**. At the callback, the director's role becomes more visible, since the director needs to see with whom he or she might ultimately be working. Based on your talent and some fortuitous coincidences, you'll land the part!

JOB
OPPORTUNITIES
DATABANK

Job Opportunities Databank

The Job Opportunities Databank contains listings for more than 210 major film and video production companies, postproduction facilities, and other companies providing services allied with film and video that offer entry-level hiring and/or internships. It is divided into two sections: Entry-Level Job and Internship Listings, which provides full descriptive entries for companies in the United States; and Additional Companies, which includes name, address, and telephone information only for companies that did not respond to our inquiries. For complete details on the information in this chapter, please consult "How to Use the Job Opportunities Databank" at the front of this directory.

Entry-Level Job and Internship Listings

21st Century Film Corp.
7000 W. 3rd St.
Los Angeles, CA 90064
Phone: (310)914-0500

Employees: 20.

▶ **Internships**

Type: The company does not offer an internship program.

Aaron Spelling Productions Inc.
5700 Wilshire Blvd.
Los Angeles, CA 90036
Phone: (213)965-5999
Fax: (213)965-5840

Business Description: Movie and television production company.

Act III Communications Inc.
1800 Century Park E.
Los Angeles, CA 90067
Phone: (310)553-3636

Business Description: Involved in television film production.

Opportunities: Hires executive personnel and support staff with previous experience.

Benefits: Benefits include medical insurance, dental insurance, and savings plan.

Application Procedures: The company does not accept unsolicited resumes. Apply in person to Joanie Bergman, Office Mgr.

▶ **Internships**

Contact: Joanie Bergman, Office Mgr.

Type: Offers paid interships to college students.

155

Action Video Inc.

6616 Lexington Ave.
Los Angeles, CA 90038
Phone: (213)461-3611
Fax: (213)460-4023

Business Description: Action Video is a television commercial postproduction company.

Employees: 46.

Benefits: Benefits include medical insurance, life insurance, vision insurance, savings plan, profit sharing, and credit union.

Human Resources: Cindy Beal.

Application Procedures: Send resume and cover letter to the department head of the position of interest.

▶ **Internships**

Type: The company does not offer an internship program.

T he director is the artistic leader of the production team and is ultimately responsible for every decision that shapes the film. Usually hired by the producer, he/she determines the style of the film and translates the script from the written page into moving images.

Source: *Getting Started in Film*

Admusic Inc.

3500 W. Olive Ave.
Burbank, CA 91505
Phone: (818)953-4100

Business Description: Provides music production services for television commercials.

Employees: 15.

Opportunities: Hires entry-level personnel with college degrees, some college course work, or previous experience, depending on the position.

Benefits: Benefits include medical insurance, life insurance, dental insurance, and vision insurance.

Human Resources: Kristine Burdorf, Office Mgr.

Application Procedures: Places newspaper

advertisements for certain openings. Send resume and cover letter.

▶ **Internships**

Type: Offers unpaid internships for college credit. Send resume and cover letter to the attention of the Office Manager.

Affiliated Models Inc.

The Affiliated Bldg.
1680 Crooks Rd.
Troy, MI 48084
Phone: (313)244-8770

Business Description: Talent agency.

Opportunities: Hires models and on-camera talent.

Human Resources: Linda Hack, Pres.

Application Procedures: Send resume listing experience and detailing all physical characteristics including height, weight, and hair color. Include four candid photographs (two head shots/two full-length). Enclose a self-addressed, stamped envelope for reply. Send to the attention of the New Talent Department.

▶ **Internships**

Type: The company does not offer an internship program.

AIMS Media

9710 De Soto Ave.
Chatsworth, CA 91311
Phone: (818)773-4300
Fax: (818)341-6700

Business Description: Engaged in movie and video distribution and production.

Employees: 57.

Opportunities: Hires entry-level office, sales, and telemarketing personnel with previous experience.

Benefits: Benefits include medical insurance and 401(k).

Human Resources: Adele Brant, Controller.

Application Procedures: Send resume and cover letter to the attention of Adrian Milder, Sales Mgr.

▶ **Internships**

Type: The company does not offer an internship program.

All American Television Inc.
205 Lexington Ave.
New York, NY 10017
Phone: (212)685-1700

Business Description: Engaged in television syndication and advertising sales.

Employees: 60.

Opportunities: Hires entry-level staff in advertising and sales. Requirements include a college degree and previous experience.

Benefits: Benefits include medical insurance, life insurance, dental insurance, and vision insurance.

Human Resources: Maria Doane, Office Mgr.

Application Procedures: Send cover letter and resume to Louise Perillo, Sr. VP, Personnel and Admin.

▶ **Internships**

Type: The company does not offer an internship program.

All Post
1133 N. Hollywood Way
Burbank, CA 91505
Phone: (818)841-7440

Employees: 230.

Application Procedures: Send resume and cover letter to Hank Smith, Dir.

▶ **Internships**

Type: The company does not offer an internship program.

Allied Film and Video
7375 Woodward Ave.
Detroit, MI 48202
Phone: (313)871-2222

Business Description: Provides video duplication services.

Employees: 750.

Opportunities: Hires accounting and finance personnel with college degrees. Also hires management information systems personnel.

Benefits: Benefits include medical insurance, life insurance, dental insurance, vision insurance, profit sharing, disability insurance, and vacation days.

Human Resources: Ed Hagden.

Application Procedures: Advertises in *Detroit Free Press* and *Detroit News*. Send resume and cover letter in response to advertisements. Unsolicited resumes are not kept on file.

▶ **Internships**

Type: The company does not offer an internship program.

AME Inc.
1133 N. Hollywood Way
Burbank, CA 91505
Phone: (818)841-7440

Business Description: Provides postproduction film services.

Employees: 230.

Opportunities: Offers entry-level preproduction positions. Previous experience and/or college course work required.

Benefits: Benefits include medical insurance.

Human Resources: Hank Smith, Dir. of Human Resources.

Application Procedures: Apply in person or send resume to the attention of Hank Smith, Dir. of Human Resources.

▶ **Internships**

Type: The company does not offer an internship program.

American Media Inc.
9900 University Ave.
West Des Moines, IA 50266-6769
Phone: (515)224-0919

Business Description: Producer of corporate training videos.

Employees: 87.

Opportunities: Hires entry-level staff in training, sales, and shipping and handling. College degree and/or previous experience required.

Benefits: Benefits include medical insurance, life insurance, dental insurance, and 401(k).

Human Resources: Melissa Chavis, Office Mgr.

Application Procedures: Send resume to Melissa Chavis, Office Mgr.

▶ **Internships**

Type: Offers unpaid internships to college students. **Number Available Annually:** 4-5.

Application Procedure: Call to schedule an interview.

American Motion Pictures

2247 15th Ave. W.
Seattle, WA 98119
Phone: (206)282-1776

Business Description: Provides motion picture duplicating and editing services.

Employees: 45.

Opportunities: Hires entry-level personnel in production and duplication capacities.

Benefits: Benefits include medical insurance, dental insurance, and profit sharing.

Human Resources: Lorraine Smith, Cust. Serv.

Application Procedures: Send resume and cover letter to Lorraine Smith.

▶ **Internships**

Contact: David Thompson, VP of Customer Services.

Type: Offers internships to full-time college seniors. Send resume and cover letter to David Thompson. **Number Available Annually:** 3.

documentaries, feature and industrial films, and more.

▶ **Internships**

Contact: Lisa Sutherland.

Type: Offers acquisitions/duplication, research, and film sales internships. Interns work a minimum of 24 hours/week. **Number Available Annually:** 20.

Duties: Acquisitions/duplication interns prepare tape re-transfers to broadcast NTSC, PAL, and VHS formats; repair, splice, and evaluate 35mm and 16mm original film elements; work in the tape library, time code formats; and do inventory work. Research interns fact check, complete computer searches, cue tape, edit, duplicate shots, log notes, and work on compilation tapes. Film sales interns research and screen cassettes, complete database searches, screen and time completed shows, return masters, time code, license, duplicate, and work on promotions.

Application Procedure: Send resume and cover letter to Lisa Sutherland.

> **J**ob growth during the 1990s is expected to slow but remain steady at about 1.5 million new jobs each year, reflecting the coming demographic changes in society. By the year 2005 the labor force should consist of nearly 151 million workers—up 21 percent from 1990.
>
> Source: *Discover the Best Jobs for You!*

Archive Films, Inc.

530 W. 25th St.
New York, NY 10001
Phone: (212)620-3955
Fax: (212)645-2137

Business Description: Founded in 1979, Archive Films, Inc. is an international supplier of motion picture stock footage for commercial, broadcast, corporate, educational, and other purposes. Maintains a database of over 10,000 films containing shot-by-shot descriptions of the footage. All footage is available on film and videotape format for use by advertising agencies, television producers, news broadcasts,

A.R.I.Q. Footage, Inc.

1 Main St.
East Hampton, NY 11937
Phone: (516)329-9200

Business Description: Serves as a library with archives of motion picture footage. Researches film and provides historical footage for various media.

Employees: 4.

Opportunities: Offers entry-level research positions.

▶ **Internships**

Contact: Joe Lauro, Pres.

Type: Offers unpaid internships to college students and graduates, graduate students, and others. Accepts international applicants. **Number Available Annually:** 2-10.

Duties: Interns conduct film research and work on film-to-tape transfer, assembly editing, and maintenance of archive library.

Application Procedure: Contact Joe Lauro.

Ariza Talent & Modeling Agency, Inc.

909 E. Semoran Blvd.
Casselberry, FL 32707
Phone: (407)332-0011

Opportunities: Hires acting and modeling talent.

Human Resources: Jeff Callender, Agent.

Application Procedures: Send resume with photograph or contact by phone.

▶ **Internships**

Type: The company does not offer an internship program.

Assistant Directors Training Program

15503 Ventura Blvd.
Encino, CA 91436-3140
Phone: (818)386-2545
Fax: (818)382-1794

Business Description: On-the-job training program offering classroom seminars on the role of the second assistant director of a motion picture.

▶ **Internships**

Type: Offers assistant director trainee positions. Trainees earn $392-$382/week and receive health insurance, placement and housing assistance, and job counseling. Open to college graduates. College credit is available. Upon completion of program, interns are able to attain free-lance work in the industry. **Number Available Annually:** 8-20. **Applications Received:** 1,500.

Duties: Trainees assist in motion picture and television production administration, attend seminars, and work with studio and production companies.

Application Procedure: Call or write to the attention of Elizabeth Stanley, administrator.

Associated Television International

650 N. Bronson Ave.
Hollywood, CA 90004
Phone: (213)871-1340

Business Description: Television production company.

Employees: 70.

Opportunities: Hires production assistants and camera operators with previous experience.

Benefits: Benefits include medical insurance and dental insurance.

Human Resources: David McKenzie, CEO.

Application Procedures: Send resume and cover letter to the attention of David McKenzie, CEO.

▶ **Internships**

Type: The company does not offer an internship program.

Atlanta Sound and Lighting Co.

2368 John Glenn Dr.
Atlanta, GA 30341
Phone: (404)455-7695

Business Description: Provides stage lighting, sound systems, and consulting for theatrical productions and conventions.

Opportunities: Hires technical staff (sound, lighting, etc.).

Human Resources: Jennifer Crumbley.

Application Procedures: Send resume and cover letter.

▶ **Internships**

Type: Has no formal internship program, but does accept volunteers.

Application Procedure: Phone or apply in person.

Atlantic Video Inc.

150 S. Gordon St.
Alexandria, VA 22304
Phone: (703)823-2800
Fax: (703)370-6748

Business Description: Provides videotape distribution and production services.

Employees: 70.

Opportunities: Hires entry-level staff in technical control and operations. College degree required and previous experience helpful.

Benefits: Benefits include medical insurance, dental insurance, and 401(k).

Human Resources: Tom Kitner, Master Control Supervisor.

Application Procedures: Send resume to Personnel Department, 650 Massachussetts Ave., Washington, DC 20001.

Audiovisual Design Studios Inc.
1823 Silas Dean Hwy.
Rocky Hill, CT 06067
Phone: (203)529-2581

Business Description: Motion picture services and production company.

Employees: 3.

Opportunities: Hires entry-level staff for computer graphics positions. Experience and educational requirements vary by position. Also hires free-lancers.

Human Resources: Joe Wall, Pres.

Application Procedures: Send resume and cover letter to Joe Wall, Pres.

▶ **Internships**

Type: The company does not offer an internship program.

T he length of the resume may also be different for the experienced candidate. Whereas a two-page document might not be appropriate for a new graduate, it can serve a valuable purpose for the veteran employee. Often, the candidate has enough relevant accomplishments and experiences to expand to a second page.

Source: *Planning Job Choices: 1994*

Bert Berdis and Company Inc.
1956 N. Cahuenga Blvd.
Hollywood, CA 90068
Phone: (213)462-7261

Business Description: Writers and producers of commercials for advertising agencies.

Opportunities: Hires performers who have agent representation.

Human Resources: Jeff Howell, Casting Dir.

Application Procedures: Company typically works through agents. Send audio cassette to Jeff Howell. No walk-ins or cold calls.

▶ **Internships**

Type: No formal internship program in place; company may hire interns for specific projects.

Big Picture Editorial Co.
15 W. 44th St., 7th Fl.
New York, NY 10036
Phone: (212)768-2666

Business Description: Involved in video editing services.

Employees: 20.

Opportunities: Hires experienced entry-level office personnel.

Benefits: Benefits include medical insurance, life insurance, dental insurance, and vision insurance.

Application Procedures: Send resume and cover letter.

▶ **Internships**

Type: The company does not offer an internship program.

Boss Film Studios
13335 Maxella Ave.
Marina Del Rey, CA 90292
Phone: (310)823-0433

Business Description: Producers of television advertisements and visual effects.

Employees: 75.

Opportunities: Offers entry-level positions in purchasing to qualified applicants.

Benefits: Benefits include medical insurance, life insurance, and credit union membership.

Application Procedures: Send resume to the attention of the human resources department.

▶ **Internships**

Type: The company does not offer an internship program.

Broadway Video Inc.
1619 Broadway
New York, NY 10019
Phone: (212)265-7600

Business Description: Television commercial postproduction company.

Officers: Andrea Baker, Dir. of Operations.

Employees: 50.

Opportunities: Offers entry-level positions in video editing. Previous experience required.

Application Procedures: Send resume to the attention of Andrea Baker, Dir. of Operations.

Bureau of National Affairs Inc. BNA Communications

9439 Key West Ave.
Rockville, MD 20850-3396
Phone: (202)452-4200

Employees: 1,700.

Opportunities: Hires entry-level staff in a variety of areas. Previous experience and educational requirements depend on position.

Benefits: Benefits include medical insurance, life insurance, dental insurance, vision insurance, savings plan, tuition assistance, profit sharing, child-care programs, elder-care programs, and transportation.

Application Procedures: Apply in-person, call, or send resume and cover letter to Carolyn Taylor, 1231 25th St., NW, Ste. 100, Washington, DC 20037.

▶ Internships

Type: Offers paid internships in legal, non-legal, editorial, and minority areas to college juniors and seniors. **Number Available Annually:** 20-30.

Application Procedure: Apply through college or university attended.

Buzzco Associates, Inc.

33 Bleeker St.
New York, NY 10012
Phone: (212)473-8800
Fax: (212)473-8891

Business Description: Animation company involved in such projects as sales films, network identification, and commercials.

▶ Internships

Contact: Candy Kugel, Dir./Prod.

Type: Offers unpaid internships to high school seniors and graduates, college students, and college graduates. Interns have the potential to move into full-time positions. **Number Available Annually:** 2-3. **Applications Received:** 10-25.

Duties: Interns run messages and provide project assistance.

Application Procedure: Contact Candy Kugel.

Cannon Pictures Inc.

8200 Wilshire Blvd.
Beverly Hills, CA 90212
Phone: (213)966-5600

Business Description: Motion picture production company.

Employees: 47.

Opportunities: Hires entry-level staff for office, mail room, and marketing positions. Must have previous experience.

Benefits: Benefits include medical insurance and dental insurance.

Application Procedures: Send resume to Cliff Townsend, Supervisor of Acct.

▶ Internships

Contact: Cliff Townsend, Supervisor of Acct.

Type: Offers paid internships to college students. **Number Available Annually:** 3.

The racial and ethnic mix of the work force in the year 2005 will be even more diverse than in the year 1990 given the differential birth and immigration rates of various racial and ethnic groups. Blacks, Hispanics, Asians, and other minority groups will represent 27 percent of the work force—up from 22 percent in 1990. These groups also will account for 35 percent of labor force entrants between 1990 and 2005.

Source: *Discover the Best Jobs for You!*

Capitol Video Communications Corp.

2121 Wisconsin Ave.
Washington, DC 20007
Phone: (202)965-7800

Officers: Joseph Rothstein, Pres.

Employees: 80.

Application Procedures: Interested candidates should forward a resume with cover letter to the personnel department.

Carolco Pictures

8800 Sunset Blvd.
Los Angeles, CA 90069
Phone: (213)850-8800

Business Description: Involved in motion

picture and videotape production and distribution.

Employees: 88.

Opportunities: Hires entry-level office personnel with some previous experience.

Benefits: Benefits include medical insurance, life insurance, dental insurance, 401(k), personal/sick days, and vacation days.

Application Procedures: Places newspaper advertisements for certain openings. Does not accept unsolicited resumes.

▶ **Internships**

Type: The company does not offer an internship program.

Castle Rock Entertainment

335 N. Maple Dr.
Beverly Hills, CA 90210
Phone: (310)285-2300

Business Description: Motion picture and video production company.

Employees: 65.

Opportunities: Hires entry-level staff for mailroom, receptionist, computer, and typing positions. Depending on position, previous experience may be required.

Human Resources: Jan Steimer.

Application Procedures: Send resume to the human resources director.

▶ **Internships**

Type: The company does not offer an internship program.

CBS Inc.

51 W. 2nd St.
New York, NY 10019
Phone: (212)975-4321

Business Description: Involved in communications and television and radio broadcasting.

Officers: Laurence A. Tisch, CEO, Pres. and Chm. of the Board; Peter W. Keegan, Senior VP and Financial Officer; Joan Showalter, VP of Human Resources.

Employees: 6,500.

CC Studios Inc.

389 Newtown Tpk.
Weston, CT 06883
Phone: (203)222-0002

Employees: 15.

Opportunities: Hires entry-level personnel in such areas as accounting, customer service, and the warehouse. Previous experience and some college course work is required.

Benefits: Benefits include medical insurance, life insurance, dental insurance, and fitness center.

Human Resources: Linda Griffin, Dir. of Operations.

Application Procedures: Send resume and cover letter to the attention of Linda Griffin.

▶ **Internships**

Contact: Joe Query, Admin. Dir.

Type: Offers internships for college students.

Celluloid Studios

1422 Delgany L St.
Denver, CO 80202
Phone: (303)595-3152

Business Description: Production agency for television commercials.

Employees: 8.

Opportunities: Previous experience and some college course work required for entry-level positions.

Benefits: Benefits include medical insurance.

Human Resources: Holly Meather, Admin.

Application Procedures: Send resume, call, or apply in person.

▶ **Internships**

Type: The company does not offer an internship program.

Chace Productions Inc.

7080 Hollywood Blvd.
201 S. Victory St.
Hollywood, CA 90028
Phone: (213)466-3946
Fax: (213)464-1893

Business Description: Chace Productions is an audio postproduction company.

Officers: Bob Heiver, President; Louis Fiore, Controller.

Employees: 30.

Opportunities: Hires experienced entry-level office personnel.

Benefits: Benefits include medical insurance, life insurance, dental insurance, and 401(k).

Human Resources: Pam Rosauer, Dir. of Human Resources.

Application Procedures: Send resume and cover letter to the attention of Bob Heiver.

▶ Internships

Type: The company does not offer an internship program.

Cherry Mellon Ibbetson and Associates Inc.
254 W. 23rd St.
New York, NY 10011
Phone: (212)727-1111

Business Description: Television commercial production company.

Employees: 1.

Opportunities: Hires free-lancers and producers. Candidates must have previous experience and a college degree.

Application Procedures: Send resume and cover letter to Kendra Eggen.

▶ Internships

Type: The company does not offer an internship program.

Cine Magnetics Inc.
650 Halstead Ave.
Mamaroneck, NY 10543
Phone: (914)698-3554

Business Description: Involved in video and film duplication and photo finishing.

Employees: 260.

Opportunities: Hires entry-level personnel in the production and technical departments.

Benefits: Benefits include medical insurance, life insurance, and a cafeteria plan.

Human Resources: Vanna Rohn.

Application Procedures: Send resume and cover letter.

▶ Internships

Type: The company does not offer an internship program.

Cintex Entertainment Inc.
345 Maple Dr.
Beverly Hills, CA 90210
Phone: (310)281-2600

Officers: Diane Milan, VP of Admin.

Employees: 10.

Opportunities: Hires entry-level personnel in the customer service department. College degree and previous experience preferred.

Benefits: Benefits include medical insurance, life insurance, dental insurance, and savings plan.

Application Procedures: Send resume and cover letter to the attention of Diane Milan, VP of Admin.

▶ Internships

Type: No formal internship program set up yet. Call for information.

Women will represent over half of all entrants into the labor force during the 1990s. While accounting for 39 percent of the labor force in 1972 and 41 percent of the labor force in 1976, women in the year 2005 will constitute over 47 percent of the labor force. By the year 2005, 4 out of 5 women between the ages of 25 and 54 will be in the labor force.

Source: *Discover the Best Jobs for You!*

Classic Video Duplication Inc.
463 Union Ave.
Westbury, NY 11590
Phone: (516)334-1441

Business Description: Commercial, industrial, and personal videotape duplication company.

Employees: 12.

Opportunities: Hires entry-level staff with previous experience.

Application Procedures: Apply in person. Send resume and cover letter to the attention of Ray Nives, President.

▶ Internships

Type: The company does not offer an internship program.

Columbia Pictures Entertainment Inc.

10202 W. Washington
Culver City, CA 90232
Phone: (310)280-8000

Business Description: Provides movie production and distribution services.

Opportunities: Hires entry-level clerical staff. Candidates must have previous experience.

Application Procedures: Send resume to Human Resources Department.

▶ **Internships**

Type: Offers paid internships for credit to college students.

Application Procedure: Send resume to Human Resources Department.

New occupations for the 1990s and beyond will center around information, energy, high-tech, healthcare, and financial industries. They promise to create a new occupational structure and vocabulary relating to computers, robotics, biotechnology, lasers, and fiber optics. And as these fields begin to apply new technologies to developing new innovations, they in turn will generate other new occupations in the 21st century.

Source: *Discover the Best Jobs for You!*

Compact Video Group Inc.

2820 W. Olive Ave.
Burbank, CA 91505
Phone: (818)840-7000

Business Description: Provides television and film production work and satellite transmission uplinking services.

Employees: 350.

Opportunities: Offers entry-level positions in accounting, payroll, billing, and general office work to college graduates.

Benefits: Benefits include medical insurance, life insurance, dental insurance, a savings plan, and 401(k).

Human Resources: Kristi Kleckner, Dir. of Human Resources.

Application Procedures: Send or fax resume to Kristi Kleckner, Dir. of Human Resources.

▶ **Internships**

Type: The company does not offer an internship program.

Complete Post Inc.

6087 Sunset Blvd.
Hollywood, CA 90028
Phone: (213)467-1244

Business Description: Provides television postproduction services.

Officers: Tony Bolm, Dir. of Operational Svcs.

Employees: 130.

Opportunities: Offers entry-level positions in the vault or shipping areas to college graduates. Candidates must have college background in television production.

Benefits: Benefits include medical insurance, dental insurance, profit sharing, and 401(k).

Application Procedures: Send resume and cover letter to Kevin Johnson.

▶ **Internships**

Type: The company does not offer an internship program.

Composite Image Systems

1144 N. Las Palmas Ave.
Hollywood, CA 90038
Phone: (213)463-8811

Business Description: Video postproduction company.

Employees: 60.

Opportunities: Hires entry-level office and accounting personnel.

Benefits: Benefits include medical insurance, life insurance, dental insurance, a savings plan, and profit sharing.

Application Procedures: Recruits personnel from other agencies. Apply to the head of the department of interest.

▶ **Internships**

Type: The company does not offer an internship program.

Cutaways Ltd.

445 E. Illinois St.
Chicago, IL 60611
Phone: (312)836-5999

Business Description: Television commercial editing company.

Employees: 7.

Opportunities: Opportunities available for experienced college graduates.

Benefits: Benefits include medical insurance, life insurance, and profit sharing.

Human Resources: Karen Schick, Business Mgr.

Application Procedures: Most hiring is done through referrals.

▶ **Internships**

Type: The company does not offer an internship program.

Cutler Productions
18425 Burbank Blvd., Ste. 508
Tarzana, CA 91356
Phone: (818)345-2166

Business Description: Cutler Productions is involved in film, radio, and television production.

Opportunities: Hires voice talent and engineering staff.

Human Resources: Shelly Brubaker.

Application Procedures: Those interested should send resume and tape to Joel Perry, Producer or Gil Christner, Producer.

▶ **Internships**

Type: The company does not offer an internship program.

Cutters Inc.
230 N. Michigan Ave.
Chicago, IL 60601
Phone: (312)644-2500
Fax: (312)644-2501

Business Description: Involved in television, commercial, and off-line editing.

Employees: 30.

Opportunities: Entry-level opportunities include clerical and receptionist positions.

Benefits: Benefits include medical insurance, life insurance, and dental insurance.

Application Procedures: Send resume to the attention of Donna Hamilton.

▶ **Internships**

Type: Offers paid internships to college students.

Application Procedure: Contact Donna Hamilton.

David Geffen Co. Film Div.
9130 Sunset Blvd.
Los Angeles, CA 90069
Phone: (310)278-9010

Business Description: Involved in motion picture and video production.

Application Procedures: Send resume and cover letter to the attention of Human Resources.

D'Elia-Wittkofski Productions
1 Market St.
Pittsburgh, PA 15222
Phone: (412)391-2900

Employees: 24.

Opportunities: Job requirements include experience in production and some college course work.

Benefits: Benefits include medical insurance, life insurance, and profit sharing.

Human Resources: Kendra Bond, Office Mgr.

Application Procedures: Send resume and cover letter to Kelly Atquaro, Operations Mgr.

▶ **Internships**

Type: Offers internships to college juniors and seniors for college credit. **Number Available Annually:** 2-3.

Application Procedure: Send resume and cover letter to Kendra Bond.

Deluxe Laboratories Inc.
1377 N. Serrano Ave.
Hollywood, CA 90027
Phone: (213)462-6171

Business Description: Motion picture film developers.

Employees: 500.

Opportunities: Offers entry-level employment to union members.

Benefits: Benefits include medical insurance, life insurance, and dental insurance.

▶ **Internships**

Type: The company does not offer an internship program.

165

Dennis Mirsch MacGuffin Films Ltd.

411 Lafayette
New York, NY 10016
Phone: (212)529-3100

Employees: 15.

Opportunities: Hires entry-level staff with previous experience.

Benefits: Benefits include medical insurance, life insurance, and dental insurance.

Application Procedures: Hiring conducted through personal contacts and by word-of-mouth. Company does not accept unsolicited resumes.

▶ **Internships**

Type: The company does not offer an internship program.

In 1992, women experienced their highest labor-force participation rate of all time—57.8 percent. They also accounted for 60 percent of total growth between 1982 and 1992.

Source: *Working Woman*

Diamond Entertainment Corp.

1395 Manassero St.
Anaheim, CA 92807
Phone: (714)693-3399
Fax: (714)693-3339

Business Description: Motion picture production company.

Employees: 85.

Opportunities: Entry-level staff are hired in the Video Tape Library. Previous experience is required.

Benefits: Benefits include medical insurance, dental insurance, life insurance, and vision insurance.

Human Resources: Sandy Foncannon.

Application Procedures: Send resume and cover letter to the attention of the human resources department.

▶ **Internships**

Type: The company does not offer an internship program.

Dick Clark Productions Inc.

3003 W. Olive Ave.
Burbank, CA 91505
Phone: (818)841-3003

Employees: 70.

Opportunities: Hires entry-level staff with previous experience in secretarial, production, and accounting areas.

Benefits: Benefits include medical insurance, life insurance, dental insurance, savings plan, 401(k), and flex plan (section 125).

Application Procedures: Call, apply in person, or send resume and samples to Terri Grahm, Asst. to Controller.

▶ **Internships**

Type: Offers unpaid internships to college juniors and seniors. **Number Available Annually:** 1-2.

Application Procedure: Send completed application to Terri Grahm.

DIR Broadcasting and Television Corp.

32 E. 57th St.
New York, NY 10022
Phone: (212)371-6850

Business Description: Involved in the production and broadcasting of radio and television programs.

Opportunities: Hires broadcast production personnel.

Benefits: Benefits include medical insurance and life insurance.

Application Procedures: Send resume and cover letter.

▶ **Internships**

Contact: Bonnie DeFilippis.

Type: Offers internships preferably to college students. **Number Available Annually:** 2.

Du-Art Film Laboratories Inc.

245 W. 55th St.
New York, NY 10019
Phone: (212)757-4580

Business Description: Involved in motion picture services and television broadcasting.

Employees: 155.

Opportunities: Hires entry-level clerical staff.

Benefits: Benefits include medical insurance, life insurance, dental insurance, and vision insurance.

Application Procedures: Send resume and application.

▶ **Internships**

Type: The company does not offer an internship program.

Duplication Factory Inc.
4275 Norex Dr.
Chaska, MN 55318
Phone: (612)448-9912

Business Description: Provides video duplication services.

Officers: Kathy Johnson.

Employees: 50.

Opportunities: Offers entry-level positions. Requirements vary by position.

Benefits: Benefits include medical insurance, life insurance, and 401(k).

Application Procedures: Call or send resume to the attention of Barry Johnson or Dick Norgaard, Plant Mgr.

▶ **Internships**

Type: The company does not offer an internship program.

Editing Concepts Inc.
345 Hudson St.
New York, NY 10014
Phone: (212)687-9030

Business Description: Motion picture film editing company.

Employees: 13.

Opportunities: Entry-level hiring varies. Previous experience required.

Benefits: Benefits include medical insurance, life insurance, dental insurance, and savings plan.

Human Resources: Bernice Rothstan.

Application Procedures: Send resume to Nancy Sinn, Asst. Dir.

▶ **Internships**

Type: The company does not offer an internship program.

Effects House Corp.
111 8th Ave.
New York, NY 10011
Phone: (212)924-9150

Business Description: Provides special effects for the motion picture industry.

Employees: 6.

Opportunities: Entry-level hiring requirements include a general knowledge of film.

Benefits: Benefits include medical insurance.

Application Procedures: Staff hiring is done through unions.

Epic Productions Inc.
4640 Lankershim
North Hollywood, CA 91602
Phone: (818)766-6888

Business Description: Theatrical film producers.

Officers: Sarah Stannard, Office Mgr.

Employees: 28.

Benefits: Benefits include medical insurance and dental insurance.

▶ **Internships**

Type: The company does not offer an internship program.

EUE Screen Gems Ltd.
220 E. 44th St.
New York, NY 10017
Phone: (212)867-4030

Business Description: Television commercial film production company.

Employees: 60.

Opportunities: Hires entry-level staff as free-lance coordinators, production coordinators, and administrative assistants. College degree required.

Benefits: Benefits include medical insurance, savings plan, and 401(k).

Human Resources: Kim Armstrong.

Application Procedures: Send resume to Chris Cooney, Exec. Prod.

▶ **Internships**

Type: Offers unpaid internships to college juniors and seniors. **Number Available Annually:** 6.

Application Procedure: Send resume to Chris Cooney.

EUE Screen Gems Ltd.
Independent Artists
16 W. 56th St.
New York, NY 10019
Phone: (212)765-4640

Business Description: Involved in television film and commercial production.

Officers: Herb Sidel, Exec. Prod.

Opportunities: Hires entry-level office personnel.

Benefits: Benefits include medical insurance and 401(k).

Application Procedures: Send resume and cover letter to the attention of Herb Sidel.

▶ **Internships**

Type: The company does not offer an internship program.

Exit Productions Inc.
180 Franklin St.
New York, NY 10013
Phone: (212)925-8750
Fax: (212)925-8810

Business Description: Provides television commercial production and print advertising services.

Employees: 10.

Opportunities: Hires advertisement production assistants with previous experience.

Benefits: Benefits include medical insurance.

Human Resources: Susan Garvey, Controller.

Application Procedures: Send resume to Renee VanDorn, Human Resources Mgr.

▶ **Internships**

Type: Offers unpaid internships. **Number Available Annually:** 1.

Application Procedure: Send resume to Renee VanDorn.

Faces and Places Inc.
1 Hidden Meadow Rd.
Weston, CT 06883
Phone: (203)221-1400

Business Description: Motion picture and television casting directors.

Employees: 2.

Benefits: Benefits include medical insurance, life insurance, and profit sharing.

▶ **Internships**

Type: The company does not offer an internship program.

Famous Artists Agency Inc.
1700 Broadway
New York, NY 10019
Phone: (212)245-3939

Business Description: Represents specific signed artists and entertainers.

Opportunities: Hires entry-level agent assistants and clerical staff.

Human Resources: Mari Vaiciunas.

Application Procedures: Send resume and cover letter to Mari Vaiciunas.

▶ **Internships**

Type: Offers paid and unpaid clerical internships for college credit. **Number Available Annually:** 1.

Application Procedure: Send resume and cover letter.

Fast Lane Productions Inc.
395 Yuma St.
Denver, CO 80223
Phone: (303)778-0045

Opportunities: Hires technical production staff with at least two years experience in sound and lighting. Candidates must also be able to lift at least 30 pounds.

Application Procedures: Apply in person or send resume and cover letter.

▶ **Internships**

Type: The company does not offer an internship program.

Film/Video Arts
817 Broadway
New York, NY 10003
Phone: (212)673-9361
Fax: (212)475-3467

Business Description: A nonprofit organization offering subsidized rates to independent producers of film and video. Also offers classes and provides film and video equipment.

Employees: 15.

Opportunities: Offers entry-level administrative and technical positions.

Application Procedures: Contact Karen Helmerson, Dep. Dir.

▶ **Internships**

Contact: Angie Cohn, Intern Coord.

Type: Offers unpaid postproduction, vault, media training, and public relations internships to high school graduates, college students and graduates, and graduate students. Applicants must be over the age of 18. College credit is available. Full-time employment possible and placement assistance provided. **Number Available Annually:** 15-18.

Application Procedure: Contact Angie Cohn.

Filmworks USA Inc.
2000 Lakewood Ave.
PO Box 6826
Atlanta, GA 30315-5013
Phone: (404)622-4488

Business Description: Involved in motion picture movie studio rental and trade shows.

Employees: 4.

Opportunities: Offers part-time positions only.

Application Procedures: Apply in person or call to request application. Send completed application to Diane Kent, Office Mgr.

▶ **Internships**

Type: Offers paid internships to college students.

Application Procedure: Contact Diane Kent.

Fincannon and Associates Inc.
201 N. Front St., Ste. 107
Wilmington, NC 28401
Phone: (919)251-1500

Business Description: Casting company for motion pictures.

Employees: 4.

Benefits: Benefits include medical insurance, life insurance, dental insurance, and retirement.

Application Procedures: Send resume and cover letter to Lisa Fincannon, Casting Dir.

▶ **Internships**

Type: Offers unpaid internships to college students. College credit is available. **Number Available Annually:** 3.

Application Procedure: Send application including name of college or university and internship representative's name to Lisa Fincannon.

Firehouse Films Inc.
38 Centre Ave.
New Rochelle, NY 10801
Phone: (914)576-2500

Business Description: Involved in television commercial film production.

Employees: 12.

Opportunities: Hires free-lance production and film personnel.

Human Resources: John Sterner, Pres.

Application Procedures: Send resume and cover letter to the attention of Barbara Klein, Production Dept.

▶ **Internships**

Type: The company does not offer an internship program.

Fries Entertainment Inc.
6922 Hollywood Blvd.
Los Angeles, CA 90028
Phone: (213)466-2266

Business Description: Producer and distributor of television programs and theatrical motion pictures.

Employees: 25.

Benefits: Benefits include medical insurance, life insurance, and dental insurance.

Human Resources: Pamela Earid, Personnel Mgr.

Application Procedures: Send resume and cover letter to the attention of Pamela Earid. Phone calls not accepted.

▶ **Internships**

Type: The company does not offer an internship program.

A rt direction is a branch of architecture in which environments are built, but seldom in their entirety and seldom to last. What the art director creates are spaces (internal and external), facades, and even entire towns. These are often seen by more people than will ever see any single building in the world. Beyond that, the art director, using only fragments of nature or architecture or manmade objects, can evoke mood, establish themes, and etch characters in films.

Source: Hollywood Art: Art Direction in the Days of the Great Studios

---

General Television Industries Inc.
13320 Northend
Oak Park, MI 48237
Phone: (313)548-2500

Business Description: Television commercial producers.

Employees: 100.

Opportunities: Offers entry-level technical and administrative positions. College degree and/or previous experience required.

Human Resources: Lorraine Peak, Dir. of Human Resources.

Application Procedures: Send resume to the attention of Lorraine Peak, Dir. of Human Resources.

▶ **Internships**

Type: Offers paid internships to college students. **Number Available Annually:** 2.

Application Procedure: Send resume and cover letter to Lorraine Peak.

Goodtimes Home Video Corp.
401 5th Ave.
New York, NY 10016
Phone: (212)951-3000

Business Description: Movie production company.

Employees: 100.

Opportunities: Offers entry-level positions. Educational requirements vary by position, however, some college course work is required.

Benefits: Benefits include medical insurance, life insurance, and profit sharing.

Application Procedures: Call, apply in person, or send resume to the attention of Lilly Rettis, Personnel Dir. Fax: (212)213-9319.

▶ **Internships**

Contact: Lilly Rettis, Personnel Dir.

Type: Offers unpaid internships to college students. College credit is available. **Number Available Annually:** 5-6.

Application Procedure: Send resume to Lilly Rettis.

Gordon Media Enterprises Co.
295 Madison Ave.
New York, NY 10017
Phone: (212)683-6854

Business Description: Radio and television recording studio.

Employees: 21.

Opportunities: Offers entry-level opportunites in duplication.

Benefits: Benefits include medical insurance, life insurance, dental insurance, and 401(k).

Application Procedures: Send resume to the attention of Steven Stephens, Gen. Mgr.

▶ **Internships**

Contact: Steven Stephens, Gen. Mgr.

Type: Offers internships to college students.

Application Procedure: Contact Steven Stephens.

Grace and Wild Studios Inc.
23689 Industrial Park
Farmington Hills, MI 48335
Phone: (313)471-6010

Business Description: Involved in film and

videotape production, film transfer, and other related services.

Employees: 68.

Opportunities: Hires entry-level shipping/receiving staff and low-level assistants with previous experience.

Benefits: Benefits include medical insurance, life insurance, dental insurance, a savings plan, and a profit sharing.

Human Resources: Keith Ness.

Application Procedures: Send resume and cover letter to the head of the department of interest.

▶ **Internships**

Type: Offers paid internships for college credit to college students. **Number Available Annually:** 1.

Hanna-Barbara Productions
3400 Cahuenga Blvd.
Los Angeles, CA 90068
Phone: (213)851-5000

Employees: 400.

Opportunities: Hires entry-level office personnel with previous experience and college degree.

Benefits: Benefits include medical insurance and 401(k).

Human Resources: LeeAnn Gibson, Human Resources Admin.

Application Procedures: Send resume and cover letter.

▶ **Internships**

Type: Offers unpaid internships for credit to college students.

Harmony Gold
7655 Sunset Blvd.
Los Angeles, CA 90046
Phone: (213)851-4900

Business Description: Television film production company.

Opportunities: Hires administration personnel with previous experience and some college course work.

Human Resources: Alexander List, Dir. of Personnel.

Application Procedures: Send resume and cover letter to the attention of Alexander List. Phone calls not accepted.

▶ **Internships**

Type: The company does not offer an internship program.

Harpo Inc.
PO Box 909715
Chicago, IL 60670
Phone: (312)633-1000

Business Description: Television film production company.

Application Procedures: Send resume and cover letter to HARPO Inc., Human Resources Department, 110 Carpenter, Chicago, IL 60607.

Hearst Entertainment Productions Inc.
1640 S. Sepulveda Blvd.
Los Angeles, CA 90025
Phone: (310)478-1700

Business Description: Television film production company.

Employees: 65.

Opportunities: Hires production assistants and administrative personnel; college degree required.

Benefits: Benefits include medical insurance, dental insurance, vision insurance, savings plan, and a 401(k) plan.

Application Procedures: Send resume and cover letter to the attention of the human resources department.

▶ **Internships**

Type: Offers unpaid internships for college credit to seniors at Pennsylvania State University. **Number Available Annually:** 2.

Application Procedure: Internships are arranged through Pennsylvania State University.

Hemdale Film Corp.
7966 Beverly Blvd.
Los Angeles, CA 90048
Phone: (213)966-3700

Employees: 45.

Opportunities: Entry-level positions include receptionists and assistants. Candidates must have previous experience.

Benefits: Benefits include medical insurance, life insurance, dental insurance, vision insurance, 401(k), and vacation and sick leave.

Human Resources: Taryn Lee, Mgr. of Personnel and Payroll.

Application Procedures: Job openings are advertised through entertainment papers and by word-of-mouth. Those interested should call or send resume and samples to Taryn Lee, Mgr. of Personnel and Payroll.

▶ **Internships**

Type: Offers unpaid internships to college students. College credit is available. General office and administrative positions are available.

Application Procedure: Call Taryn Lee.

The restructuring of the American work force will mean that this country's best businesses will be giving their workers—in particular, women—more responsibility, pushing that responsibility downward, making use of frontline workers, and achieving a greater degree of flexibility. It will mean relying on the motivation and loyalty of workers as their key competitive strategy. It will be what makes them unique and capable of delivering a better product, a higher quality product—and a bigger profit for themselves, their shareholders, and their workers.

Source: *Working Woman*

Hollywood Film and Video Inc.
6060 Sunset Blvd.
Hollywood, CA 90028
Phone: (213)464-2181
Fax: (213)464-0893

Business Description: Develops and prints motion picture film.

Benefits: Benefits include medical insurance and a pension plan.

Application Procedures: Send resume and cover letter to Dottie Nardone, Controller.

▶ **Internships**

Type: The company does not offer an internship program.

Hollywood Rental Company Inc.
7848 N. San Fernando Rd.
Sun Valley, CA 91352
Phone: (213)849-1326

Employees: 200.

Opportunities: Hires entry-level staff in a variety of areas.

Benefits: Benefits include medical insurance, life insurance, dental insurance, and 401(k).

Application Procedures: Send application and resume to the human resources department.

▶ **Internships**

Type: The company does not offer an internship program.

Image Entertainment Inc.
9333 Oso Ave.
Chatsworth, CA 91311
Phone: (818)407-9100

Business Description: Involved in formatting and licensing of movie laser disks.

**Image Transform Inc.
Compact Video Group Inc.**
4142 Lankershim Blvd.
North Hollywood, CA 91602
Phone: (818)985-7566

Employees: 350.

Opportunities: Hires entry-level office personnel with computer experience.

Benefits: Benefits include medical insurance, life insurance, dental insurance, savings plan, and 401(k).

Application Procedures: Send application to the attention of the Human Resources Department.

▶ **Internships**

Type: The company does not offer an internship program.

Imagine Films Entertainment Inc.
1925 Century Park E.
Los Angeles, CA 90067
Phone: (310)277-1665

Business Description: Motion picture production company.

Opportunities: Hires entry-level staff in various areas. A three- or four-year degree is preferred.

Three or more years of previous work experience is acceptable.

Benefits: Benefits include medical insurance, life insurance, dental insurance, vision insurance, savings plan, and tuition assistance.

Human Resources: Robin Barris, Mgr. Dir.

Application Procedures: Maintains a job hotline at 310-277-1665, ext. 846; apply in person or through direct phone contact; send resume and cover letter.

▶ **Internships**

Type: Offers a paid internship program to college juniors and seniors. College credit is available. **Number Available Annually:** 1.

Application Procedure: Send resume or phone Robin Barris.

International Producers Services

3518 Cahuenga Blvd. W.
Los Angeles, CA 90068
Phone: (213)851-3595

Business Description: Television commercial production company.

Employees: 6.

Opportunities: Offers entry-level positions to production assistants.

Application Procedures: Send resume.

▶ **Internships**

Type: The company does not offer an internship program.

International Video Services

1501 Broadway
New York, NY 10036
Phone: (212)730-1411

Business Description: Provides videotape editing and duplication facilities.

Employees: 6.

Opportunities: Entry-level staff are hired as interns in the film transfer area.

Benefits: Benefits include medical insurance.

Human Resources: Kim Flynn, Office Mgr.

Application Procedures: Call or send resume and cover letter to Kim Flynn, Office Mgr.

▶ **Internships**

Type: Offers unpaid internships. Full-time employment is possible.

Application Procedure: Call or send resume to Kim Flynn.

J2 Communications

10850 Wilshire Blvd., No. 1000
Los Angeles, CA 90024
Phone: (310)474-5252

Employees: 8.

Opportunities: Hires experienced entry-level office personnel.

Benefits: Benefits include medical insurance and life insurance.

Application Procedures: Apply in person or send resume and cover letter to the human resources department.

▶ **Internships**

Type: The company does not offer an internship program.

Jim Henson Productions Inc.

117 E. 69th St.
New York, NY 10021
Phone: (212)794-2400

Employees: 200. Includes employees in Los Angeles, New York, and London.

Opportunities: Hires entry-level staff as assistants, receptionists, and in administrative positions. Requirements vary by position.

Benefits: Benefits include medical insurance, dental insurance, 401(k), and vacation, sick, and personal days.

Human Resources: Debbie McClellan.

Application Procedures: Send resume and cover letter to human resources in response to advertisements placed in trade magazines.

▶ **Internships**

Type: Offers paid internships to college students or those with industry experience. Positions available in production and public relations. College credit is available to public relations interns. **Number Available Annually:** 4.

Application Procedure: Send resume in response to advertisements. Mail to Human Resources, 5358 Melrose Ave., W. Bldg., 3rd Fl., Hollywood, CA 90038.

Kings Road Entertainment, Inc.
1901 Ave. of the Stars
Los Angeles, CA 90067
Phone: (213)552-0057

Business Description: Motion picture production company.

Kushner-Locke Co.
11601 Wilshire Blvd.
Los Angeles, CA 90025
Phone: (213)445-1111

Business Description: Producer of television programs and movies.

Today's new technology, in such forms as robot welders on auto assembly lines, is wiping out jobs. But economic historians point out that new technology in the long run has always created more jobs than it has destroyed, and should do so again.

Source: *Time*

Landsburg Co.
11811 W. Olympic Blvd.
Los Angeles, CA 90064
Phone: (310)478-7878

Employees: 25.

Opportunities: Entry-level positions include assistant to the executive secretary and couriers; college degree required.

Benefits: Benefits include medical insurance and dental insurance.

Human Resources: Jenny Levy, Personnel Dept.

Application Procedures: Send completed application, resume, and cover letter to the personnel department.

▶ **Internships**

Type: Offers internships for college credit to juniors and seniors. Send resume and cover letter to the attention of the Manager of Creative Affairs. **Number Available Annually:** 8.

Laser Edit East Inc.
Laser-Pacific Media Corp.
304 E. 45th St.
New York, NY 10017
Phone: (212)983-3255

Business Description: Television postproduction and editing company.

Employees: 25.

Opportunities: Hires entry-level staff in postproduction engineering. College degree required.

Benefits: Benefits include medical insurance, life insurance, dental insurance, vision insurance, savings plan, tuition assistance, and profit sharing.

Application Procedures: Send resume and cover letter to Gary Sharfin, Gen. Mgr.

▶ **Internships**

Type: The company does not offer an internship program.

Laser-Pacific Media Corp.
540 N. Hollywood Way
Burbank, CA 91505
Phone: (818)842-1111

Business Description: Film editing company.

Officers: Seana Harrison, Accountant.

Employees: 225.

Opportunities: Hires technical personnel; college degree required.

Benefits: Benefits include medical insurance, dental insurance, life insurance, vision insurance, savings plan, tuition assistance, profit sharing, elder-care programs, and child-care programs.

Application Procedures: Send resume and cover letter to the attention of Seana Harrison, Accountant.

▶ **Internships**

Type: The company does not offer an internship program.

Limelight Commercials Co.
806 Lexington Ave.
Los Angeles, CA 90038
Phone: (213)464-5808

Employees: 17.

Opportunities: Hires entry-level staff in a

variety of areas. Requirements depend on position.

Benefits: Benefits include medical insurance, life insurance, and savings plan.

Human Resources: Wendy Ford, Prod. Coord.

Application Procedures: Send resume and cover letter to Wendy Ford, Prod. Coord.

▶ **Internships**

Type: The company does not offer an internship program.

Limelite Video Inc.
7355 NW 41st St.
Miami, FL 33166
Phone: (305)593-6969

Business Description: Provides video postproduction services.

Officers: Margaret Schwartz.

Employees: 60. Includes employees at Miami and New York locations.

Opportunities: Offers entry-level office and technical positions. Previous experience required.

Benefits: Benefits include medical insurance, dental insurance, and vision insurance.

Application Procedures: Send resume and demo reel to the attention of the human resources department.

▶ **Internships**

Type: The company does not offer an internship program.

Lorimar-Warner Bros. Inc.
4000 Warner Blvd.
Tower, 8th Fl.
Burbank, CA 91505
Phone: (818)954-6000

Business Description: Engaged in motion picture and television production and distribution.

Benefits: Benefits include medical insurance, life insurance, dental insurance, and savings plan.

Application Procedures: Call the job hotline at (818)954-5400 for available positions. Send resume to Human Resources Department.

▶ **Internships**

Type: Offers paid internships to college students. **Number Available Annually:** 5-6.

Application Procedure: Send resume to Human Resources Department.

Lucasfilm Ltd. Lucasfilm Digital Commercial Productions Lucasfilm Ltd.
PO Box 2459
San Rafael, CA 94912
Phone: (415)662-1800

Business Description: Commercial production company.

Employees: 170.

Opportunities: Hires entry-level staff in a number of areas. Educational requirements and experience vary by position.

Benefits: Benefits include medical insurance, life insurance, dental insurance, vision insurance, savings plan, tuition assistance, and profit sharing.

Human Resources: Jim Cruzat, Human Resources Asst.

Application Procedures: Send resume to Human Resources Department. Positions are sometimes advertised in magazines and newspapers.

▶ **Internships**

Type: Offers internships for credit to college juniors. **Number Available Annually:** 20.

Application Procedure: Send resume to Human Resources Department.

MagneTech Corp.
3941 SW 47th Ave.
Fort Lauderdale, FL 33314
Phone: (305)354-2145

Business Description: Provides audio and videotape duplication services.

Employees: 65.

Benefits: Benefits include medical insurance.

Application Procedures: Send resume and cover letter to the attention of Human Resources.

▶ **Internships**

Type: Offers unpaid internships.

Manhattan Transfer-Edit Inc.
545 5th Ave.
New York, NY 10017
Phone: (212)687-4000

Business Description: A postproduction facility involved in tape transfering and editing.

Officers: Peggy Pellicanl, Dir. of Admin.

Opportunities: Hires entry-level staff with previous experience in various areas.

Benefits: Benefits include medical insurance, life insurance, dental insurance, and 401(k).

Application Procedures: Send resume and cover letter to the attention of Director of Administration.

▶ Internships

Type: The company does not offer an internship program.

The big corporation of the future will consist of a relatively small core of central employees and a mass of smaller firms working for it under contract. And even within the central core, there will be much shifting around, more hiring of people for specific, temporary assignments.

Source: *Time*

Mary Perillo Inc.
125 Cedar St., 8S
New York, NY 10006
Phone: (212)608-3943

Business Description: Produces film and video products, video art, music productions (including videos), and commercials. Works include *Sesame Street* shorts.

Employees: 3.

Opportunities: Offers entry-level clerical positions.

Application Procedures: Contact Mary Perillo.

▶ Internships

Contact: Molly Maguire, Office Mgr.

Type: Offers unpaid production internships to high school students and graduates and college students. College credit is available. Full-time employment possible. Placement assistance provided. **Number Available Annually:** 1-2. **Applications Received:** 50.

Duties: Production interns perform office, library, and production tasks and dubbing.

Application Procedure: Contact Molly Maguire.

Maxfilms
PO Box 901251
Palmdale, CA 93590
Phone: (805)272-5832

Business Description: Film, television, and documentary producers.

Employees: 6.

▶ Internships

Contact: Mr. Sid Glenar, VP of Production.

Type: Internships are available for the following positions (during production times only): assistant to producer; asssistant to director; camera assistant; editing assistant; assistant to art director; and actors. Interns are paid minimum wage and receive hands-on production experience. **Number Available Annually:** 10-12. **Applications Received:** 500.

Application Procedure: Send letter and resume. For acting internships, send photo as well.

Mayhew Productions
139 W. 21st St.
New York, NY 10011
Phone: (212)752-3010

Business Description: Film production company.

Officers: Wess Christopher, CEO.

Opportunities: Hires entry-level staff in the shipping department. Candidates must have previous experience.

Benefits: Benefits include medical insurance, life insurance, dental insurance, and 401(k).

Application Procedures: Send resume and cover letter to Wess Christopher, CEO.

▶ Internships

Type: The company does not offer an internship program.

MCA Inc.
100 Universal City Plz.
Universal City, CA 91608
Phone: (818)777-1000

Business Description: Involved in motion

picture production and record and book publishing.

Officers: L.R. Wasserman, CEO and Chm. of the Board; Harold M. Haas, VP of Finance.

Employees: 18,000.

Medcom Inc.
PO Box 3225
Garden Grove, CA 92642
Phone: (714)891-1443

Business Description: Provides film and video production services.

Employees: 75.

Opportunities: Hires entry-level office personnel with previous experience and some college course work.

Application Procedures: Send resume and cover letter to the attention of Debby Soelberg, Human Resources Mgr.

▶ **Internships**

Type: Offers unpaid internships to college juniors and seniors.

Media Loft Inc.
333 N. Washington Ave.
Minneapolis, MN 55401
Phone: (612)375-1086

Business Description: Involved in slide and videotape presentations.

Employees: 11.

Opportunities: Hires entry-level administrative assistants with previous computer experience and/or a college degree.

Benefits: Benefits include medical insurance and life insurance.

Application Procedures: Send resume to Jeff Harrington, Pres.

▶ **Internships**

Type: Offers paid internships to college students.

Application Procedure: Contact Jeff Harrington.

Media Network
39 W. 14th St., Ste. 403
New York, NY 10011
Phone: (212)929-2663

Business Description: Established in 1979, Media Network is a nonprofit publisher of film

and video guides and a quarterly newsletter. Focuses on social issues and change.

Employees: 6. Includes full- and part-time employees.

Benefits: Benefits include medical insurance and dental insurance.

▶ **Internships**

Contact: Yvonne Navaro, Internship Contact.

Type: Offers unpaid internships. **Number Available Annually:** 4-5.

Duties: Interns assist in creating a video library and in the development of projects. Other duties include working on a newsletter, researching, writing for media guides, cataloguing information, and new media research and review work.

Application Procedure: Contact Yvonne Navaro to apply.

Merv Griffin Enterprises
9860 Wilshire Blvd.
Beverly Hills, CA 90210
Phone: (310)859-0188

Opportunities: Offers entry-level positions for receptionists and runners.

Benefits: Benefits include medical insurance, dental insurance, and savings plan.

Human Resources: Megan Kelleher, Personnel.

Application Procedures: Send resume and cover letter to Megan Kelleher, Personnel.

▶ **Internships**

Type: The company does not offer an internship program.

MGM-UA Communications Co.
MGM-UA Film Group
1000 Washington Blvd.
Culver City, CA 90232
Phone: (310)280-6000

Business Description: Motion picture and video producers.

MJI Broadcasting
1290 Avenue of the Americas
New York, NY 10104
Phone: (212)245-5010

Business Description: Involved in radio program syndication.

Opportunities: Hires entry-level production staff.

Benefits: Benefits include medical insurance, life insurance, and dental insurance.

Application Procedures: Send resume to Eric Sheffield, Dir. of Admin.

▶ **Internships**

Type: Offers unpaid internships to college students.

Application Procedure: Send resumes to Eric Sheffield.

L ook to small and medium-size companies. They have been the traditional engines of job creation even during the era of supposed domination by the corporate elephants, and though they have been lagging in hiring lately, many experts expect that to change.

Source: *Time*

Modern Talking Picture Service Inc.
Modern TV Division
5000 Park St. N.
St. Petersburg, FL 33709
Phone: (813)541-7571

Business Description: Provides public relations programming.

Employees: 60.

Opportunities: Hires entry-level staff in the warehouse and data entry areas. Candidates must have previous experience.

Benefits: Benefits include medical insurance and life insurance.

Human Resources: Sue Johnson.

Application Procedures: Apply in person.

▶ **Internships**

Type: The company does not offer an internship program.

Morgan Creek Productions
1875 Century Park E., Ste. 200
Los Angeles, CA 90067
Phone: (310)284-8884

Business Description: Motion picture producers.

Employees: 35.

Opportunities: Offers entry-level opportunities. College degree and/or previous experience required.

Benefits: Benefits include medical insurance, life insurance, and a savings plan.

Application Procedures: Send resume to the attention of Richard Kupfer, Admin.

▶ **Internships**

Type: Offers unpaid internships to college students. College credit is available. **Number Available Annually:** 3-4.

Application Procedure: Send resume to Richard Kupfer.

Motion Picture Laboratories Inc.
781 S. Main St.
Memphis, TN 38106
Phone: (901)774-4944

Business Description: Video posting and videocassette duplication company.

Employees: 52.

Opportunities: Hires entry-level staff as clerks. Candidates must have previous experience.

Benefits: Benefits include medical insurance, life insurance, and savings plan.

Human Resources: Larry Jackson, VP.

Application Procedures: Apply in person or send resume and cover letter to Larry Jackson, VP.

▶ **Internships**

Type: Offers unpaid internships to college students. **Number Available Annually:** 2.

Application Procedure: Apply through college or university attended.

MTM Enterprises Inc.
4024 Redford Ave.
Studio City, CA 91604
Phone: (818)760-5000

Business Description: Engaged in television production and distribution.

Employees: 55.

Opportunities: Hires entry-level office personnel with previous experience.

Benefits: Benefits include medical insurance, life insurance, dental insurance, vision insurance, savings plan, tuition assistance, and 401(k).

Human Resources: Lynn Perkins, Supervisor of Personnel.

Application Procedures: Send resume and cover letter to the attention of Lynn Perkins. Applications can be filled out on site.

▶ Internships

Type: Offers unpaid internships for college credit to college seniors and graduate students. **Number Available Annually:** 70-75.

National Video Center/Recording Studios Inc.
460 W. 42nd St.
New York, NY 10036
Phone: (212)279-2000

Business Description: Provides videotape production and editing services.

Employees: 200.

Opportunities: Hires entry-level personnel with college degree in communications.

Benefits: Benefits include medical insurance, life insurance, dental insurance, vision insurance, and a pension plan.

Human Resources: Elliot Minor, Controller.

Application Procedures: Send applications to the personnel department.

▶ Internships

Type: The company does not offer an internship program.

National Video Industry Inc.
15 W. 17th St.
New York, NY 10011
Phone: (212)691-1300

Business Description: Videotape postproduction facility.

Benefits: Benefits include medical insurance, life insurance, dental insurance, and vision insurance.

Human Resources: Ivy Schaefer.

Application Procedures: Those interested in entry-level editing positions should send resume to Ivy Schaefer.

▶ Internships

Type: The company does not offer an internship program.

NBA Entertainment
645 5th Ave.
New York, NY 10022
Phone: (212)826-7000

Employees: 400.

Opportunities: Hires entry-level staff in the marketing and legal areas. Candidates must have college degree.

Benefits: Benefits include medical insurance, life insurance, dental insurance, savings plan, profit sharing, and 401(k).

Human Resources: Loretta Hackett, Personnel.

Application Procedures: Send resume to Gordon Frank, Consultant.

▶ Internships

Contact: Seth Sylvan, Asst. Dir. of Public Rel.

Type: Offers paid internships to college students.

Application Procedure: Send cover letter and resume to Seth Sylvan.

New Line Cinema Corp.
888 7th Ave.
New York, NY 10106
Phone: (212)239-8880
Fax: (212)239-9104

Business Description: Producer and distributor of theatrical motion pictures and video tapes.

Employees: 160.

Benefits: Benefits include medical insurance, dental insurance, multi-employer defined benefit pension plan, an employee stock ownership plan, incentive compensation to certain executive employees, an incentive stock plan, and a stock option plan for all full-time employees.

Human Resources: Diana Demarco, VP of Admin.

Application Procedures: Send resume and cover letter to the attention of Human Resources.

▶ Internships

Type: Offers unpaid internships for credit to college students. **Number Available Annually:** 30-60.

Application Procedure: Call the Intern

Administrator or send a letter of interest to Steve Harris.

New World Entertainment Ltd.
1440 S. Sepulveda Blvd.
Los Angeles, CA 90025
Phone: (310)444-8100

Employees: 115.

Opportunities: Hires office and marketing personnel with previous experience.

Benefits: Benefits include medical insurance, life insurance, accidental death and dismemberment insurance, and long-term disability.

Application Procedures: Send resume and cover letter to the attention of the human resources department.

▶ **Internships**

Type: The company does not offer an internship program.

Get as much education as possible. Never mind the tales of college graduates working as bellboys—even though such stories are true. On no opinion are the experts so unanimous as that the future belongs to the knowledge worker, master of his PC, fiber-optics whatsit, E-mail gizmo, and whatever takes its place.

Source: *Time*

NewVisions Inc.
12 Rte. 17 N., Ste. 302
Paramus, NJ 07652
Phone: (201)712-9500

Opportunities: Hires entry-level clerical personnel with previous experience.

Benefits: Benefits include medical insurance and dental insurance.

Human Resources: John Talbut, Mgr. Dir.

Application Procedures: Contact the company for more information.

▶ **Internships**

Type: The company does not offer an internship program.

Nightingale-Conant Corp.
7300 N. Lehigh Ave.
Chicago, IL 60648
Phone: (312)588-6217

Business Description: Involved in audio and video cassette production.

Officers: Vic Conant, CEO; Sidney Lemer, VP of Finance.

Employees: 275.

Northwest Film Center
1219 SW Park Ave.
Portland, OR 97205
Phone: (503)221-1156

Business Description: Serves the Northwest as a media arts center that provides film and video education, publications, library programs, and exhibits.

Employees: 15.

Application Procedures: Does not accept unsolicited resumes.

▶ **Internships**

Contact: Dan Eichler, Intern. Coord.

Type: Offers unpaid program assistantships to high school students and graduates, college students and graduates, graduate students, and others. College credit is available. Internships emphasize public relations/marketing. Placement assistance is provided. **Number Available Annually:** 1-4. **Applications Received:** 30.

Application Procedure: Contact Dan Eichler.

Application Deadline: August 25 for fall; December 1 for winter; May 1 for summer.

Northwest Teleproductions Inc.
4455 W. 77th St.
Minneapolis, MN 55435
Phone: (612)835-4455

Business Description: Provides full-service videotape and film production services.

Employees: 109.

Opportunities: Hires personnel in accounting and production departments; college degree and previous experience required.

Benefits: Benefits include medical insurance, life insurance, savings plan, and profit sharing.

Human Resources: Linda VanVickle, Asst. Controller; Jim Steffen, Treas. & Sec.

Application Procedures: In production, send resume and cover letter to the attention of Jim Steffen; in accounting, send resume and cover letter to the attention of Linda VanVickle.

▶ **Internships**

Type: The company does not offer an internship program.

O'Connor-Burnham Productions

6 Executive Park NE, Ste. 101
Atlanta, GA 30329
Phone: (404)329-8500

Business Description: Videotape and film production services.

Officers: Jennifer Buck.

Employees: 22.

Opportunities: Offers entry-level production positions to college graduates.

Benefits: Benefits include medical insurance and dental insurance.

Application Procedures: Call, apply in person, or send resume to the attention of the production director.

▶ **Internships**

Type: Offers unpaid internships to college seniors.

Application Procedure: Send cover letter and resume to the attention of the production coordinator.

Ohlmeyer Communications Co.

962 N. La Cienega Blvd.
Los Angeles, CA 90069
Phone: (310)659-8557

Business Description: Engaged in television show production.

Employees: 30.

Opportunities: When hiring, previous experience and/or college course work are required.

Application Procedures: Send resume to the attention of Diane Reiss, Mgr. of Admin.

▶ **Internships**

Type: Offers internships.

Application Procedure: Call or write for internship information.

Orion Pictures Corp.

1325 Avenue of the Americas
New York, NY 10019
Phone: (212)505-0051

Business Description: Major motion picture production company.

Employees: 137.

Opportunities: Hires entry-level staff in all areas. Previous experience required.

Benefits: Benefits include medical insurance, life insurance, dental insurance, savings plan, and profit sharing.

Application Procedures: Send resume and cover letter to the attention of Cathy Houser, VP of Admin.

▶ **Internships**

Type: Offers unpaid internships to college students. College credit is available. **Number Available Annually:** 10-12.

Application Procedure: Send resume and cover letter to Cathy Houser.

Orion Pictures Corp.
Orion Television Entertainment

1888 Century Park E.
Los Angeles, CA 90067
Phone: (310)282-0550

Business Description: Involved in the production of motion pictures.

Opportunities: Hires personnel in marketing, legal, and home video areas. College degree and previous experience required.

Benefits: Benefits include medical insurance, dental insurance, and savings plan.

Human Resources: Cathy Houser, VP of Human Resources & Admin.

Application Procedures: Send resume and cover letter to the attention of Cathy Houser.

▶ **Internships**

Contact: Cathy Houser.

Type: Offers paid internships for college students. **Number Available Annually:** 5-15.

Pacific Tile and Art Studio

6350 Santa Monica Blvd.
Los Angeles, CA 90038
Phone: (213)464-0121

Business Description: Involved in television and motion picture titles.

Employees: 100.

Benefits: Benefits include medical insurance, life insurance, dental insurance, and vision insurance.

Human Resources: Craig Dodson, Controller.

Application Procedures: Send resume and cover letter to the attention of Craig Dodson.

▶ Internships

Type: The company does not offer an internship program.

To keep up with fast-changing technology and workplace requirements, some analysts say, workers can expect to change careers—not just jobs, careers—three or four times during their working lives. That may be extreme, but experts say a high-tech worker must be ready to go back to school and learn new skills, on his or her own if an employer will not finance it, as a minimum of every five to 10 years.

Be prepared to work in small groups or on your own. Even on assembly lines, work teams rather than masses of undifferentiated laborers are the order of the day. The trend is likely to go much further among knowledge workers.

Source: *Time*

Palestrini Film Editing Inc.
575 Lexington Ave.
New York, NY 10022
Phone: (212)752-3348

Business Description: Involved in film editing.

Employees: 35.

Opportunities: Hires entry-level assistants who've had college course work in film editing.

Benefits: Benefits include medical insurance, life insurance, dental insurance, savings plan, and profit sharing.

Human Resources: Ethyl Rubinstein, Dir. of Operations.

▶ Internships

Type: Offers paid internships for credit to college students. Number Available Annually: 4-5.

Application Procedure: Send resume to Ethyl Rubinstein.

Paramount Communications Inc.
15 Columbus Circle
New York, NY 10023
Phone: (212)373-8000

Business Description: Involved in television and motion picture production and distribution, television station and cable network operations, and book publishing.

Officers: Martin S. Davis, CEO and Chm. of the Board; Ronald L. Nelson, Exec. VP and CFO; William F. Ashcroft, VP of Human Resources.

Employees: 12,000.

Opportunities: Account assistant positions in the public relations department require a college degree.

Human Resources: William F. Ashcroft, VP of Human Resources.

Application Procedures: Contact Human Resources for more information.

Paramount Pictures Corp.
5555 Melrose Ave.
Los Angeles, CA 90038
Phone: (213)956-5000
Fax: (213)956-8496

Business Description: A subsidiary of Paramount Communications Inc. involved in motion picture production and operation of indoor theaters.

Officers: Sherry Lansing, Chm. of the Board; Patrick B. Purcell, Exec. VP and CFO; William Hawkins, Sr. VP of Human Resources.

Employees: 2,350.

Human Resources: William Hawkins, Sr. VP of Human Resources.

Photomagnetic Sound Studios Inc. Editing Concepts Inc.
222 E. 44th St.
New York, NY 10017
Phone: (212)687-9030

Business Description: Sound studio for television and motion picture productions.

Opportunities: Hires photographers with previous experience.

Benefits: Benefits include medical insurance.

Application Procedures: Send resume and cover letter to the attention of Studio Manager.

▶ **Internships**

Type: The company does not offer an internship program.

Pinnacle Systems Inc.
870 W. Maude
Sunnyvale, CA 94086
Phone: (408)970-9787

Business Description: Designs and manufactures digital video effects for television program production.

Officers: Art Chadwick, CFO.

Employees: 35.

Opportunities: Offers sales, technical, and engineering positions. College degree and/or previous experience required.

Benefits: Benefits include medical insurance, life insurance, and dental insurance.

Application Procedures: Send resume to the attention of Lori Hoch, Admin. Asst.

▶ **Internships**

Type: The company does not offer an internship program.

Pioneer Video Manufacturing Inc.
PO Box 4368
Carson, CA 90749
Phone: (310)518-0710

Opportunities: Hires production personnel with previous experience; some college course work preferred.

Benefits: Benefits include medical insurance, dental insurance, savings plan, and tuition assistance.

Application Procedures: Apply in person or send resume and cover letter to the attention of Human Resources.

▶ **Internships**

Type: The company does not offer an internship program.

Post Group Inc.
6335 Homewood Ave.
Los Angeles, CA 90028
Phone: (213)462-2300
Fax: (213)463-0836

Business Description: Provides videotape postproduction services.

Praxis Film Works Inc.
6918 Tujunga Ave.
North Hollywood, CA 91605
Phone: (818)508-0402

Business Description: Involved in television commercial production.

Employees: 15.

Opportunities: Hires production and stage crew staff with previous experience.

Benefits: Benefits include medical insurance and life insurance.

Human Resources: Joyce Parent.

Application Procedures: Send resume and cover letter to the attention of production office.

▶ **Internships**

Type: The company does not offer an internship program.

Producers Color Service Inc.
24242 Northwestern Hwy.
Southfield, MI 40875
Phone: (313)352-5353

Business Description: Movie production company.

Employees: 225.

Opportunities: Hires entry-level production staff.

Benefits: Benefits include medical insurance, life insurance, dental insurance, vacation, and a savings plan.

Human Resources: Lori Tunney.

Application Procedures: Send resume and cover letter to Gregg Tiryakian, Dir. of Recruiting.

▶ **Internships**

Type: Offers paid internships.

Application Procedure: Send resume and cover letter to Gregg Tiryakian.

Production Masters Inc.
834 N. 7th Ave.
Phoenix, AZ 85007
Phone: (602)254-1600
Fax: (602)495-9949

Business Description: A videotape production company.

Officers: David Case, Pres.

Employees: 30.

Opportunities: Hires entry-level office personnel, audio and visual personnel, and editors with previous experience and a college degree.

Benefits: Benefits include medical insurance, life insurance, dental insurance, and 401(k).

Application Procedures: Send resume and cover letter to the attention of Personnel Office.

▶ **Internships**

Contact: Richard Dwyer, Camera Dir.

Type: Offers unpaid internships for college credit. Send resume and cover letter to the attention of Richard Dwyer.

F or the young performer who is looking to build a career in show business, representation by a qualified professional is the only way to find paying work.

Source: *The Young Performer's Guide*

Professional Video Services Corp.
2030 M St.
Washington, DC 20036
Phone: (202)775-0894
Fax: (202)775-1288

Business Description: Videotape production and video equipment rental company.

Employees: 50.

Opportunities: Hires entry-level office and building services staff. College degree, some college course work, or previous experience helpful but not essential.

Benefits: Benefits include medical insurance, life insurance, dental insurance, savings plan, and tuition assistance.

Human Resources: Roger Sullivan, Dir. of Production; Melanie Ierardi, Office Mgr.

Application Procedures: Send resume and cover letter.

▶ **Internships**

Type: Offers unpaid internships for college credit to students. **Number Available Annually:** 1.

Propaganda Films
940 N. Mansfield
Los Angeles, CA 90038
Phone: (213)462-6400

Business Description: Engaged in television, video, and commercial film production.

Opportunities: Hires entry-level producers and assistants. College degree and/or previous experience may be required depending on position.

Benefits: Benefits include medical insurance, dental insurance, and savings plan.

Application Procedures: Contact the department in your area of interest.

▶ **Internships**

Contact: Linda Alderete, Dir. of Adm. in Human Resources.

Type: Offers unpaid internships to college students. College credit is available.

Application Procedure: Send resume and cover letter to Linda Alderete.

Public Interest Video Network
4704 Overbrook Rd.
Bethesda, MD 20816
Phone: (301)656-7244
Fax: (301)656-0327

Business Description: The media center is a nonprofit organization that produces public television programming and videos. Targets nonprofit organizations interested in social issues.

Employees: 3.

Opportunities: Offers entry-level production assistant positions. Some production experience and writing skills required.

Application Procedures: Send resume and cover letter.

▶ **Internships**

Contact: Arlen Slobodow, Dir.

Type: Offers unpaid production assistant positions to college students and graduate students. College credit is available. Placement assistance and job counseling provided. Full-time employment is possible. **Number Available Annually:** 2. **Applications Received:** 12.

Duties: Production assistants work in the areas of field production, research, and distribution.

Application Procedure: Contact Arlen Slobodow.

Pyramid Teleproductions Databank

6305 N. O'Connor St., Ste. 103
Irving, TX 75039
Phone: (214)869-3330

Business Description: Videotape postproduction services.

Employees: 45.

Opportunities: Offers entry-level positions to experienced couriers and receptionists.

Benefits: Benefits include medical insurance, life insurance, dental insurance, and vision insurance.

Application Procedures: Send resume to the attention of Dan Hill, Post-Production Coord.

▶ **Internships**

Type: The company does not offer an internship program.

R. Greenberg Associates Inc. Speedy/RCA

350 W. 39th St.
New York, NY 10018
Phone: (212)239-6767

Business Description: Involved in television broadcasting.

Employees: 80.

Opportunities: Hires entry-level office and administration personnel with college degree and previous experience.

Benefits: Benefits include medical insurance, life insurance, dental insurance, and vision insurance.

Human Resources: Cece Critchley, Head of Bus. Affairs.

▶ **Internships**

Type: The company does not offer an internship program.

Raycom Inc.

PO Box 33367
Charlotte, NC 28233
Phone: (704)331-9494

Business Description: Producer of live, televised sporting events.

Benefits: Benefits include medical insurance and life insurance.

Application Procedures: Send resume to Vanessa Holliman, Secretary. Send tapes to Peter Rolfe, Production Dept. Mgr.

▶ **Internships**

Contact: Vanessa Holliman, Secretary.

Type: Offers paid internships to college graduates.

Application Procedure: Send resume to Vanessa Holliman.

Rebo Group

530 W. 25th St., 2nd Fl.
New York, NY 10001
Phone: (212)989-9466

Business Description: Videotape production company.

Employees: 20.

Opportunities: Hires entry-level staff with previous experience and some college course work.

Benefits: Benefits include medical insurance.

Human Resources: Kathleen Scott, Mgr. Dir.

▶ **Internships**

Type: The company does not offer an internship program.

Red Dog Films Inc.

11727 Mississippi Ave.
Los Angeles, CA 90025
Phone: (310)478-7070

Business Description: Commercial film production company.

Officers: Sue Crain, Production Mgr.

Employees: 4.

Opportunities: Hires free-lance personnel.

Benefits: Free-lancers receive a pension plan.

Application Procedures: Send resume and cover letter to the attention of Sue Crain.

▶ **Internships**

Type: The company does not offer an internship program.

Republic Pictures Corp.
12636 Beatrice St.
Los Angeles, CA 90066
Phone: (310)306-4040
Fax: (310)301-0221

Business Description: Independent producer and worldwide distributor of feature and television films; also sells video cassettes in North America and markets theatrical and video rights to international licenses. Maintains library of over 4,000 hours of films and television programs.

To recent college grad with No Work Experience: Look back on your college career. Were you active in student government? How about other campus organizations? What did you do for these organizations? For example, did you coordinate events, prepare budgets, or lead an organization?

Next, look at the papers you wrote, projects, and case studies. What research and analytical skills were required? You should be able to develop a list of skills to base your resume on.

Source: *Detroit Free Press*

Resolution Inc.
19 Gregory Dr.
South Burlington, VT 05403
Phone: (802)862-8881
Fax: (802)865-2308

Business Description: Provides videotape production and duplication services.

Employees: 200.

Opportunities: Hires entry-level production personnel.

Benefits: Benefits include medical insurance, life insurance, dental insurance, savings plan, and disability insurance.

Application Procedures: Apply in person or send resume and cover letter to the attention of Nancy Hopper, Payroll/Benefits Admin.

▶ **Internships**

Type: Offers internships for college students. Send resume and cover letter to the attention of the payroll/benefits administrator.

RHI Entertainment Inc.
156 W. 56th St.
New York, NY 10019
Phone: (212)977-9001
Fax: (212)977-9049

Business Description: Independent producer of long-form television programming, such as movies-of-the-week and mini-series, for network or cable television. The company distributes its original productions and the acquired programming in its library to both domestic and international media and acquires distribution rights from third parties to expand its library.

Employees: 30.

RKO Pictures Inc.
1801 Ave. of the Stars, Ste. 448
Los Angeles, CA 90067
Phone: (310)277-0707

Business Description: Motion picture developing company.

Employees: 15.

Opportunities: Hires entry-level office personnel and administrative assistants with previous experience.

Benefits: Benefits include medical insurance.

Application Procedures: Send resume and cover letter.

▶ **Internships**

Type: Offers paid internships to graduate students.

Application Procedure: Send resume and cover letter.

Rosetti Films Inc.
143 E. 19th St.
New York, NY 10003
Phone: (212)505-1160

Business Description: Provides television commercial production services.

Opportunities: Hires free-lance production assistants.

▶ **Internships**

Type: The company does not offer an internship program.

RW Lynch Company Inc.
2333 San Ramon Valley Blvd., Ste. 300
San Ramon, CA 94583
Phone: (510)837-3877

Employees: 50.

Opportunities: Hires clerical and customer service personnel with previous experience.

Benefits: Benefits include medical insurance, life insurance, dental insurance, vision insurance, and 401(k).

Human Resources: Ellen Evans, Personnel Mgr.

Application Procedures: Call or send resume and cover letter to the attention of Ellen Evans, Personnel Mgr.

▶ **Internships**

Type: The company does not offer an internship program.

Saban Productions
4000 W. Alameda St.
Burbank, CA 91505
Phone: (818)972-4800

Business Description: Television film production company.

Employees: 150.

Benefits: Benefits include medical insurance, life insurance, dental insurance, vision insurance, savings plan, and pharmacy coverage.

Human Resources: Lisa Kranz.

Application Procedures: Send resume and cover letter to the human resources department.

▶ **Internships**

Type: Offers paid internships to college seniors for credit. Send resume and cover letter to the human resources department. **Number Available Annually:** 1-2.

Santa Clarita Studio Corp.
25135 Anza Dr.
Valencia, CA 91355
Phone: (805)294-2000

Opportunities: Hires entry-level staff in production areas.

Application Procedures: Send resume.

SBK Pictures Inc.
711 Montgomery Ave.
Narberth, PA 19072
Phone: (215)667-7171

Business Description: Provides broadcast design and production services for television and radio commercials.

Application Procedures: Hires free-lancers. Contact Brian McMulty, Production Mgr.

▶ **Internships**

Type: The company does not offer an internship program.

Second City Comedy Marketing Group Inc.
1616 N. Wells St.
Chicago, IL 60614
Phone: (312)664-4032

Business Description: Television commercial production.

Officers: Karen Crane, Controller.

Employees: 200.

Opportunities: Offers entry-level positions to high school graduates.

Benefits: Benefits include medical insurance, dental insurance, and a savings plan.

Application Procedures: Apply in person or send resume and samples to the attention of Mr. Kelly Leonard, Assoc. Producer.

▶ **Internships**

Contact: Mr. Kelly Leonard, Assoc. Producer.

Type: Offers unpaid internships. College credit is available. **Number Available Annually:** 2.

Application Procedure: Write to Kelly Leonard to request an application.

Simon and Kumin Casting
1600 Broadway
New York, NY 10009
Phone: (212)245-7670

Business Description: Involved in casting for television, film, and theatre.

Employees: 5.

Opportunities: Hires entry-level office staff with previous experience. New hires must start as interns.

Benefits: Benefits include medical insurance,

life insurance, dental insurance, and vision insurance.

Human Resources: Alyssa Roth, Assoc. Casting Dir.

Application Procedures: Send resume and cover letter to Alyssa Roth, Assoc. Casting Dir.

▶ **Internships**

Type: Offers paid internships. **Number Available Annually:** 3-4.

Application Procedure: Send resume to Alyssa Roth.

If you truly want to accomplish things, part of your job is to identify the people with power and influence and identify what areas they control. Even if you are powerful, say a department head, you will not be able to accomplish your agenda if other key power people are not working with you, or if they are actively working against you.

Source: *Detroit Free Press*

Society for Visual Education Inc.
1345 Diversey Pkwy.
Chicago, IL 60614-1299
Phone: (312)525-1500

Benefits: Benefits include medical insurance, life insurance, and dental insurance.

Human Resources: Maria Paloma, Human Resources Contact; Roberta Kushen, Dir. of Human Resources.

Application Procedures: Send cover letter and resume to Roberta Kushen, Dir. of Human Resources.

SOS Productions Inc.
753 Harmon Ave.
Columbus, OH 43223
Phone: (614)221-0966

Business Description: Videotape production company.

Employees: 30.

Opportunities: Hires entry-level staff in clerical and studio production areas. Candidates must have previous experience.

Benefits: Benefits include medical insurance, life insurance, dental insurance, and 401(k).

Application Procedures: Send resume and cover letter to Ron Shkolnik, Pres.

▶ **Internships**

Contact: Mark Jacobson, Studio Mgr.

Type: Offers internships for credit to college students. **Number Available Annually:** 2-3 per school quarter.

Application Procedure: Contact Mark Jacobson.

The Sound Tracker
PO Box 9063
Seattle, WA 98109
Fax: (206)781-1103

Business Description: Established in 1980, The Sound Tracker provides nature-sound-recording services. Maintains a nature-sound archive.

▶ **Internships**

Type: Offers unpaid internships to high school seniors, college graduates, and graduate students. College credit is available. Placement and housing assistance is provided. Full-time positions are possible. **Number Available Annually:** 2.

Duties: Interns work in field management and archive inventory.

Application Procedure: Contact by fax or mail Gordon Hempton, sound tracker/recording artist.

Spelling Entertainment Group Inc.
1 E. 4th St.
Cincinnati, OH 45202
Phone: (513)579-2482
Fax: (513)579-2580

Business Description: Engaged in the development, production, and distribution of television series, series pilots, made for TV movies, and television mini-series. Also produces films that are financed and distributed by major studios and licenses merchandising and music rights associated with television and properties.

Officers: Carl H. Lindner, CEO and Chm. of the Board; Fred J. Runk, VP, CFO and Treasurer; S.

Craig Lindner, Pres. and COO; Larry Otto, VP of Human Resources.

Employees: 500.

Human Resources: Larry Otto, VP of Human Resources.

Application Procedures: Send resume and cover letter.

Terry Heffernan Films
352 6th St.
San Francisco, CA 94103
Phone: (415)626-1999

Business Description: Photography and film direction company.

Employees: 5.

Benefits: Benefits include medical insurance, life insurance, dental insurance, vision insurance, tuition assistance, profit sharing, and a pension plan.

Application Procedures: Check classified advertisements.

TI-IN Network Inc.
1000 Central Pkwy. N.
San Antonio, TX 78230
Phone: (210)490-3900

Business Description: Television film production company.

Employees: 565.

Opportunities: Hires accounting and marketing personnel with college degrees.

Benefits: Benefits include medical insurance, life insurance, dental insurance, and stock purchase plan.

Human Resources: Ellen Hillis; Tammy Elliott.

Application Procedures: Send resume, cover letter, and application to the head of the department of interest.

▶ **Internships**

Type: Offers production internships for college credit.

Time Warner Inc.
75 Rockefeller Plz.
New York, NY 10019
Phone: (212)484-8000

Business Description: Involved in movie and video production, music, book, and periodical publishing, and cable television operation. In Time Warner's filmed entertainment areas, Warner Bros. is involved in theatrical movie releases, as well as syndication programming and international distribution of television programming. Also operates Warner Bros. Home Video.

Officers: Steven J. Ross, CEO and Chm. of the Board; Bert W. Wasserman, Exec. VP and CFO.

Employees: 44,000.

Benefits: Benefits include an employee stock ownership plan, a 401(k) plan, and profit sharing. Time Warner operates a child care facility at its headquarters that is to be used as a temporary, back-up source of day care.

Human Resources: Susan Geisenheimer, Human Resources Dir.

Application Procedures: Send resume and cover letter.

Todd-AO Corp.
172 Golden Gate Ave.
San Francisco, CA 94102
Phone: (415)928-3200

Business Description: Movie postproduction sound services.

Officers: John Sherwood, Pres.

Employees: 13.

Opportunities: Offers secretarial, production, performing, and executive positions. Previous experience and/or college degree required.

Benefits: Benefits include medical insurance and life insurance.

Application Procedures: Performing positions advertised in trade magazines, newspapers, and at job agencies. Performers should apply in person. Other applicants should send resumes to John Sherwood, Pres.

▶ **Internships**

Type: The company does not offer an internship program.

Todd-AO/Glen Glenn Studios
900 Seward St.
Hollywood, CA 90038
Phone: (213)962-4000

Business Description: Provides movie postproduction and sound services.

Employees: 160.

Opportunities: Hires entry-level staff for clerical and receptionist positions. Requirements vary by position.

Benefits: Benefits include medical insurance and life insurance.

Application Procedures: Send resume to the human resources department.

▶ **Internships**

Type: Offers paid internships. College credit is available.

Application Procedure: Write to the human resources department.

Travisano DiGiacoma Films

155 W. 19th St.
New York, NY 10011
Phone: (212)255-2225

Business Description: Involved in television commercial production.

Employees: 13.

Opportunities: Hires personnel with previous experience in film production.

Benefits: Benefits include medical insurance.

Application Procedures: Send resume and cover letter to the attention of Melissa Roche, Office Mgr.

▶ **Internships**

Type: The company does not offer an internship program.

Twentieth Century-Fox Film Corp.

10201 W. Pico Blvd.
Los Angeles, CA 90064
Phone: (310)277-2211
Fax: (310)203-2979

Business Description: Major motion picture production company.

Employees: 2,000.

Opportunities: Hires entry-level computer and office personnel.

Benefits: Benefits include insurance and 401(k).

Human Resources: Gia Santos, Dir. of Human Resources.

Application Procedures: Places newspaper advertisements for certain openings; send resume and cover letter.

▶ **Internships**

Type: The company does not offer an internship program.

Universal Belo

PO Box 655237
Dallas, TX 75265
Phone: (214)977-7038

Business Description: Developers of television shows and commercials.

Human Resources: Jeff Lamb, Dir. of Human Resources.

Application Procedures: For application information, contact Mark Rapier. Phone: (214)977-7121.

Varitel Video

3575 Cahuenga Blvd. W.
Los Angeles, CA 90068
Phone: (213)850-1165

Business Description: Provides video postproduction services.

Employees: 75.

Opportunities: Offers production assistant positions to college graduates.

Benefits: Benefits include medical insurance, life insurance, dental insurance, and a savings plan.

Application Procedures: Send resume to Frank Lide, VP of Operations.

▶ **Internships**

Type: Offers unpaid internships to college students.

Application Procedure: Send resume and cover letter to Frank Lide.

Vaughn Communications Inc.

7951 Computer Ave. S
Minneapolis, MN 55435
Phone: (612)832-3100

Business Description: Involved in videotape duplication and rental of video production equipment.

Officers: Paul Laidlaw, Personnel Dept.

Employees: 425.

Opportunities: Offers positions in upper management; college degree and/or previous experience required.

Benefits: Benefits include medical insurance, life insurance, dental insurance, savings plan, tuition assistance, profit sharing, 401(k), and stock options.

Application Procedures: Apply in person or send resume to the personnel department.

▶ **Internships**

Type: Offers paid and unpaid internships to both college and vocational students. College credit is available. **Number Available Annually:** 2.

Application Procedure: Send resume or application to the attention of Paul Laidlaw.

VCA Teletronics Inc. New York
231 E. 55th St.
New York, NY 10022
Phone: (212)355-1600

Business Description: Provides postproduction film services.

Employees: 200.

Opportunities: Hires entry-level staff with previous experience in shipping.

Benefits: Benefits include medical insurance, life insurance, dental insurance, and 401(k).

Application Procedures: Send resume to Wes Christopher, CEO.

▶ **Internships**

Type: The company does not offer an internship program.

VCI Home Video Communications Inc.
6535 E. Skelly Dr.
Tulsa, OK 74145
Phone: (918)622-6460

Officers: Betty Scott, Exec. Asst.

Employees: 9.

Opportunities: Offers entry-level positions in a variety of areas. Previous experience required, college degree preferred.

Benefits: Benefits include medical insurance and life insurance.

Application Procedures: Send resume to the attention of Robert A. Blair.

▶ **Internships**

Type: The company does not offer an internship program.

Verrex Corp.
1130 Rte. 22 W
Mountainside, NJ 07092
Phone: (908)232-7000

Business Description: Provides contract services of audiovisual, sound, and recording specialties.

Opportunities: Hires entry-level clerical personnel with previous experience.

Benefits: Benefits include medical insurance and dental insurance.

Application Procedures: Send resume and cover letter to the attention of Jeannie Fulford, Office Mgr.

▶ **Internships**

Type: The company does not offer an internship program.

"**W**hen would be the best month to send my resume?" a reader asks. The best time is right now. Much more important is following up with a polite but persistent phone call, about a week after your resume arrives.

Source: *Detroit Free Press*

Video 5000 Ltd.
211 E. 43rd St.
New York, NY 10017
Phone: (212)867-8800

Business Description: Video postproduction company.

Employees: 3.

Opportunities: Hires entry-level video editors with previous experience.

Benefits: Benefits include medical insurance, dental insurance, vision insurance, vacation and sick leave.

Human Resources: Queen Lyons.

Application Procedures: Send resume, cover letter, and samples to Chuck DeLaney.

▶ **Internships**

Type: The company does not offer an internship program.

VideoWorks Inc.
Electric Picture Works
24 W. 40th St.
New York, NY 10018
Phone: (212)869-2500

Business Description: Involved in graphics, special effects, and commercials on videotape.

Opportunities: Hires entry-level staff in all areas.

Benefits: Benefits include medical insurance, life insurance, dental insurance, and vision insurance.

Human Resources: Steven Villante, Vice Pres.

Application Procedures: Send resume to Steve Villante, Vice Pres.

▶ Internships

Type: The company does not offer an internship program.

Visual Management Group Inc.
700 W. Pete Rose Way
Cincinnati, OH 45203
Phone: (513)784-1600

Business Description: Provides motion picture postproduction services.

Employees: 15.

Opportunities: Hires entry-level, part-time staff in tape operations. Candidates must have college degree and previous experience.

Benefits: Benefits include medical insurance and dental insurance.

Human Resources: Amy Radebaugh, Bus. Mgr.

Application Procedures: Send resume and cover letter to Randy Hisle, Dir. of Oper. and Eng.

▶ Internships

Type: Offers unpaid internships to college students in the film industry. **Number Available Annually:** 2.

Application Procedure: Contact Randy Hisle.

Walt Disney Co.
500 S. Buena Vista St.
Burbank, CA 91521
Phone: (818)560-1000

Business Description: Involved in amusement park operations, motion picture production for the theatrical film, and the television and video industries.

Officers: Michael D. Eisner, CEO and Chm. of the Board; Richard D. Nanula, Senior VP and CFO; Michael W. Buckhoff, VP of Human Resources.

Employees: 58,000.

Human Resources: Michael W. Buckhoff, VP of Human Resources.

Application Procedures: Send resume and cover letter.

Warner Bros. Inc.
4000 Warner Blvd.
Burbank, CA 91522
Phone: (818)954-6000

Business Description: Major motion picture production and distribution company.

Opportunities: Hiring is based on interviews conducted by agents.

Application Procedures: Send resume and cover letter.

Warner Bros. Studio Facilities
Human Resources Dept.
1041 N. Formosa Ave.
West Hollywood, CA 90046
Phone: (213)850-2571

Business Description: Division of Warner Bros. Inc.

Opportunities: Hires entry-level clerical staff; college degree and previous experience required.

Benefits: Benefits include medical insurance, dental insurance, savings plan, and tuition assistance.

Application Procedures: Check jobline at (818)954-5400 for openings. Send resume and cover letter to the human resources department, 4000 Warner Blvd., Bldg. 33, Burbank, CA 91522.

▶ Internships

Contact: Shelly Driba, Human Resources.

Type: Offers internship program.

Application Procedure: Send resume and cover letter to Shelly Driba.

West Coast Video Duplicating Inc.
385 Valley Dr.
Brisbane, CA 94005
Phone: (415)468-7330
Fax: (415)468-1386

Business Description: Provides videotape and disc reproduction services.

Employees: 980.

Opportunities: Hires entry-level production staff with previous experience.

Benefits: Benefits include medical insurance, life insurance, dental insurance, vision insurance, and vacation days.

Human Resources: Mr. Landon.

Application Procedures: Apply in person.

▶ **Internships**

Type: The company does not offer an internship program.

Weston Woods Studio
Weston Woods
Weston, CT 06883
Phone: (203)226-3355

Business Description: Involved in the production of children's films.

Employees: 25.

Opportunities: Hires entry-level office and production personnel.

Human Resources: Linda Griffin, Dir. of Operations.

Application Procedures: Send resume and cover letter to the attention of Linda Griffin.

▶ **Internships**

Contact: Cari Best, Editorial Dir.

Type: Offers unpaid internships.

Will Vinton Productions Inc.
1400 NW 22nd St.
Portland, OR 97210
Phone: (503)225-1130

Business Description: Engaged in animation, commercials, and video production.

Employees: 50.

Opportunities: Hires entry-level office personnel.

Benefits: Benefits include medical insurance, life insurance, dental insurance, vision insurance, and tuition assistance.

Application Procedures: Send resume and cover letter to the attention of Personnel Department.

▶ **Internships**

Type: The company does not offer an internship program.

Talk to the experts. Informational interviews are not just for students. Find out who is succeeding at what you do and request an interview. A few conversations with established professionals can compress an education into a few hours.

Source: *Detroit Free Press*

Wilshire Court Productions
1840 Century Park E., Ste. 400
Los Angeles, CA 90067
Phone: (310)557-2444

Business Description: Engaged in cable television program production.

Employees: 45.

Opportunities: Hires production and development assistants with college degrees.

Benefits: Benefits include medical insurance, life insurance, dental insurance, and vision insurance.

Application Procedures: Production assistant applicants should send resume and cover letter to the attention of Dean Simon, Office Mgr.

▶ **Internships**

Type: Offers paid internships to college students. **Number Available Annually:** 3.

Application Procedure: Send resume and cover letter to the department of interest.

Windsor Video
Unitel Video Inc.
8 W. 38th St.
New York, NY 10018
Phone: (212)944-9090

Business Description: Engaged in videotape postproduction services.

Employees: 100.

Opportunities: Hires entry-level office staff with previous experience and some college course work.

Benefits: Benefits include medical insurance, life insurance, dental insurance, and profit sharing.

Application Procedures: Send resume and cover letter to the attention of Lillian Morales, Operations Mgr. Asst.

▶ **Internships**

Type: Offers summer internships for college credit. Transportation is provided. **Number Available Annually:** 2.

When hit with a layoff, the first risk workers face is panic. They roll up in a ball and don't do anything for weeks. Or they deny their loss of earnings by going on a spending spree. Panic is normal, as are anger and tears. But it's crucial to get an early grip on your finances—to see how many months you can go without work.

Source: *Detroit Free Press*

WRS Motion Picture and Video Laboratories
1000 Napor Blvd.
Pittsburgh, PA 15205-1501
Phone: (412)937-7700

Employees: 180.

Opportunities: Hires entry-level staff in all areas. Previous experience required.

Benefits: Benefits include medical insurance, life insurance, dental insurance, vision insurance, savings plan, tuition assistance, profit sharing, and 401(k) plan.

Human Resources: Mary Sokol.

Application Procedures: Send resume to Jim Potter, Human Resource Mgr.

Zanuck Co.
202 N. Canon Dr.
Beverly Hills, CA 90210
Phone: (310)274-0261

Business Description: Motion picture production company.

Employees: 6.

Opportunities: Hires entry-level principals and assistants with college degrees and previous experience.

Benefits: Benefits include medical insurance, life insurance, dental insurance, and savings plan for full-time employees.

▶ **Internships**

Type: The company does not offer an internship program.

Additional Companies

Anderson Soft-Teach Corp.
983 University Ave.
Los Gatos, CA 95030
Phone: (408)399-0100

Associates and Ferren
PO Box 609
Wainscott, NY 11975
Phone: (516)537-7800

Barry and Enright Productions
703 Marco Pl.
Santa Monica, CA 90401
Phone: (310)556-1000

Buena Vista Home Video
500 S. Buena Vista St.
Burbank, CA 91521
Phone: (818)560-0044

CEL Communications Inc.
633 3rd Ave.
New York, NY 10017
Phone: (212)557-3400

Children's Television Workshop
1 Lincoln Plaza
New York, NY 10023
Phone: (212)595-3458

Fayette Products Inc.
400 W. Erie St.
Chicago, IL 60610
Phone: (312)944-1690

Group W Productions, Inc.
3801 Barham Blvd.
Los Angeles, CA 90068
Phone: (213)850-3800

HBO Studio Productions Inc.
120A E. 23rd St.
New York, NY 10010
Phone: (212)512-7800

HKM Productions Inc.
1641 N. Ivar Ave.
Hollywood, CA 90028
Phone: (213)465-9494

Jack Morton Productions Inc.
641 Avenue of the Americas
New York, NY 10011
Phone: (212)727-0400

KLM Video Inc.
5420 Butler Rd.
Bethesda, MD 20816
Phone: (301)986-7944

Kultur International Films Inc.
121 Hwy. 36
West Long Branch, NJ 07764
Phone: (908)229-2343

Library of Solutions Inc.
530 Walnut St., 13th Fl.
Philadelphia, PA 19106
Phone: (215)574-2000

Media Associates Inc.
7400 Fullerton Rd., Ste. 105
Springfield, VA 22153
Phone: (703)866-6100

Midwest Media Artists Access Center
2388 University Ave.
St. Paul, MN 55114
Phone: (612)646-6104
Fax: (612)646-3879

Raleigh TV and Film Inc.
5300 Melrose Ave.
Hollywood, CA 90038
Phone: (213)466-3111

Select Media Communications Inc.
152 W. 57th St.
New York, NY 10019
Phone: (212)765-1020

Stephen J. Cannell Productions Inc.
7083 Hollywood Blvd.
Hollywood, CA 90028
Phone: (213)465-5800

As a rule of thumb, you'll need one month of job search for every $10,000 in salary you seek, although older people or those in bad job markets may find that their search goes on much longer.

Source: *Detroit Free Press*

Technicolor Inc.
4050 Lankershim Blvd.
North Hollywood, CA 91608
Phone: (818)769-8500

Television Production Services
3514 Chamblee Dunwoody
Atlanta, GA 30341
Phone: (404)452-8700

Twentieth Century Fox Film Corp. CBS-Fox Video
1211 Avenue of the Americas
New York, NY 10036
Phone: (212)819-3200

U-Edit Video Inc.
1002 N. Central Expwy., Ste. 689
Richardson, TX 75080
Phone: (214)690-3348

Unitel Video Inc.
515 W. 57th St.
New York, NY 10019
Phone: (212)867-4600

White Production Archives Inc.
12213 S. Pulaski Rd.
Alsip, IL 60658
Phone: (708)535-1540

CAREER
RESOURCES

Career Resources

The Career Resources chapter covers additional sources of job-related information that will aid you in your job search. It includes full, descriptive listings for sources of help wanted ads, professional associations, employment agencies and search firms, career guides, professional and trade periodicals, and basic reference guides and handbooks. Each of these sections is arranged alphabetically by organization, publication, or service name. For complete details on the information provided in this chapter, consult the introductory material at the front of this directory.

Sources of Help Wanted Ads

Advance Job Listings
PO Box 900
New York, NY 10020

Affirmative Action Register for Effective Equal Opportunity Recruitment
AAR, Inc.
8356 Olive Blvd.
St. Louis, MO 63132
Phone: (314)991-1335

Green, Warren H., editor. Published monthly. $15.00/year. Provides listing of state, university, and other publicly-funded positions directed to women, minorities, veterans, and handicapped job seekers.

American Film
BPI Communications, Inc.
6671 Sunset Blvd.
Ste. 1514
Hollywood, CA 90028
Phone: (213)856-5350

$24.00/year (includes membership in the American Film Institute); $2.50/single issue.

Art Direction
10 East 39th St.
New York, NY 10016
Phone: (212)889-6500
Fax: (212)889-6504

Monthly. $27.50/year; $4.00/single issue.

Audio
1633 Broadway
New York, NY 10019
Phone: (212)767-6330

Monthly. $19.94/year; $2.75/issue.

Audio Visual Communications
PTN Publishing Co.
445 Broad Hollow Rd.
Melville, NY 11747
Phone: (516)845-2700
Fax: (516)845-7109

Twelve times/year. $60.00/year; $6.00/single issue.

AV Video
Montage Publishing, Inc.
25550 Hawthorne Blvd.
Ste. 314
Torrance, CA 90505
Phone: (213)373-9993

Monthly. $15.00/year.

T he entertainment industry is one of the largest—and fastest growing—occupational fields in the world. TV and movie production companies are constantly seeking dedicated, motivated Production Assistants to enter this field. Once you have joined the fellowship of entertainment professionals, you can advance as far as your skills and knowledge will take you.

Source: *How to Break into the Film Business: The Production Assistant's Handbook*

Back Stage
Back Stage Publications Inc.
330 W. 42nd St.
New York, NY 10036
Phone: (212)947-0020

Weekly. $50.00/year. Newspaper reporting on entertainment, films, and television commercials.

BFF News
Black Filmmaker Foundation (BFF)
Tribeca Film Center
375 Greenwich
Ste. 600
New York, NY 10013
Phone: (212)941-3944
Fax: (212)941-3943

Monthly. Free to members. Includes job and internship listings, calls for entries, and calendar of events.

Billboard Magazine
BPI Communications, Inc.
1515 Broadway
39th Fl.
New York, NY 10036
Phone: (212)764-7300

Timothy White, editor-in-chief. Weekly. $178.00/year. International magazine of music and home entertainment geared toward professionals in the music industry and related fields.

The Black Collegian
1240 S. Broad St.
New Orleans, LA 70125
Phone: (504)821-5694

Quarterly. $10.00/year; $5.00/year for students; $2.50/issue. Career and job-oriented publication for black college students.

Broadcast Opportunities
Broadcast Foundation of College/University Students
89 Longview Rd.
Port Washington, NY 11050
Phone: (516)883-2897

Periodic.

Broadcasting
Broadcasting Publications
1705 DeSales St., NW
Washington, DC 20036
Phone: (202)659-2340

Weekly. $70.00/year; $2.00/issue.

Career Woman
Equal Opportunity Publications, Inc.
44 Broadway
Greenlawn, NY 11740

Three times/year. $13.00/year. Recruitment magazine for women. Provides free resume service and assists women in identifying employers and applying for positions.

Creative Register
American Center for Design (ACD)
233 E. Ontario
Ste. 500
Chicago, IL 60611
Phone: (312)787-2018
Fax: (312)649-9518

Monthly. Referral service bulletin.

CSI National Career Network

Computer Search International Corporation
(CSI)
7926 Jones Branch Dr., Ste. 120
McLean, VA 22102
Phone: (302)749-1635

Online database that contains job listings from potential employers and candidate resumes from executive recruiting firms. Covers more than 40 technical and managerial job categories.

Directory of Internships

Ready Reference Press
PO Box 5249
Santa Monica, CA 90409
Phone: (213)474-5175

$95.00. Lists internship opportunities in many fields of interest, including, but not limited to arts, journalism, public relations, education, law, environmental affairs, business, engineering, and computer science. In addition, cites summer internship opportunities, work/study programs, and specialized opportunities for high school and undergraduate students. Indexed by subject, geography, and program.

Equal Opportunity Magazine

Equal Opportunity Publications
44 Broadway
Greenlawn, NY 11740

Three times/year. $13.00/year. Minority recruitment magazine. Includes a resume service.

The Hollywood Reporter

6715 Sunset Blvd.
Hollywood, CA 90028
Phone: (213)464-7411

Daily, Monday - Friday. $116.00/year; $180.00/year in New York City; $335.00/year outside N.Y.C. Film, TV, and entertainment trade newspaper.

How

F & W Publications, Inc.
1507 Dana Ave.
Cincinnati, OH 45207
Phone: (513)531-2222
Toll-free: 800-283-0963
Fax: (513)531-1843

Bimonthly. $41.00/year; $7.00/single issue.

In Motion

1203 West St.
Annapolis, MD 21401
Phone: (301)269-0605
Fax: (301)263-4615

Monthly. $24.95/year; $4.00/single issue.

International Women's Writing Guild Network

International Women's Writing Guild
(IWWG)
Box 810
Gracie Station
New York, NY 10028
Phone: (212)737-7536

Six times/year. Free to members. Lists employment opportunities, awards, and calendar of events. Helps women writers publish their work.

> **Y**ou must discard the traditional image of corporate security and paternalism and replace it with an image of yourself as a free agent skills broker.
> You must change your goal of working your way up the corporate ladder to a goal of moving from one project to another, to several different employers, and possibly even changing industries.
>
> Source: *Detroit Free Press*

Internship and Job Opportunities in New York City and Washington, D.C.

The Graduate Group
86 Norwood Rd.
West Hartford, CT 06117

$27.50.

Internships: On-the-Job Training Opportunities for All Types of Careers

Peterson's Guides, Inc.
20 Carnegie Center
PO Box 2123
Princeton, NJ 08543-2123
Phone: (609)243-9111
Fax: (609)243-9150

Annual, December. $27.95, plus $3.00 shipping. Covers: 850 corporations, social service organizations, government agencies, recreational facilities (including parks and forests), entertainment industries, and science and research facilities which offer about 50,000 apprenticeships and internships in 23 different career areas. Entries include: Organization name, address, name of contact; description of internship offered, including duties, stipend, length of service; eligibility requirements; deadline for application and application procedures. Arrangement: Classified by subject (arts, communications, business, etc.). Indexes: Subject/organization name, geographical.

> **I**n all cases, the people with an edge will be those who know how to use a computer to do their jobs more efficiently, who can present ideas cogently, and who work well in teams.
>
> Source: *U.S. News & World Report*

The Job HUNTER
University of Missouri-Columbia
Career Planning and Placement Center
100 Noyes Bldg.
Columbia, MO 65211

Biweekly. $75.00/year; $50.00/six months. Lists opportunities for college graduates with 0-3 years experience in many fields. Includes information on internships and summer jobs.

Jobs in Arts and Media Management: What They Are and How to Get One!
American Council for the Arts
1285 Avenue of the Americas
New York, NY 10019
Phone: (212)245-4510

Langley, Stephen, and Abruzzo, James. 1986. $19.95. Includes lists of about 150 sources of information on job opportunities in the arts, including organizations offering internships, job listings, graduate programs, and short-term study; professional groups concerned with theater, music, dance, opera, museum and gallery management, film, and telecommunication management. (Does not include popular music performing or music recording.) Entries include: For internships - Organization name,

address, phone, description, requirements. For job referral associations and periodicals - Association or publisher name, address, fields covered, services offered, turn-around time, average number of jobs, cost of subscription or dues, comments. Arrangement: Classified by type of source.

Location Production Guide
PO Box 617024
Orlando, FL 32861-7024
Phone: (407)295-1094
Fax: (407)293-4948

Twice/year. $12.00/year; $6.95/single issue.

Millimeter
Penton Publishing
1100 Superior Ave.
Cleveland, OH 44112
Phone: (216)696-7000
Fax: (216)696-1267

Monthly. $50.00/year; $7.00/single issue.

The National Ad Search
National Ad Search, Inc.
PO Box 2083
Milwaukee, WI 53201

Fifty issues/year. $235.00/year; $145.00/six months; $75.00/three months. Contains listings of 'over 2,000 current career opportunities from over 72 employment markets.'

National Business Employment Weekly
Dow Jones and Company, Inc.
PO Box 300
Princeton, NJ 08543
Phone: (609)520-4000

Weekly. $199.00/year; $112.00/six months. Newspaper containing help wanted advertising from four regional editions of the *Wall Street Journal*. Includes statistics and articles about employment opportunities and career advancements.

National Directory of Arts Internships
National Network for Artist Placement
935 West Ave. 37
Los Angeles, CA 90065
Phone: (213)222-4035

Biennial, odd years. $35.00, postpaid, payment

with order. Includes about 800 internship opportunities in dance, music, theater, art, design, film, and video. Provides name of sponsoring organization, address, name of contact; description of positions available, eligibility requirements, stipend or salary (if any), application procedures. Classified by discipline.

National Directory of Internships

National Society for Internships and
Experiential Education
3509 Haworth Dr.
Ste. 207
Raleigh, NC 27609
Phone: (919)787-3263

Biennial, fall of odd years. $22.00, plus $2.50 shipping. Covers: Over 30,000 educational internship opportunities in 75 fields with over 2,650 organizations in the United States for youth and adults. Entries include: Organization name, address, phone, contact name, description of internship opportunities, including application procedures and deadlines, remuneration, and eligibility requirements. Arrangement: Classified by type of organization. Indexes: Geographical, organization name, career field.

National Employment Listing Service Bulletin

Sam Houston State University
College of Criminal Justice
Huntsville, TX 77341

Monthly. $30.00/year for individuals; $65.00/year for institutions/agencies.

New England Employment Week

PO Box 806
Rockport, ME 04856

Opportunity Report

Job Bank, Inc.
PO Box 6028
Lafayette, IN 47903
Phone: (317)447-0549

Biweekly. $252.00/year. Lists 3,000-4,000 positions across the United States, from entry-level to upper management, in a variety of occupational fields. Ads are derived from newspapers, primarily in growth markets. Ads

contain position description, employment requirements, and contact information.

Peterson's Job Opportunities for Business and Liberal Arts Graduates

Peterson's Guides, Inc.
PO Box 2123
Princeton, NJ 08543-2123
Phone: (609)243-9111

Compiled by the Peterson's staff. 1993. $20.95 paperback. 300 pages. Lists hundreds of organizations that are hiring new business, humanities, and social science graduates in the areas of business and management. Explores how to match academic backgrounds to specific job openings. Provides information about opportunities for experienced personnel as well. Includes data on starting locations by city and state, summer jobs, co-op jobs, internships, and international assignments.

Post

Post Pro Publishing
25 Willowdale Ave.
Port Washington, NY 11050
Phone: (516)767-2500
Fax: (516)767-9335

Monthly. $40.00/year; $5.00/single issue.

Video Systems

9221 Quivira Rd.
PO Box 12901
Overland Park, KS 66212
Phone: (913)888-4664

Monthly. Free to qualified subscribers. $45.00/year.

Where the Jobs Are: A Comprehensive Directory of 1200 Journals Listing Career Opportunities

Garrett Park Press
PO Box 190
Garrett Park, MD 20896
Phone: (301)946-2553

1989. $15.00; $14.00, prepaid. Contains list of approximately 1,200 journals that publish advertisements announcing job opportunities. Arranged alphabetically. Indexes: Occupational field.

Professional Associations

Academy of Motion Picture Arts and Sciences

8949 Wilshire Blvd.
Beverly Hills, CA 90211
Phone: (310)247-3000
Fax: (310)247-9619

Motion picture producers, directors, writers, cinematographers, editors, actors, and craftsmen. Presents awards for outstanding achievements in motion picture production. Bestows student film awards and screenwriting fellowships. **Membership:** 5,210. **Publication(s):** *Academy Players Directory*, 3x/year. • *Annual Index of Motion Picture Credits.*

Academy of Science Fiction, Fantasy, and Horror Films

334 W. 54th St.
Los Angeles, CA 90037
Phone: (213)752-5811

Actors, writers, producers, directors, special effects people, and other individuals connected with the film industry; persons in the field of education. **Membership:** 3,000. **Purpose:** Recognizes artists in the science fiction, fantasy, and horror genres in the fields of acting, music, direction, writing, cinematography, special effects, makeup, film criticism, set decoration and design, stop motion animation, publicity, and advertising. Conducts lectures and seminars. **Publication(s):** *Academy of Science Fiction, Fantasy, and Horror Films—Newsletter*, quarterly.

Actors' Equity Association (AEA)

165 W. 46th St.
New York, NY 10036
Phone: (212)869-8530
Fax: (212)719-9815

Membership: AFL-CIO. **Purpose:** Represents professional actors and stage managers. Maintains Actors' Equity Foundation that makes awards and grants to organizations or charities that work in the best interests of theatre. **Publication(s):** *Equity News*, monthly.

Actor's Fund of America

1501 Broadway
Ste. 518
New York, NY 10036
Phone: (212)221-7300
Fax: (212)764-0238

Membership: Human service organization of the entertainment industry. Activities: Sponsors survival jobs program to provide employment for those between engagements. Provides emergency financial assistance to those in need; makes available social services, counseling and psychotherapy, health and education services, and nursing home care and retirement housing. Conducts substance abuse programs and blood drives.

African-American Film and Television Association

6565 Sunset Blvd., Ste. 301
Hollywood, CA 90028
Phone: (213)466-8221

Entertainment networking organization. Conducts seminars in film production, distribution, etc.

American Center for Design (ACD)

233 E. Ontario
Ste. 500
Chicago, IL 60611
Phone: (312)787-2018
Fax: (312)649-9518

Membership: Design professionals, educators, and students. Activities: Offers placement service. Acts as informational, technical, and educational resource to the design community. Sponsors The 100 Show, an annual national design exhibition. Conducts workshops and seminars; bestows awards; provides specialized education. Maintains design gallery and 700 volume reference library.

American Cinema Editors

1041 N. Formosa Ave.
West Hollywood, CA 90046
Phone: (213)850-2900
Fax: (213)850-2922

Invitational society of professional motion picture and television film editors. **Membership:** 335. **Purpose:** Sponsors production and distribution of motion picture films on film editing entitled Basic Principles of

Film Editing, and Interpretation and Values. Presents annual ACE Eddie Award for best film editing. Conducts Visiting Editor program at schools. **Publication(s):** *American Cinemeditor*, quarterly.

American Film Institute

John F. Kennedy Center for the Performing Arts
Washington, DC 20566
Phone: (202)828-4000

Nonprofit, nongovernmental corporation dedicated to preserving and developing the nation's artistic and cultural resources in film and video. **Membership:** 135,000. **Purpose:** To catalog and preserve America's film heritage; to make grants available to film and videomakers for the production and films and to award internships on major motion picture productions; to act as a bridge between learning a craft and practicing a profession, through an intensive two-year course in filmmaking and film theory; to promote the study of film as an art form with its own aesthetics, history, and techniques through seminars for film teachers and special materials. **Publication(s):** *American Film*, monthly. • *Guide to College Film Courses*, periodic.

American Film Marketing Association

12424 Wilshire Blvd., Ste. 600
Los Angeles, CA 90025-1040
Phone: (310)447-1555
Fax: (310)447-1666

Independent producers and distributors of feature length theatrical films; private and governmental organizations involved in selling film rights to domestic and foreign territories. **Membership:** 115. **Publication(s):** *Newsletter*, quarterly.

American Institute of Graphic Arts (AIGA)

1059 3rd Ave.
New York, NY 10021
Phone: (212)752-0813
Toll-free: 800-548-1634
Fax: (212)755-6749

Membership: Graphic designers, art directors, illustrators, packaging designers, and craftsmen involved in printing and allied graphic fields.

Purpose: Sponsors exhibits and projects in the public interest. Annually awards medal for distinguished achievement in the graphic arts. Sponsors traveling exhibitions. Operates gallery. Maintains library of design books and periodicals; offers slide archives. **Publication(s):** *AIGA Journal of Graphic Design*, quarterly. • *AIGA Membership Directory*, biennial. • *AIGA News*, bimonthly. • *Graphic Design USA*, annual.

The most successful employees of the future will be mid-level decision makers who can use their own computer support systems. They will have specialized knowledge and expertise, and will be able to shift from one company to another, and industry to industry.

Source: *Detroit Free Press*

American Society of Cinematographers

17892 N. Orange Dr.
Hollywood, CA 90028
Phone: (213)969-4333
Fax: (213)876-4973

Professional directors of motion picture and television photography and others affiliated with cinematography. **Membership:** 279. **Publication(s):** *American Cinematographer Magazine*, monthly. • Also publishes *American Cinematographer Manual* • *ASC Cinema Workshop* • *Light on Her Face* • *American Cinematographer Video Manual*.

Associated Actors and Artistes of America

165 W. 46th St.
New York, NY 10036
Phone: (212)869-0358

Membership: International body consisting of 7 national unions within the performing arts field, each autonomous in its particular jurisdiction. Members are: Actors' Equity Association; American Federation of Television and Radio Artists; American Guild of Musical Artists; American Guild of Variety Artists; Hebrew Actors' Union; Italian Actors' Union; Screen Actors Guild; Screen Extras' Guild.

Associated Writing Programs (AWP)

Old Dominion University
1411 N. 49th St.
Norfolk, VA 23529-0079
Phone: (804)683-3839

Membership: Writers; students and teachers in writing programs; editors, publishers, and creative and professional writers. Activities: Helps writers get published and find jobs; and enhances the quality of literary education. Operates placement service. Sponsors competitions.

Association for Independent Video and Filmmakers

625 Broadway, 9th Fl.
New York, NY 10012
Phone: (212)473-3400

Independent film and videomakers, producers, directors, writers, and individuals involved in film and television. **Membership:** 4,500. **Publication(s):** *The Independent*, 10x/year. • *The Next Step*, periodic. • Also publishes *Directory of Film and Video Productions in Latin America and the Caribbean* • *Guide to Film and Video Distributors* • *Guide to International Film and Video Festivals* • *Ship Shape Shipping*, and books and pamphlets.

Association of Audio-Visual Technicians (AAVT)

2378 S. Broadway
Denver, CO 80210
Phone: (303)698-1820
Fax: (303)777-3261

Membership: Individuals who produce audiovisual materials, train audiovisual technicians, or repair audiovisual and video systems. Activities: Offers placement services. Professional association that acts as a clearinghouse for information and communications between its members and the rest of the audio-visual materials industry. Conducts service seminars.

Association of Entertainment Industry Computer Professionals

1341 Ocean Ave.
Box 361
Santa Monica, CA 90401

Computer people working at studios or production companies, people who use computers to write and prepare budgets, graphics, and musical scores.

Association of Freelance Professionals

3607 W. Magnolia Blvd., No. 6
Burbank, CA 91505
Phone: (818)842-7797
Fax: (818)842-8226

Publication(s): *Freelancer*, newsletter.

Association of Visual Communicators

8130 La Mesa Blvd., No. 406
La Mesa, CA 91941-6437
Phone: (619)461-1600

Media producers, managers, and creative and technical people in industry, government, education, and technical, promotional, and enrichment fields. **Membership:** 5,000. **Purpose:** Sponsors seminars and competitions. Bestows awards. **Publication(s):** *Association of Visual Communicators—Membership Directory*, annual. • *Visions*, quarterly.

Black American Cinema Society

3617 Monclair St.
Los Angeles, CA 90018
Phone: (213)737-3292

Faculty members, students, senior citizens, and film and jazz enthusiasts. **Membership:** 1,350. **Purpose:** To bring about an awareness of the contributions made by blacks to the motion picture industry in silent films, early talkies, and short and feature films. Provides financial support to independent black filmmakers. **Publication(s):** *Black Talkies Souvenir Book*, annual. • *Mayme Clayton Gold Tournament Souvenir Book*, annual.

Black Filmmaker Foundation

Tribeca Film Center
375 Greenwich, Ste. 600
New York, NY 10013
Phone: (212)941-3944
Fax: (212)941-3943

Serves as a media arts center. Fosters audience development by programming local, national, and international film festivals. Conducts seminars and workshops. **Membership:** 3,000.

Publication(s): *Annual Report* • *BFF News*, monthly. • *Blackface*, quarterly.

Black Stuntmen's Association (BSA)

8949 W. 24th St.
Los Angeles, CA 90034
Phone: (213)870-9020

Membership: Men and women, ages 18 to 50, who are members of the Screen Actors Guild and the American Federation of Television and Radio Artists. Activities: Offers placement service. Serves as an agency for stuntpeople in motion pictures and television. Conducts stunt performances at various local schools. Maintains library of television and motion picture films. Plans to operate school for black stuntpeople.

Broadcast Designers Association

251 Kearny St., Ste. 611
San Francisco, CA 94108
Phone: (415)788-2324
Fax: (415)788-7622

Designers, artists, art directors, illustrators, photographers, animators, and other professionals in the television industry; educators and students; commercial and industrial companies that manufacture products related to design. **Membership:** 1,006. **Purpose:** To assist television designers by disseminating educational information. Informs members of new design trends, graphic/technical information, and state-of-the-art equipment and materials. Bestows awards. **Publication(s):** *BDA Update*, 10x/year. • *Scanlines*, quarterly. • Also publishes a series of television design books.

Casting Society of America

6565 Sunset Blvd., Ste. 306
Los Angeles, CA 90028
Phone: (213)463-1925

Cinewomen

9903 Santa Monica Blvd., Ste. 461
Beverly Hills, CA 90212
Phone: (310)855-8720

Nonprofit networking organization for women. **Purpose:** To provide support for women professionally and emotionally at any stage in their career.

Council of Writers Organizations (CWO)

c/o WIW
220 Woodward Bldg.
733 15th St. NW
Washington, DC 20005
Phone: (202)347-4973

Membership: Twenty-four organizations representing 35,000 writers. Activities: Maintains referral service. Serves as an umbrella agency for organizations representing writers. Provides a means of sharing information among organizations and their members as well as a voice for professional writers.

Strategy: Until recently, most advice on career development focused on how to move up the corporate ladder. All that changed in the late 1980s, as corporate America began a series of cutbacks and layoffs that resulted in a broader, flatter hierarchy. Lateral moves were no longer taboo, and were even encouraged; some Fortune 500 corporations began using them as a way to keep valued employees challenged and motivated.

In fact, one of the trends in the personnel business is a new horizontal structure called "broad banding," in which employees are loosely organized into a few broad job categories, rather than the dozens of titles in traditional systems.

Source: *Working Woman*

Directors Guild of America (DGA)

7920 Sunset Blvd.
Hollywood, CA 90046
Phone: (310)289-2000
Fax: (310)289-2029

Membership: Independent. **Purpose:** Negotiates agreements for members. Bestows awards. **Publication(s):** *Directory of Members*, annual. • *Newsletter*, monthly.

Fastbreak Syndicate, Inc. (FSI)

PO Box 1626
Orem, UT 84059
Phone: (801)785-1300

Membership: Freelancers including writers, graphic artists, and photographers. Activities:

Operates placement service. Seeks to enhance the profitability of freelance work and to facilitate the exchange of information and the marketing of finished works, using a computer network. Sponsors competitions for beginning freelancers; bestows awards. Maintains library and archive. Plans to conduct regional workshops and seminars.

According to the Association of Part-Time Professionals, 20 million Americans are working part-time. More than 4.5 million are part-time professionals, whose ranks have swelled more than 50 percent the past decade.

Source: *Detroit Free Press*

Graphic Artists Guild (GAG)

11 W. 20th St., 8th Fl.
New York, NY 10011
Phone: (212)463-7730
Fax: (212)463-8779

Membership: Graphic, textile, and needleart designers; cartoonists, computer artists, production artists, and illustrators. **Purpose:** Promotes professional and economic interests of graphic artists. Seeks to establish standards for ownership rights, reproduction rights, business pratices, and copyrights. Has grievance procedure for members in disputes. Maintains artist-to-artist hot line, placement service, speakers' bureau, and 700 volume library. Provides legal and accounting referrals and discount program for products and services. Offers specialized education in business school courses and seminars. Bestows biennial Walter Hortens Memorial Awards for distinguished service and outstanding client. **Publication(s):** *Directory of Illustration*, annual. • *Graphic Artists Guild Handbook: Pricing and Ethical Guidelines*, biennial. • *Graphic Artists Guild— National Newsletter*, quarterly. • *Graphic Artists Guild—The Update*, monthly.

Independent Feature Project

132 W. 21st St., 6th Fl.
New York, NY 10011
Phone: (212)243-7777
Fax: (212)243-3882

Independent film producers and directors.

Membership: 2,000. **Purpose:** Promotes the production and distribution of independent feature films. Conducts seminars. **Publication(s):** *Off Hollywood Report*, quarterly.

Interactive Multimedia Association

3 Church Cir., Ste. 800
Annapolis, MD 21401-1933
Phone: (410)626-1380

Organizations and institutions that produce and use interactive multimedia technology or optical media systems (computer programs utilizing laser discs); those providing services to the industry. **Membership:** 190. **Purpose:** To expand markets for interactive products and services. Encourages greater public awareness of the industry and demonstrates uses and values of the technology. Promotes improved government relations by developing procurement guidelines for product development and supporting legislation that would create resources for developing information technologies. Bestows awards. **Publication(s):** *Interactive Industry News*, monthly. • *Who's Who in Interactive Media*, annual. • Also publishes *The Power of Multimedia: A Guide to Interactive Technology in Education and Workforce Training* and *Recommended Practices for Interactive Video Portability* (books).

International Animated Film Society (ASIFA)

PO Box 787
Burbank, CA 91503
Phone: (818)842-8330

Professional animators, fans, and students of animation. **Purpose:** To advance and promote understanding and quality of animation. Provides search and rescue referral service to restore and repair damaged cells (individual celluloid frames); certifies authenticity of artwork that may have been used in animated films. Conducts demonstrations on the production and sale of cells. Bestows annual Annie Award for best animated film and filmmaker categories; sponsors open houses at animation studios. **Publication(s):** *Inbetweener*, monthly. • Also publishes *Annie Awards Annual Program Book*.

International Association of Independent Producers

PO Box 2801
Washington, DC 20013
Phone: (202)775-1113

Individuals and firms associated with the motion picture and recording industry. Sponsors apprentice programs, workshops, and scholarships. Offers placement service. **Membership:** 3,400. **Publication(s):** *Communication Arts International*, quarterly. • *Film and Recording Production*, annual. • *Newsletter*, 8x/year.

International Communications Industries Association

3150 Spring St.
Fairfax, VA 22031
Phone: (703)273-7200
Fax: (703)278-8082

Dealers, manufacturers, producers, and suppliers of audiovisual, video, and microcomputer products and materials. **Membership:** 1,500. **Purpose:** Bestows awards for innovative use of audiovisuals, industry contributions, and advancing media use. **Publication(s):** *Communications Industries Report*, monthly. • *Equipment Directory of Video, Computer and Audio-Visual Products*, annual. • *ICIA Membership Directory*, annual.

International Documentary Association

1551 S. Robertson Blvd., Ste. 201
Los Angeles, CA 90035
Phone: (310)284-8422
Fax: (310)785-9334

Individuals and organizations involved in nonfiction film and video. **Membership:** 1,000. **Purpose:** To promote nonfiction film and video; to encourage the progress of the documentary arts and sciences; to support the efforts of nonfiction film and videomakers throughout the world. Bestows awards. **Publication(s):** *International Documentary*, monthly. • *Membership Directory*, biennial.

International Graphics, Inc.

c/o Stan Corfman
Marathon Oil Co.
539 S. Main St.
Findlay, OH 45840
Phone: (419)422-2121

Membership: Graphic communicators whose principal means of livelihood is derived from the practice of industrial, scientific and technical art, graphic design, computer graphics, and those areas of photography, motion pictures, and television that deal with the creation and preparation of visual graphics. Activities: Offers placement service and specialized education. Sponsors competitions; bestows awards; compiles statistics. Affiliated with Council of Communication Societies.

International Interactive Communications Society

PO Box 1862
Lake Oswego, OR 97035
Phone: (503)649-2065
Fax: (503)649-2309

Professionals in the fields of training and education, computer science, instructional design, marketing, multimedia production, and communications. **Membership:** 1,900. **Purpose:** Promotes the advancement of interactive technologies. Fosters communication and exchange of ideas among members. Sponsors workshops, seminars, and other educational programs. **Publication(s):** *IICS Reporter*, monthly. • *Interact*, 3x/year. • *Membership Directory*, annual.

International Teleproduction Society

350 5th Ave., Ste. 2400
New York, NY 10118
Phone: (212)629-3266

Companies involved in teleproduction (the making of audio and videotapes). Encourages interest in videotapes and videotape production; conducts public seminars. **Membership:** 350. **Publication(s):** *Handbook on Recommended Standards and Procedures*, periodic. • *Membership Directory*, periodic.

International Television Association

6311 N. O'Connor Rd., LB 51
Irving, TX 75039
Phone: (214)869-1112
Fax: (214)869-2980

Individuals engaged in video communications needs analysis, scriptwriting, producing, directing, consulting, and operations management in the videotape and nonbroadcast television fields. **Membership:** 9,500. **Purpose:** Seeks to advance the arts and sciences of the field for professionals working outside of the broadcast area. Sponsors workshops, seminars, conferences, and Annual Video Festival. Bestows awards. **Publication(s):** *International Television Association—Handbook of Forms*, periodic. • *International Television Association—Membership Directory*, annual. • *International Television News*, 10x/year. • *Video Systems Magazine*, monthly. • Also publishes *Tracking Trends in Corporate Video* (book).

No matter how technically proficient they may be, many midlevel managers will find they have no other place to go but into business for themselves. Entrepreneurship has blossomed during these days of downsizing: preliminary Internal Revenue Service figures for 1990, the most current year for which data are available, show that taxpayers filed nearly 14.7 million "sole proprietorship" forms, a 23 percent jump over 1985.

Source: U.S. News & World Report

International Women's Writing Guild (IWWG)

Box 810
Gracie Station
New York, NY 10028
Phone: (212)737-7536

Membership: Women writers interested in expressing themselves through the written word professionally and for personal growth. Activities: Conducts talent bank, a job placement effort to place women in writing-related work. Participates in international network. Sponsors writing conferences and regional weekend writing workshops. Facilitates manuscript submissions to New York literary agents. Maintains health insurance program at group rates; offers legal referral services; bestows Artist of Life Award.

Models and Photographers of America (MPA)

PO Box 25099
Colorado Springs, CO 80936-5099

Membership: Freelance and professional models and photographers; those employed in modeling-related fields (film producers, actresses, make-up artists, art directors, lab technicians, publishers, modeling agents, and students). Activities: Maintains placement service and biographical archives. Operates automated data bank containing models' and photographers' portfolios. Provides for communication among members; recognizes outstanding talent in the profession. Conducts surveys; compiles statistics. Bestows Model of the Year and Photographer of the Year awards in the fashion, figure, and glamour categories.

Motion Picture Association of America

1600 Eye St. NW
Washington, DC 20006
Phone: (202)293-1966

Principal producers and distributors of motion pictures in the United States. Seeks to establish and maintain high moral and artistic standards in the industry. **Membership:** 9.

National Academy of Recording Arts and Sciences

303 N. Glenoaks Blvd., Ste. 140
Burbank, CA 91502-1178
Phone: (213)849-1313

Vocalists, conductors, composers, musicians, arrangers, recording producers, studio engineers, art directors, album designers, and others engaged in creative work for the production of commercially-released recordings. **Membership:** 7,000. **Publication(s):** *Grammy Magazine*, periodic. • *The Grammy Winners Book*, annual. • *The Recording Academy News*. • *Program Book*.

National Association of Broadcast Employees and Technicians (NABET)

7101 Wisconsin Ave., Ste. 800
Bethesda, MD 20814
Phone: (301)657-8420
Fax: (301)657-9478

Membership: AFL-CIO. **Publication(s):** *News*, bimonthly.

National Council for Culture and Art (NCCA)

1600 Broadway
Ste. 611C
New York, NY 10019
Phone: (212)757-7933

Membership: Artists, civic and business leaders, professional performers, and visual arts organizations. Activities: Offers placement services and employment opportunities. Sponsors art programs and spring and fall concert series. Operates Opening Night, a cable television show. Bestows annual Monarch Award and President's Award, and sponsors annual Monarch Scholarship Program. Provides children's services; conducts charitable program; maintains hall of fame. Plans to conduct Minority Playwrights Forum, Dance Festival U.S.A., Vocal and Instrumental Competition, Film and Video Festival, and Concerts U.S.A.

National Press Photographers Association (NPPA)

3200 Croasdaile Dr.
Ste. 306
Durham, NC 27705
Phone: (919)383-7246
Fax: (919)383-7261

Membership: Professional news photographers and others whose occupation has a direct professional relationship with photojournalism, the art of news communication by photographic image through publication, television film, or theater screen. Activities: Maintains job placement and National Student Intern program committees. Sponsors annual television-newsfilm workshop and annual cross-country (five locations) short course. Conducts annual competition for newsphotos and for television-newsfilm, and monthly contest for still clipping and television-newsfilm. Maintains audiovisual library of tapes, recordings, and slides on aspects of photojournalism.

Producers Guild of America

400 S. Beverly Dr., Rm. 211
Beverly Hills, CA 90212
Phone: (310)557-0807

Motion picture television producers. **Membership:** 450.

Recording Industry Association of America

1020 19th St. NW, Ste. 200
Washington, DC 20036
Phone: (202)775-0101

Companies that manufacture sound recordings for home use. **Membership:** 75. **Publication(s):** *Inside the Recording Industry-A Statistical Overview*, annual. • *Newsletter*, quarterly. • *Report*, annual.

Screen Actors Guild (SAG)

7065 Hollywood Blvd.
Hollywood, CA 90028
Phone: (213)465-4600
Fax: (213)856-6603

Screen actors' labor union. **Membership:** 75,000. **Publication(s):** *Screen Actor*, quarterly. Covers union activities, general interest topics, and includes book reviews and obituaries. $7.00/year for nonmembers. • *Screen Actor Hollywood*, quarterly. Regional newsletter. Covers official business of the guild and general interest topics.

Screen Extras Guild

3629 Cahuenga Blvd. W.
Los Angeles, CA 90068
Phone: (213)851-4301

Membership: 5,300.

Show Business Association (SBA)

1501 Broadway
New York, NY 10036
Phone: (212)354-7600

Membership: Writers, performers, producers, editors, directors, designers, artists, and audiences in the entertainment field. Activities: Operates placement service. Participates in political campaigns and the drafting of related legislation; lobbies at city, state, and national levels; conducts training programs in the arts field. Sponsors competitions and bestows monetary awards annually for excellence; maintains biographical archives; compiles statistics. Maintains library of 24,000 volumes. Publications include: *How to Produce a Show and Film* (annual), *Angels* (listing of investors for shows, films, and art programs), *Summer Theatres* (annual), *Models Guide* (annual), and *Show Business* (weekly tabloid).

Don't hesitate to take any work that is offered to you. What you need is experience, and one way to get it, may be by working for free. Sometimes, freebies (or "spec", as it is called) offer free "on the job training", which can help you gain experience. Though this training period is not easy, if you are committed to finding a job and are just starting out, it is an option that could be worth your time.

Source: *How to Break into the Film Business: The Production Assistant's Handbook*

Society of Broadcast Engineers (SBE)
PO Box 20450
Indianapolis, IN 46220
Phone: (317)253-1640
Fax: (317)253-0418

Membership: Broadcast engineers, students, and broadcast professionals in closely allied fields. **Purpose:** Promotes professional abilities of members and provides information exchange. Maintains certification program; represents members' interests before the Federal Communications Commission and other governmental and industrial groups. **Publication(s):** *Membership Directory*, periodic. • *President's Newsletter*, quarterly.

Society of Motion Picture and Television Art Directors
11365 Ventura Blvd., Ste. 315
Studio City, CA 91604
Phone: (818)762-9995

Supervisors of the design, construction, and decor of motion pictures and settings. **Membership:** 400.

Society of Motion Picture and Television Engineers
595 W. Hartsdale Ave.
White Plains, NY 10607
Phone: (914)761-1100

Professional engineers and technicians in motion pictures, television, and allied arts and sciences. **Membership:** 9,000. **Publication(s):** *Directory*, annual. • *Journal*, monthly. • *News and Notes*, monthly. Also publishes technical reports and books.

Stuntmen's Association of Motion Pictures
4810 Whitsett Ave.
North Hollywood, CA 91607
Phone: (818)766-4334

Men who do stunt work in motion pictures and television and who belong to the Screen Actors Guild and/or the American Federation of Television and Radio Artists. **Membership:** 135. **Purpose:** Association's activities are primarily fraternal and charitable. Seeks to improve working conditions for stuntmen and encourages members to uphold high professional standards. **Publication(s):** *Stuntmen's Directory*, annual.

Stuntwomen's Association of Motion Pictures
5215 Lankershim Blvd., Ste. 8
North Hollywood, CA 91601
Phone: (213)462-1605

Stunt actresses and stunt coordinators who belong to the Screen Actors Guild and/or the American Federation of Television and Radio Artists. **Membership:** 21.

United Scenic Artists (USA)
575 8th Ave.
New York, NY 10018
Phone: (212)581-0300

Labor union providing contracts and benefits for professional scenic designers, scenic artists, costume and lighting designers, diorama and display workers, mural artists, and costume painters employed by TV, theatre, motion picture studios, and producers of commercials. **Membership:** 2,000. **Publication(s):** *Directory*. Monthly.

University and College Designers Association (UCDA)

210 N. Ironwood Dr.
South Bend, IN 46615
Phone: (219)288-8232
Fax: (219)237-1818

Membership: Colleges, universities, junior colleges, or technical institutions that have an interest in visual communication design; individuals who are involved in the active production of such communication design or as teachers or students of these related disciplines. Activities: Maintains placement service. Purposes are to: aid, assist, and educate members through various programs of education; improve members' skills and techniques in communication and design areas such as graphics, photography, signage, films, and other related fields of communication design; be concerned with the individual members' relationships within their own institutions as well as the larger communities in which they serve; aid and assist members in their efforts to be professionals in their respective fields through programs of education and information. Sponsors competitions; bestows awards.

University Film and Video Association (UFVA)

c/o Donald J. Zirpola
Loyola Marymount University
Communication Arts Dept.
Los Angeles, CA 90045
Phone: (213)338-3033
Fax: (213)641-3964

Membership: Professors and video/filmmakers concerned with the production and study of film and video in colleges and universities. Activities: Operates placement service. Conducts research programs; presents annual grants; bestows scholarships and awards. Affiliated With: University Film and Video Foundation.

Women in Film

6464 Sunset Blvd., Ste. 530
Hollywood, CA 90028
Phone: (213)463-6040
Fax: (213)463-0963

Membership: 1,500. **Purpose:** To support women in the film and television industry and to serve as a network for information on qualified women in the entertainment field. Conducts workshops featuring lectures and discussions on such areas as directing, producing, contract negotiation, writing, production development, acting, and technical crafts. **Publication(s):** *WIF Directory*, annual. • *WIF Reel News*, monthly.

Writers Guild of America

8955 Beverly Blvd.
West Hollywood, CA 90048
Phone: (213)550-1000

Labor union for writers in the fields of motion pictures, television, and radio. Represents members in collective bargaining and other labor matters. **Membership:** 6,600. **Purpose:** To obtain adequate domestic and foreign copyright legislation and to promote better copyright relations between the United States and other countries. Bestows awards; sponsors research programs. **Publication(s):** *Journal*, monthly. • *Writers Guild Directory*, periodic.

Employment Agencies and Search Firms

Austin Employment Agency

71-09 Austin St.
Forest Hills, NY 11375
Phone: (718)268-2700

Employment agency.

Beautiful People International

3240 University Ave.
Madison, WI 53705
Phone: (608)238-6372

Places staff in variety of temporary assignments.

Bert Davis Associates, Inc.

400 Madison Ave.
New York, NY 10017
Phone: (212)838-4000

Executive search firm.

Blair Personnel of Parsippany, Inc.
1130 Rte. 46
Box 5306
Parsippany, NJ 07054
Phone: (201)335-6150

Employment agency. Focuses on regular and temporary placement.

Calvert Associates, Inc.
202 E. Washington St.
Ste. 304
Ann Arbor, MI 48104
Phone: (313)769-5413

Employment agency.

> **A** lateral move often involves compromise in salary or title. To compensate, the job has to offer great training, experience, or exposure. You must be convinced that the position will help you develop valuable skills that will make you more marketable for your next big move.
>
> Source: *Working Woman*

Capitol Search Employment Services
915 Clifton Ave.
Clifton, NJ 07013
Phone: (201)779-8700

Employment agency. Second location in Ridgewood, NJ.

Chaloner Associates
Box 1097
Back Bay Station
Boston, MA 02117
Phone: (617)451-5170
Fax: (617)451-8160

Executive search firm.

Claremont-Branan, Inc.
2150 Parklake Dr.
Ste. 212
Atlanta, GA 30345
Phone: (404)491-1292

Employment agency. Executive search firm.

Consultants and Designers Inc.
360 W. 31st St.
New York, NY 10001
Phone: (212)563-8400

Places staff in temporary positions.

Creative Options/Temporary Options
1730 K St., NW
Washington, DC 20006
Phone: (202)785-8367

Employment agency. Places staff on a regular and temporary basis.

Fuller Williams Placement
406 W. 34th
Kansas City, MO 64111
Phone: (816)931-8236

Employment agency.

Helen Edwards and Staff Agency
2500 Wilshire Blvd.
Ste. 1018
Los Angeles, CA 90057
Phone: (213)388-0493

Employment agency.

Howard-Sloan Associates, Inc.
545 5th Ave.
New York, NY 10017
Phone: (212)661-5250
Fax: (212)687-5760

Executive search firm.

I.D.E.A. of Charleston, Inc.
PO Box 11100
Charleston, SC 29411
Phone: (803)723-6944

Employment agency. Places individuals on a temporary or regular basis.

Kathy Clarke Model and Talent Agency
2030 E. 4th St.
Ste. 102
Santa Ana, CA 92705
Phone: (714)667-0222

Employment agency.

LaserType
12788 Highway 9
Ste. 6
Boulder Creek, CA 95006
Phone: (208)338-9080

Employment agency.

The Pathfinder Group
295 Danbury Rd.
Wilton, CT 06897
Phone: (203)762-9418

Employment agency. Executive search firm. Recruits staff in a variety of fields.

Printers Placement
1609 Gessner
Box 904
Houston, TX 77080
Phone: (713)973-4904

Employment agency. Provides regular or temporary placement of staff.

Production Associates
5530 S. 79th, East Place
Tulsa, OK 74145
Phone: (918)622-7038

Employment agency.

Randolph Associates, Inc.
PO Box 1586
Boston, MA 02104-1586
Phone: (617)227-2554

Employment agency. Provides regular or temporary placement of staff.

Remer-Ribolow and Associates
275 Madison Ave.
Ste. 1605
New York, NY 10016
Phone: (212)808-0580

Employment agency.

RitaSue Siegel Associates, Inc.
18 E. 48th St.
New York, NY 10017
Phone: (212)308-0700
Fax: (212)308-0805

Executive search firm.

Staff Inc.
2121 Cloverfield Blvd.
Ste. 133
Santa Monica, CA 90404
Phone: (213)829-5447

Employment agency.

Career Guides

300 New Ways to Get a Better Job
Bob Adams, Inc.
260 Center St.
Holbrook, MA 02343
Phone: (617)767-8100
Fax: (617)767-0994

Baldwin, Eleanor. $7.95. Advocates a job search approach designed to meet the changing nature of the job market.

Given the growing enthusiasm with which companies are using the independent databanks, anyone who is launching a job hunt should probably consider signing on with one. The cost is fairly low—typically $20 to $50 for a six- to 12-month listing. (Often, applicants are sent a lengthy application form that subs for a resume.)

Source: *U.S. News & World Report*

---

850 Leading USA Companies
Jamenair Ltd.
PO Box 241957
Los Angeles, CA 90024
Phone: (213)470-6688

Studner, Peter K. $49.95. Compatible with IBM and IBM-compatibles.

A-Job Hunting We Will Go
McGraw Hill Book Co.
Continuing Education Program
1221 Avenue of the Americas
New York, NY 10020
Phone: (212)997-6572

Video cassette. 3/4' U-matic. 21 minutes. Part of a ten-part series entitled *The Career*

215

Development Video Series, which offers a step-by-step approach to finding a job and planning a career.

Acting Professionally: Raw Facts About Careers in Acting

Mayfield Publishing Co.
1240 Villa St.
Mountain View, CA 94041
Phone: (415)960-3222
Fax: (415)960-0328

Robert Cohen. Fourth edition, 1990.

Start building your network. It's always easier to build one when you're working, because the topic of unemployment won't cloud your interaction. The easiest way is to involve yourself in an industry association, but don't overlook church groups, charities, and political organizations. Don't just join, participate. Make yourself known. Cultivate friendships, not just contact.

Become known as a doer. I've run across folks who say they don't have time. Make time. It's your future at stake. No one said it would be easy.

Source: *Detroit Free Press*

The Actor: A Practical Guide to a Professional Career

Donald I. Fine, Inc.
19 W. 21st St.
New York, NY 10010
Phone: (212)727-3270
Fax: (212)727-3277

Eve Brandstein and Joanna Lipari. 1987. Topics covered include auditions, networking, and restarting a stalled career.

Actor/Actress

Careers, Inc.
PO Box 135
Largo, FL 34649-0135
Phone: (813)584-7333

1992. Four-page brief offering the definition, history, duties, working conditions, personal qualifications, educational requirements, earnings, hours, employment outlook, advancement, and careers related to this position.

Actors and Actresses

Chronicle Guidance Publications, Inc.
66 Aurora St. Extension
PO Box 1190
Moravia, NY 13118-1190
Phone: (315)497-0330
Toll-free: 800-622-7284

1991. Career brief describing the nature of the job, working conditions, hours and earnings, education and training, licensure, certification, unions, personal qualifications, social and psychological factors, location, employment outlook, entry methods, advancement, and related occupations.

The American Almanac of Jobs and Salaries

Avon Books
105 Madison Ave.
New York, NY 10016
Phone: (212)481-5600
Toll-free: 800-247-5470

John Wright, editor. Revised and updated, 1990. A comprehensive guide to the wages of hundreds of occupations in a wide variety of industries and organizations.

The Berkeley Guide to Employment for New College Graduates

Ten Speed Press
PO Box 7123
Berkeley, CA 94707
Phone: (415)845-8414

Briggs, James I. $7.95. 256 pages. Basic job-hunting advice for the college student.

Best of the National Business Employment Weekly

Consultants Bookstore
Templeton Rd.
Fitzwilliam, NH 03447
Phone: (603)585-2200
Fax: (603)585-9555

$5.00/booklet. Booklets summarizing the best articles from the *National Business Employment Weekly* on a variety of job hunting topics.

Broadcast Technician

Careers, Inc.
PO Box 135
Largo, FL 34649-0135
Phone: (813)584-7333

1991. Two-page occupational summary card

describing duties, working conditions, personal qualifications, training, earnings and hours, employment outlook, places of employment, related careers, and where to write for more information.

Career Choices for the 90's for Students of Art

Walker and Co.
720 5th Ave.
New York, NY 10019
Phone: (212)265-3632
Toll-free: 800-289-2553
Fax: (212)307-1764

1990. Describes alternative careers for students of art. Offers information about job outlook and competition for entry-level candidates. Includes a bibliography and an index.

Career Employment Opportunities Directory

Ready Reference Press
PO Box 5249
Santa Monica, CA 90409
Phone: (213)474-5175

Four-volume set. $190.00/set; $47.50/volume. Volume 1 covers the liberal arts and social sciences; Volume 2 covers business administration; Volume 3 covers engineering and computer sciences; Volume 4 covers the sciences. Directory of employers and career opportunities in each field. Provides information about company benefits and special programs. Indexed by subject and geography.

The Career Fitness Program: Exercising Your Options

Gorsuch Scarisbrick, Publishers
8233 Via Paseo del Norte
Ste. F-400
Scottsdale, AZ 85258

Sukiennik et al. 1989. $16.00. 227 pages. Textbook, with second half devoted to the job search process.

The Career Guide—Dun's Employment Opportunities Directory

Dun's Marketing Services
Dun and Bradstreet Corporation
Three Sylvan Way
Parsippany, NJ 07054-3896
Phone: (201)605-6000

Annual, December. $450.00; $385.00 for public libraries (lease basis). Covers: More than 5,000 companies that have a thousand or more employees and that provide career opportunities in sales, marketing, management, engineering, life and physical sciences, computer science, mathematics, statistics planning, accounting and finance, liberal arts fields, and other technical and professional areas; based on data supplied on questionnaires and through personal interviews. Also covers personnel consultants; includes some public sector employers (governments, schools, etc.) usually not found in similar lists. Entries include: Company name, location of headquarters and other offices of plants; entries may also include name, title, address, and phone of employment contact; disciplines or occupational groups hired; brief overview of company; discussion of types of positions that may be available; training and career development programs; benefits offered. Arrangement: Companies are alphabetical; consultants are geographical. Indexes: Geographical, Standard Industrial Classification code.

Career Information Center

Macmillan Publishing Co.
866 3rd Ave.
New York, NY 10022
Phone: (818)898-1391
Toll-free: 800-423-9534

Richard Lidz and Linda Perrin, editorial directors. Fifth edition, 1993. A multi-volume set that profiles over 600 occupations. Each occupational profile describes job duties, educational requirements, advancement possibilities, employment outlook, working conditions, earnings and benefits, and where to write for more information.

Career Information System (CIS)
National Career Information System
1787 Agate St.
Eugene, OR 97403
Phone: (503)686-3872

Includes information on job search techniques and self-employment options. Also provides extensive career planning information.

The road to success has also been widened by a decade of radical changes in office life. The star businesses of the '80s were not corporate giants, long on control and conformity; they were freewheeling, entrepreneurial outfits that encouraged individuality. As companies like Ben & Jerry's and Microsoft became pop icons, their success gave millions of Americans the subversive idea that serious work did not demand total suppression of self. Employees began asking for flexible schedules and other rule bending because they knew that such arrangements worked elsewhere.

Source: *Working Woman*

Career Opportunities for Writers
Facts on File, Inc.
460 Park Ave., S.
New York, NY 10016-7382

Rosemary Ellen Guiley. 1993. Sourcebook on over 100 careers for writers from various fields.

Career Opportunities in Art
Facts on File, Inc.
460 Park Ave., S.
New York, NY 10016-7382

Susan H. Haubenstock and David Joselit. 1993. Guidebook containing valuable information on obtaining practical employment in art-related fields. Includes contact information for degree programs as well as professional associations.

Career Opportunities in Television, Cable and Video
Facts on File, Inc.
460 Park Ave., S.
New York, NY 10016-7382

Maxine K. Reed and Robert M. Reed. 1993.

Career Opportunities in the Music Industry
Facts on File, Inc.
460 Park Ave., S.
New York, NY 10016
Phone: (212)683-2244
Toll-free: 800-322-8755

Shelly Field. 1990. Discusses approximately 80 jobs in music, including the performing arts, business, and education. Each job description provides basic career information, salary, employment prospects, advancement opportunities, education, training, and experience required.

Career Placement Registry (CPR)
Career Placement Registry, Inc.
302 Swann Ave.
Alexandria, VA 22301
Phone: (703)683-1085
Fax: (703)683-0246

Online database that contains brief resumes of job candidates currently seeking employment. Comprises two files, covering college and university seniors and recent graduates, and alumni, executives, and others who have already acquired substantial work experience. Entries typically include applicant name, address, telephone number, degree level, function, language skills, name of school, major field of study, minor field of study, occupational preference, date available, city/area preference, special skills, citizenship status, employer name, employer address, description of duties, position/title, level of education, civil service register, security clearance type/availability, willingness to relocate, willingness to travel, salary expectation, and overall work experience. Available online through DIALOG Information Services, Inc.

Career Strategies—From Job Hunting to Moving Up
Association for Management Success
2360 Maryland Rd.
Willow Grove, PA 19090

Six video cassettes. Kennedy, Marilyn Moats. $36.95/each. $203.70/set. 30 minutes each. Covers the following topics: planning the job hunt, networking, resumes, interviewing, negotiating salaries and benefits, and moving up on the job.

Careering and Re-Careering for the 1990's

Consultants Bookstore
Templeton Rd.
Fitzwilliam, NH 03447
Phone: (603)585-6544
Fax: (603)585-9555

Krannich, Ronald. 1989. $13.95. 314 pages. Details trends in the marketplace, how to identify opportunities, how to retrain for them, and how to land jobs. Includes a chapter on starting a business. Contains index, bibliography, and illustrations.

Careers and the College Grad

Bob Adams, Inc.
260 Center St.
Holbrook, MA 02343
Phone: (617)767-8100
Fax: (617)767-0994

Ranno, Gigi. 1992. $12.95. 64 pages. An annual resource guide addressing the career and job-hunting interests of undergraduates. Provides company profiles and leads.

Careers in the Graphic Arts

Rosen Publishing Group, Inc.
29 E. 21st St.
New York, NY 10010
Phone: (212)777-3017

Virginia Lee Robertson. Revised edition, 1993. Discusses a career in graphic arts; outlines educational requirements, training, and skills needed to become an illustrator, layout artist, designer, and paste-up artist. Gives job hunting advice and describes how to write a resume, prepare the portfolio, and interview preparation. Gives a state-by-state listing of schools offering graphic arts.

Cartoonist

Careers, Inc.
PO Box 135
Largo, FL 34649-0135
Phone: (813)584-7333

1991. Four-page brief offering the definition, history, duties, working conditions, personal qualifications, educational requirements, earnings, hours, employment outlook, advancement, and careers related to this position.

Cartoonists

Chronicle Guidance Publications, Inc.
66 Aurora St. Extension
PO Box 1190
Moravia, NY 13118-1190
Phone: (315)497-0330
Toll-free: 800-622-7284

1992. Career brief describing the nature of the job, working conditions, hours and earnings, education and training, licensure, certification, unions, personal qualifications, social and psychological factors, location, employment outlook, entry methods, advancement, and related occupations.

> nstead of advancing in your specialty, you transfer elsewhere in the company or take temporary assignments. These moves broaden your skills and your perspective, which might help promote you in the future.
>
> Source: *Detroit Free Press*

Chronicle Career Index

Chronicle Guidance Publications
PO Box 1190
Moravia, NY 13118-1190
Phone: (315)497-0330

Annual. $14.25. Provides bibliographic listings of career and vocational guidance publications and other resources. Arrangement: Alphabetical by source. Indexes: Occupation; vocational and professional information.

The College Board Guide to Jobs and Career Planning

The College Board
45 Columbus Ave.
New York, NY 10023-6992
Phone: (212)713-8000

Joyce S. Mitchell. 1990. Covers a variety of careers. Each career profile contains information on salaries, related careers, education needed, and sources of additional information.

College Majors and Careers: A Resource Guide to Effective Life Planning

Garrett Park Press
PO Box 190C
Garrett Park, MD 20896
Phone: (301)946-2553

Paul Phifer. 1987. Lists 60 college majors, with definitions; related occupations and leisure activities; skills, values, and personal attributes needed; suggested readings; and a list of associations.

As a Production Assistant, you are expected to assist. As valuable as you may think your advice may be to others, it is probably better to keep it to yourself. Once you move up the ladder, you can do things your way, but for the time being, listen and learn, learn, learn.

Source: *How to Break into the Film Business: The Production Assistant's Handbook*

College Recruitment Database (CRD)

Executive Telecom System, Inc.
College Park North
9585 Valparaiso Ct.
Indianapolis, IN 46268
Phone: (317)872-2045

Online database that contains resume information for graduating undergraduate and graduate students in all disciplines at all colleges and universities for recruitment purposes. Enables the employer to create and maintain a private 'skill' file meeting selection criteria. Typical entries include student identification number, home and campus addresses and telephone numbers, schools, degrees, dates of attendance, majors, grade point averages, date available, job objective, curricular statement, activities/honors, and employment history. Available online through the Human Resource Information Network.

Coming Alive from Nine to Five

Mayfield Publishing
1240 Villa St.
Mountain View, CA 94041

Micheolzzi, Betty N. 1988. $12.95. In addition to general job-hunting advice, provides special information for women, young adults, minorities, older workers, and persons with handicaps.

The Complete Guide to Finding Jobs in Government

Planning/Communications
7215 Oak Ave.
Dept. CCI
River Forest, IL 60305
Phone: (708)366-5200

Lauber, Daniel. 1989. $14.95. 183 pages. A comprehensive resource for the governmental job market, featuring job-matching services; job hotlines; internships; sources of advertisements; and sources of local, state, federal, Canadian, and international opportunities.

Compu-Job

Cambridge Career Products
723 Kanawha Blvd., E.
Charleston, WV 25301

Menu-driven program designed to take the user through the job search process, from determining career alternatives to identifying openings, applying for employment, and interviewing.

CPC Annual

College Placement Council
62 Highland Ave.
Bethlehem, PA 18017

Annual, fall. Provides a directory of opportunities and employers in many fields, including health, engineering, sciences, computer fields, administration, and business. Offers job-hunting guidance.

The Director's Voice

Theatre Communications Group
355 Lexington Ave.
New York, NY 10017
Phone: (212)697-5230

Arthur Bartow. 1988. Includes interviews with 21 directors who reveal their methods for collaborating with actors, designers, musicians, and playwrights. They also discuss how their training and early influences, as well as imagination and command of craft, impact their productions.

Effective Job Search Strategies

Robert Ehrmann Productions
4741 Calle Camarada
Santa Barbara, CA 93110

Video casssette. $150.00. 26 minutes. Two college seniors, one of whom is handicapped, are advised of job search strategies and resources by a college job counselor.

The Elements of Job Hunting

Bob Adams, Inc.
260 Center St.
Holbrook, MA 02343
Phone: (617)767-8100
Fax: (617)767-0994

Noble, John. $4.95. Concisely focuses on the key components of job hunting.

The Encyclopedia of Career Choices for the 1990s: A Guide to Entry Level Jobs

Walker and Co.
720 5th Ave.
New York, NY 10019
Phone: (212)265-3632
Toll-free: 800-289-2553
Fax: (212)307-1764

1990. Describes entry-level careers in a variety of industries. Presents qualifications required, working conditions, salary, internships, and professional associations.

Encyclopedia of Careers and Vocational Guidance

J. G. Ferguson Publishing Co.
200 W. Monroe, Ste. 250
Chicago, IL 60606
Phone: (312)580-5480

William E. Hopke, editor-in-chief. Eighth edition, 1990. Four-volume set that profiles 900 occupations and describes job trends in 76 industries. Includes career description, educational requirements, history of the job, methods of entry, advancement, employment outlook, earnings, conditions of work, social and psychological factors, and sources of further information.

The Experienced Hand: A Student Manual for Making the Most of an Internship

Carroll Press
43 Squantum St.
Cranston, RI 02920
Phone: (401)942-1587

Stanton, Timothy and Ali, Kamil. 1987. $6.95. 88 pages. Guidance for deriving the most satisfaction and future benefit from an internship.

For years, firms intent on boosting productivity have been revising their reward systems. Across-the-board salary increases have lost favor as companies have based raises and bonuses on how many defect-free widgets a worker turns out or how well a department meets its goals. The latest trend, driven in part by the desire to make do with fewer workers, is to tie wages to the mastery of new tasks.

Source: *U.S. News & World Report*

Exploring Careers in Computer Graphics

Rosen Publishing Group, Inc.
29 E. 21st St.
New York, NY 10010
Phone: (212)777-3017
Toll-free: 800-237-9932

Richard Masterson. Revised edition, 1990. Explores careers in computer graphics describing educational preparation and job-hunting strategies. Includes information on applications such as CAD/CAM and business. Appendices include a glossary, trade journals, associations, colleges, and a bibliography.

Exploring Careers in Video

Rosen Publishing Group, Inc.
29 E. 21st St.
New York, NY 10010
Phone: (212)777-3017
Toll-free: 800-237-9932

Paul Allman. Revised edition, 1989. Describes various careers available in television, including the job of writer, and tells how to acquire necessary training and preparation. Covers work in network and cable TV, industrial television, and commercial production.

Exploring Nontraditional Jobs for Women
Rosen Publishing Group, Inc.
29 E. 21st St.
New York, NY 10010
Phone: (212)777-3017
Toll-free: 800-237-9932

Rose Neufeld. Revised edition, 1989. Describes occupations where few women are found, including the job of camera operator. Covers job duties, training routes, where to apply for jobs, tools used, salary, and advantages and disadvantages of the job.

> **T**he person who mentions money first loses the negotiating edge. Ever play blackjack? You don't know what the dealer's hole card is, but your cards are face up. Who's got the advantage? The dealer. You can be the dealer if you're a shrewd negotiator. Don't give answers about compensation that pin you down. Asking the salary range for the position or responding in terms of total compensation (i.e., base plus profit-sharing/bonus/commission) gives you latitude.
>
> Source: *Detroit Free Press*

For the Working Artists: A Survival Guide
c/o Warren Christianson
935 W. Ave. 37
Los Angeles, CA 90065
Phone: (213)222-4035

Judith Luther and Eric Vollmer. Second edition, updated by Eric Vollmer, 1991.

Get a Better Job!
Peterson's Guides, Inc.
PO Box 2123
Princeton, NJ 08543-2123
Phone: (609)243-9111

Rushlow, Ed. 1990. $11.95. 225 pages. Counsels the reader on job search techniques. Discusses how to win the job by bypassing the Personnel

Department and how to understand the employer's system for screening and selecting candidates. Written in an irreverent and humorous style.

The Hand That Holds the Camera: Interviews With Women Film and Video Directors
Garland Publishing Co., Inc.
717 5th Ave., Ste. 2500
New York, NY 10022
Phone: (212)751-7447
Toll-free: 800-627-6273

Lynn Fieldman Miller. 1988. Contains interviews with women directors who describe their own work and experiences in a traditionally male occupation.

High-Impact Telephone Networking for Job Hunters
Bob Adams, Inc.
260 Center St.
Holbrook, MA 02343
Phone: (617)767-8100
Fax: (617)767-0994

Armstrong, Howard. 1992. $6.95. Examines the challenges associated with phone networking, shows the reader how to use "positive errors" to generate referrals, and offers hints on how to deal with "getting the runaround". Includes advice on how to ask for the meeting and addresses long-distance job searches by phone.

Hot New Niche: Executive Temporaries
Consultants Bookstore
Templeton Rd.
Fitzwilliam, NH 03447
Phone: (603)585-2200
Fax: (603)585-9555

1991. $10.00. List of firms placing executives in temporary positions. Provides specialty and contact information.

How to Be a Working Actor: An Insider's Guide to Finding Jobs in Theatre, Film, and Television
M. Evans and Co.
216 E. 49th St.
New York, NY 10017
Phone: (212)688-2810

Mari Lyn Henry and Lynne Rogers. Second

edition, 1989. Gives advice on putting together a portfolio, finding leads, and dealing with agents and managers. Covers unions, interviewing, auditions, and screen tests.

How to Find and Get the Job You Want

Johnson/Rudolph Educational Resources, Inc.
1004 State St.
Bowling Green, KY 42101

1989. $20.50. 160 pages. Aimed at the college student.

How to Get a Better Job in This Crazy World

Crown Publishers, Inc.
225 Park Ave., S.
New York, NY 10003
Phone: (212)254-1600

Half, Robert. $17.95.

How to Get a Good Job and Keep It

VGM Career Horizons
4255 W. Touhy Ave.
Lincolnwood, IL 60646-1975
Phone: (708)679-5500

Bloch, Deborah Perlmutter. 1993. $7.95. Aimed at the recent high school or college graduate, this guide provides advice on finding out about jobs, completing applications and resumes, and managing successful interviews.

How to Get a Job

Business Week Careers
PO Box 5810
Norwalk, CT 06856-9960

Video cassette. $34.95. 70 minutes. Job search skills presented from the viewpoint of career planning and placement professionals, CEOs, and others.

How to Get and Get Ahead on Your First Job

VGM Career Horizons
4255 West Touhy Ave.
Lincolnwood, IL 60646-1975
Phone: (708)679-5500

Bloch, Deborah Perlmutter. 1988. $7.95. 160 pages. Details in step-by-step ways how to go about finding that first job, apply for it, write the winning resume, and manage the successful interview.

Women Directors: The 80% Impact

Call them pragmatic: Women who sit on the boards of directors today are more likely to consider corporate women's advancement a business issue than a personal mission, says Catalyst, the New York-based research organization. In a new survey of 162 female directors of the Fortune 1000, 80 percent say they've had an impact on their companies' sensitivity to issues that affect women. Comparing its research with a 1977 Burson-Marsteller study of 31 women directors, Catalyst found that the pool of women with business credentials has, not surprisingly, expanded. While the vast majority in 1977 came from academia, the arts, and nonprofits, more then 40 percent now have solid experience in the corporate sector.

Source: *Working Woman*

How to Get Hired Today!

VGM Career Horizons
4255 W. Touhy Ave.
Lincolnwood, IL 60646-1975
Phone: (708)679-5500

Kent, George, E. 1991. $7.95. Directed at individuals who know the type of job they are looking for. Focuses the reader on activities that are likely to lead to a job and eliminates those that won't. Shows how to establish productive contacts and discover, evaluate, and pursue strong job leads.

How to Get Interviews from Job Ads

Elderkin Associates
PO Box 1293
Dedham, MA 02026

Elderkin, Kenton W. 1989. $19.50. 256 pages.

Outlines how to select and follow up ads to get the job. Includes unique ways to get interview offers and how to incorporate the use of a computer and a fax machine in arranging interviews. Illustrated.

How to Land a Better Job
VGM Career Horizons
4255 West Touhy Ave.
Lincolnwood, IL 60646-1975
Phone: (708)679-5500

Lott, Catherine S., and Lott, Oscar C. 1989. $7.95. 160 pages. Tells the job seeker how to enhance his or her credentials, overcome past weaknesses, uncover job leads, get appointments, organize an appealing resume, and score points in interviews. A special section devoted to getting a better job without changing companies covers the process of transferring departments and gives pointers on moving up to the boss's job.

I t's your property. Remember that your work experience still belongs to you, no matter who took credit in the short run. This isn't simply a goody-goody statement to make you feel better. Besides adding to your expertise and experience, your work belongs to you because you can take credit for it on your resume. So make sure you record the accomplishments from your internship on your resume and save documentation or examples that will prove you did the work.

It's always good to keep an up-to-date work journal and to save your work samples.

Source: *Detroit Free Press*

How to Locate Jobs and Land Interviews
The Career Press, Inc.
180 5th Ave.
PO Box 34
Hawthorne, NJ 07507

French, Albert L. $9.95. Shows readers how to tap into the unadvertised, hidden job market and guides them through the resume, cover letter, and interview preparation process.

How to Market Your College Degree
VGM Career Horizons
4255 W. Touhy Ave.
Lincolnwood, IL 60646-1975
Phone: (708)679-5500

Rogers, Dorothy, and Bettinson, Craig. 1992. $12.95. Provides a guide to self-marketing as a key component of an effective job search. Helps job seekers to develop a strategic marketing plan that targets niches with needs that match their skills, differentiate themselves from the competition by positioning themselves against other candidates, evaluate their potential worth from the employer's perspective, and manage their careers as they move up the career ladder or into another field.

How to Seek a New and Better Job
Consultants Bookstore
Templeton Rd.
Fitzwilliam, NH 03447
Phone: (603)585-6544
Fax: (603)585-9555

Gerraughty, William. 1987. $5.95. 64 pages. Presents information on cover letters, resumes, and mailings. Includes a self-analysis, fifty-six questions asked by interviewers, and a variety of forms and lists.

How to Sell Yourself as an Actor
Sweden Press
Box 1612
Studio City, CA 91614
Phone: (818)995-4250

K. Callan. Second edition, completely revised, 1990.

Internships: 50,000 On-the-Job Training Opportunities for Students and Adults
Peterson's Guides, Inc.
PO Box 2123
Princeton, NJ 08543-2123
Phone: (609)243-9111
Toll-free: 800-338-3282

Brian C. Rushing, editor. Eleventh edition, 1991. Lists internship opportunities under five broad categories: communications, creative arts, human services, international affairs, and public affairs. Includes a special section on internships in Washington, DC. For each internship program, gives the name, phone number, contact person, description, eligibility requirements, and application procedure.

Job and Career Building
Ten Speed Press
PO Box 7123
Berkeley, CA 94707
Phone: (415)845-8414

Germann, Richard, and Arnold, Peter. $7.95. 256 pages.

The Job Bank Series
Bob Adams, Inc.
260 Center St.
Holbrook, MA 02343
Phone: (617)767-8100
Fax: (617)767-0994

$12.95/volume. There are eighteen volumes in the Job Bank Series, each covering a different job market. Volumes exist for the following areas: Atlanta, Boston, Chicago, Dallas/Fort Worth, Denver, Detroit, Florida, Houston, Los Angeles, Minneapolis, New York, Ohio, Philadelphia, Phoenix, San Francisco, Seattle, St. Louis, and Washington DC. Each directory lists employers and provides name, address, telephone number, and contact information. Many entries include common positions, educational backgrounds sought, and fringe benefits provided. Cross-indexed by industry and alphabetically by company name. Profiles of professional associations, a section on the region's economic outlook, and listings of executive search and job placement agencies are included. Features sections on conducting a successful job search campaign and writing resumes and cover letters.

The Job Hunt
Ten Speed Press
PO Box 7123
Berkeley, CA 94707
Phone: (415)845-8414

Nelson, Robert. $3.95. 64 pages. A compact guide with a direct, question-and-answer format with space for notations.

The Job Hunter's Final Exam
Surrey Books, Inc.
230 E. Ohio St.
Ste. 120
Chicago, IL 60611
Phone: (312)661-0050

Camden, Thomas. 1990. $10.95. 140 pages. Helps job seeker quiz self about resumes, interviews, and general job-hunting strategies.

Job Hunters Survival Kit
The Guidance Shoppe
2909 Brandemere Dr.
Tallahassee, FL 32312
Phone: (904)385-6717

Includes two interactive software programs: *The Skill Analyzer* and *The Resume Writer*. $149.95. Compatible with Apple II-plus, IIe, IIc; TRS—80 III/4; and IBM.

The Job Hunter's Workbook
Peterson's Guides, Inc.
PO Box 2123
Princeton, NJ 08543-2123
Phone: (609)243-9111

Taggart, Judith; Moore, Lynn; and Naylor, Mary. $12.95. 140 pages. Deals with such job-seeking topics as assessing personal strengths, networking, interviewing and answering interview questions, dealing with salaries and benefits, and preparing resumes, cover letters, and portfolios. A combination of self-assessment exercises, work sheets, checklists, and advice.

Job Hunting for Success
Ready Reference Press
PO Box 5249
Santa Monica, CA 90409
Phone: (213)474-5175

Set of three video cassettes. Aimed at the student job hunter. Focuses on the importance of knowing yourself, your interests, aptitudes, and other characteristics. Describes job openings in a variety of areas, including apprenticeship, clerical, on-the-job training, and summer employment. Helps prepare the student for the career planning and job search process.

Job Search: Career Planning Guidebook

Brooks/Cole Publishing Company
Marketing Dept.
511 Forest Lodge Rd.
Pacific Grove, CA 93950

Lock. 1992. 248 pages. Assists the reader in a production job search.

Job prospectors still must make careful judgements and be ready to alter course again. With American business undergoing such upheaval, today's hot field could conceivably be cold—or glutted—in a few short years. Somehow, though, the challenge of learning new skills seems to endow people with the necessary courage.

Source: *U.S. News & World Report*

The Job Search Handbook

Bob Adams, Inc.
260 Center St.
Holbrook, MA 02343
Phone: (617)767-8100
Fax: (617)767-0994

Noble, John. $6.95. 144 pages. Identifies and provides advice on the essential elements of the job search, including networking, cover letters, interviewing, and salary negotiation. Aimed at first-time entrants to the job market, those looking for a job in a new field, and middle-level professionals looking to take their next step up.

Job Search: The Total System

Consultants Bookstore
Templeton Rd.
Fitzwilliam, NH 03447
Phone: (603)585-6544
Fax: (603)585-9555

Dawson, Kenneth and Dawson, Sheryl. 1988. $14.95. 244 pages. A guide that shows how to link networking, resume writing, interviewing, references, and follow-up letters to land the job. Thirty resumes are included.

Job Seeker's Guide to Private and Public Companies

Gale Research Inc.
835 Penobscot Bldg.
Detroit, MI 48226
Phone: (313)961-2242
Fax: (313)961-6241

Annual. Four volumes. $95.00 per volume; $350.00 per set. Covers over 15,000 employers in all industries. Each volume covers a specific regional area. Entries include: Company name, address, phone, fax; number of employees; company history; description; main products, services, or accounts; parent company; names and titles of key personnel; employee information; job titles; benefits and features of employment; human resources contacts; and application procedures. Arrangement: Geographical by state, then by city. Indexes: Industry, cumulative corporate name index.

Jobs Rated Almanac: Ranks the Best and Worst Jobs by More Than a Dozen Vital Criteria

Pharos Books
200 Park Ave.
New York, NY 10166
Phone: (212)692-3863
Toll-free: 800-521-6600

Les Krantz. Second edition, 1992. Ranks 250 jobs by environment, salary, outlook, physical demands, stress, security, travel opportunities, and geographic location. Includes jobs the editor feels are the most common, most interesting, and the most rapidly growing.

Jobs! What They Are—Where They Are—What They Pay

Simon & Schuster, Inc.
Simon & Schuster Bldg.
1230 Avenue of the Americas
New York, NY 10020
Phone: (212)698-7000

Snelling, Robert O. and Snelling, Anne M. 1989. Describes duties and responsibilities, earnings, employment opportunities, training, and qualifications.

Journeying Outward: A Guide to Career Development

Delmar Publishers, Inc.
2 Computer Dr., W.
PO Box 15015
Albany, NY 12212-5015
Phone: (518)459-1150
Fax: (518)459-3552

Lynton, Jonathan. 1989. 224 pages. Examines the correct way to present oneself in the job search, covering appearance, interviewing, writing a resume, and completing a job application. Resume writing section illustrates models of various resume formats. Includes sections on planning the job search and working the plan.

Joyce Lain Kennedy's Career Book

VGM Career Horizons
4255 West Touhy Ave.
Lincolnwood, IL 60646-1975
Phone: (708)679-5500

Kennedy, Joyce Lain. Co-authored by Dr. Darryl Laramore. 1992. $17.95 paperback. $29.95 hardcover. 448 pages. Guides the reader through the entire career-planning and job-hunting process. Addresses how to find the kinds of jobs available and what to do once the job is secured. Provides a number of case histories to give examples.

Just Around the Corner: Jobs and Employment

Cambridge Career Products
723 Kanawha Blvd. E.
Charleston, WV 25301

Video cassette. Beta, VHS, 3/4' U-matic. 30 minutes. The many different aspects of work are explored in this series of 8 cassettes. Tips on good and bad job habits are given, how to fill out a job application, and how to act on a job interview are explained. Program titles: 1. Effective Job Behavior I. 2. Effective Job Behavior II. 3. Employment Agencies I. 4. Employment Agencies II. 5. Job Interviews I. 6. Job Interviews II. 7. Equal Employment Opportunity/Discrimination I. 8. Equal Employment Opportunity/Discrimination II.

Liberal Arts Jobs

Peterson's Guides, Inc.
PO Box 2123
Princeton, NJ 08543-2123
Phone: (609)243-9111

Nadler, Burton Jay. 1989. $9.95. 110 pages. Presents a list of the top 20 fields for liberal arts majors, covering more than 300 job opportunities. Discusses strategies for going after those jobs, including guidance on the language of a successful job search, informational interviews, and making networking work.

Seeking to link education with specific, real-world goals, companies are sending fewer managers to off-the-shelf programs—a change that may be causing many B-schools to lose participants. Corporate customers, which spend nearly $15 million a year on formal training programs for managers and professionals, are demanding that learning lead to immediate changes on the job. Some companies are sticking with business schools for custom programs, such as the one for Bell Atlantic at Wharton. The school now draws half its executive-education revenues from such custom programs. Others are designing their own in-house courses, often cherry-picking some of the best professors and consultants to teach them.

Source: *Business Week*

Moody's Corporate Profiles

Moody's Investors Service, Inc.
Dun and Bradstreet Company
99 Church St.
New York, NY 10007
Phone: (212)553-0300
Fax: (212)553-4700

Provides data on more than 5,000 publicly held companies listed on the New York Stock Exchange or the American Stock Exchange or NMS companies traded on the National Association of Securities Dealers Automated Quotations. Typical record elements: Company name, address, phone, D-U-N-S number, Moody's number, stock exchange, line of business analysis, annual earnings and dividends per share, and other financial and stock trading data. Available through DIALOG Information Services, Inc.

The Music Business: Career Opportunities and Self-Defense

Crown Publishers, Inc.
225 Park Ave. S.
New York, NY 10003
Phone: (212)254-1600

Dick Weissman. New, revised, updated edition, 1990.

Music Careers

Careers, Inc.
PO Box 135
Largo, FL 34649-0135
Phone: (813)584-7333

1992. Four-page brief offering the definition, history, duties, working conditions, personal qualifications, educational requirements, earnings, hours, employment outlook, advancement, and careers related to this position.

Film actors may come to a screen career with a broad background of stage work or with no previous dramatic work at all. Guided by the director, the actor must discover the characterization created by the writer and work collaboratively with his or his fellow actors.

Source: *Getting Started in Film*

Network Your Way to Job and Career Success

Consultants Bookstore
Templeton Rd.
Fitzwilliam, NH 03447
Phone: (603)585-6544
Fax: (603)585-9555

Krannich, Ron, and Krannich, Caryl. 1989. $11.95. 180 pages. Based on a comprehensive career planning framework, each chapter outlines the best strategies for identifying, finding, and transforming networks to gather information and obtain advice and referrals that lead to job interviews and offers. Includes exercises, sample interviewing dialogues, and a directory of organizations for initiating and sustaining networking activities.

Occupational Outlook Handbook

Bureau of Labor Statistics
441 G St., NW
Washington, DC 20212
Phone: (202)523-1327

Biennial, May of even years. $22.00 hardcover. $17.00 paperback. Contains profiles of various occupations, which include description of occupation, educational requirements, market demand, and expected earnings. Also lists over 100 state employment agencies and State Occupational Information Coordinating Committees that provide state and local job market and career information; various occupational organizations that provide career information. Arranged by occupation; agencies and committees are geographical. Send orders to: Superintendent of Documents, U.S. Government Printing Office, Washington, D.C. 20402 (202-783-3238).

Online Hotline News Service

Information Intelligence, Inc.
PO Box 31098
Phoenix, AZ 85046
Phone: (602)996-2283

Online database containing five files, one of which is Joblines, which features listings of employment and resume services available in voice, print, and online throughout North America. Joblines focuses on the online, library automation, and information-related fields.

The Only Job Hunting Guide You'll Ever Need

Poseidon Press
Simon and Schuster Bldg.
1230 Avenue of the Americas
New York, NY 10020
Phone: (212)698-7290

Petras, Kathryn, and Petras, Ross. 1989. $10.95. 318 pages. Covers the full range of the job search process.

Only You Can Decide: The First Key to Career Planning and Job Hunting

McGraw Hill Book Company
Continuing Education Program
1221 Avenue of the Americas
New York, NY 10020
Phone: (212)997-6572

Video cassette. 3/4' U-matic. 28 minutes. Part of

a ten-part series entitled *The Career Development Video Series,* which offers a step-by-step approach to finding a job and planning a career.

Opportunities in Acting Careers
National Textbook Co.
4255 W. Touhy Ave.
Lincolnwood, IL 60646-1975
Phone: (708)679-5500
Toll-free: 800-323-4900

Dick Moore. Revised edition, 1993. Describes acting positions in show business; discusses how much actors earn, unions, working with agents, and schools. Gives advice on how to get started. Includes a bibliography.

Opportunities in Broadcasting
VGM Career Horizons
4255 W. Touhy Ave.
Lincolnwood, IL 60646-1975
Phone: (312)679-5500
Toll-free: 800-323-4900

Elmo Israel Ellis. 1992.

Opportunities in Music Careers
National Textbook Co.
4255 W. Touhy Ave.
Lincolnwood, IL 60646-1975
Phone: (708)679-5500
Toll-free: 800-323-4900

Robert Gerardi. 1991. Includes a bibliography.

Opportunities in Television and Video Careers
VGM Career Horizons
4255 W. Touhy Ave.
Lincolnwood, IL 60646
Phone: (312)679-5500

Shonan F.R. Noronha. 1988.

Opportunities in Writing Careers
National Textbook Co.
4255 W. Touhy Ave.
Lincolnwood, IL 60646-1975
Phone: (708)679-5500
Toll-free: 800-323-4900

Elizabeth Foote-Smith. 1989. Describes writing career opportunities. Covers articles, novels, short stories, nonfiction books, reviews, and interviews. Also includes information on playwrights, poets, journalists, and broadcasters. Discusses educational preparation. Includes a bibliography.

Out of Work But Not Alone
Self-Help Clearinghouse
Publications Dept.
St. Clares - Riverside Medical Center
Pocono Rd.
Denville, NJ 07834
Phone: (201)625-9565

1984. $9.00.

All companies desire to hire the best people possible. In these years of limited hiring and reduced work forces, there are still many good jobs available. In any year, the best candidates get jobs offers; in fact, they usually have multiple offers. By preparing for your on-campus and on-site interviews as much as possible, you can place yourself among the best.

Source: *Planning Job Choices: 1994*

The Overnight Job Change Strategy
Ten Speed Press
PO Box 7123
Berkeley, CA 94707
Phone: (415)845-8414

Asher, Donald. 1993. Subtitled *How to Plan a Comprehensive, Systematic Job Search in One Evening.* Incorporates sales and marketing techniques into a six-stage job search process.

The Perfect Job Reference
Consultants Bookstore
Templeton Rd.
Fitzwilliam, NH 03447
Phone: (603)585-2200
Fax: (603)585-9555

Allen, Jeffrey, G. 1990. $9.95. Step-by-step methods for securing a written or verbal recommendation.

Peterson's Job Opportunities for Business and Liberal Arts Graduates 1993

Peterson's
PO Box 2123
Princeton, NJ 08543-2123
Phone: (609)243-9111

Compiled by the Peterson's staff. 1993. $20.95 paperback. 300 pages. Lists hundreds of organizations that are hiring new business, humanities, and social science graduates in the areas of business and management. Explores how to match academic backgrounds to specific job openings. Provides information about opportunities for experienced personnel as well. Includes data on starting locations by city and state, summer jobs, co-op jobs, internships, and international assignments.

You can also use "One day at a time" to keep you plugging away at your long-term goals. "One day at a time" can get you through any enterprise so big or complicated or long-range that it would discourage or terrify you to look at it in its entirety. Do you wonder how the great achievers and visionaries of the world accomplish so much? They do it one day at a time.

Source: *Detroit Free Press*

Professional's Job Finder

Planning/Communications
7215 Oak Ave.
River Forest, IL 60305-1935
Phone: (708)366-5297

$15.95. Discusses how to use sources of private sector job vacancies in a number of specialties and state-by-state, including job-matching services, job hotlines, specialty periodicals with job ads, salary surveys, and directories. Covers a variety of fields from health care to sales. Includes chapters on resume and cover letter preparation and interviewing.

Rejection Shock

McGraw Hill Book Company
Continuing Education Program
1221 Avenue of the Americas
New York, NY 10020
Phone: (212)997-6572

Video cassette. 3/4′ U-matic. 28 minutes. Part of

a ten-part series entitled *The Career Development Video Series*, which offers a step-by-step approach to finding a job and planning a career. Provides viewers with ways to handle frustration, anxiety, and despair in job hunting.

The Right Place at the Right Time

Ten Speed Press
PO Box 7123
Berkeley, CA 94707
Phone: (415)845-8414

Wegmann, Robert G. $11.95. 192 pages. A comprehensive approach to career planning and job seeking developed to find the right job in the new economy.

Skills in Action: A Job-Finding Workbook

University of Akron
Adult Resource Center
Akron, OH 44325

Selden, J.H. $5.50. 75 pages. Workbook format; aimed at job seekers looking for initial or transitional employment.

Super Job Search: The Complete Manual for Job-Seekers and Career-Changers

Jamenair Ltd.
PO Box 241957
Los Angeles, CA 90024
Phone: (213)470-6688

Studner, Peter. $22.95. 352 pages. A step-by-step guidebook for getting a job, with sections on getting started, how to present accomplishments, networking strategies, telemarketing tips, and negotiating tactics.

Taking Charge of Your Career Direction

Brooks/Cole Publishing Company
Marketing Dept.
511 Forest Lodge Rd.
Pacific Grove, CA 93950

Lock. 1992. 377 pages. Provides guidance for the job search process.

U.S. Employment Opportunities: A Career News Service

Washington Research Associates
7500 E. Arapaho Plaza
Ste. 250
Englewood, CO 80112
Phone: (303)756-9038
Fax: (303)770-1945

Annual; quarterly updates. $184.00. List of over 1,000 employment contacts in companies and agencies in the banking, arts, telecommunications, education, and 14 other industries and professions, including the federal government. Entries include: Company name, name of representative, address, description of products or services, hiring and recruiting practices, training programs, and year established. Classified by industry. Indexes: Occupation.

VGM's Careers Encyclopedia

National Textbook Co.
4255 W. Touhy Ave.
Lincolnwood, IL 60646-1975
Phone: (708)679-5500
Toll-free: 800-323-4900

Third edition, 1991. Profiles 200 occupations. Describes job duties, places of employment, working conditions, qualifications, education and training, advancement potential, and salary for each occupation.

What Color Is Your Parachute?

Ten Speed Press
PO Box 7123
Berkeley, CA 94707
Phone: (415)845-8414

Bolles, Richard N. 1993. $12.95 paperback. $18.95 hardcover. Subtitled: *A Practical Manual for Job-Hunters and Career-Changers.* One of the best-known works on job hunting, this book provides detailed and strategic advice on all aspects of the job search.

Where Do I Go from Here with My Life?

Ten Speed Press
PO Box 7123
Berkeley, CA 94707
Phone: (415)845-8414

Crystal, John C., and Bolles, Richard N. $11.95.

272 pages. A planning manual for students of all ages, instructors, counselors, career seekers, and career changers.

Where the Jobs Are: The Hottest Careers for the '90s

The Career Press, Inc.
180 5th Ave.
PO Box 34
Hawthorne, NJ 07507

Satterfield, Mark. 1992. $9.95. Provides a look at current trend in the job market and the industries that offer the greatest opportunity for those entering the work force or making a career change. Contains advice on career pathing opportunities and breaking into the field.

> **W**here it has so far spread, skill-based pay is helping to satisfy many would-be ladder climbers who have no room to advance. People can increase their earnings by making themselves more valuable in their current jobs—or perhaps by moving laterally to new assignments—without getting bigger titles.
>
> Source: *U.S. News & World Report*

Where to Start Career Planning

Peterson's
PO Box 2123
Princeton, NJ 08543-2123
Phone: (609)243-9111

Lindquist, Carolyn Lloyd, and Miller, Diane June. 1991. $17.95. 315 pages. Lists and describes the career-planning publications used by Cornell University's Career Center, one of the largest career libraries in the country. Covers more than 2,000 books, periodicals, and audiovisual resources on topics such as financial aid, minority and foreign students, overseas employment and travel, resources for the disabled, second careers, study-and-work options, summer and short-term jobs, women's issues, and careers for those without a bachelor's degree. Includes a bibliographic title index.

Who's Hiring Who?

Ten Speed Press
PO Box 7123
Berkeley, CA 94707
Phone: (415)845-8414

Lathrop, Richard. $9.95. 268 pages. Provides advice on finding a better job faster and at a higher rate of pay.

Work in the New Economy: Careers and Job Seeking into the 21st Century

The New Careers Center
1515 23rd St.
Box 297-CT
Boulder, CO 80306

1989. $15.95.

The Working Actor: A Guide to the Profession

Viking Penguin
375 Hudson St.
New York, NY 10014
Phone: (212)366-2000

Katinka Matson, editor. Revised edition, 1993.

Writer

Careers, Inc.
PO Box 135
Largo, FL 34649-0135
Phone: (813)584-7333

1992. Four-page brief offering the definition, history, duties, working conditions, personal qualifications, educational requirements, earnings, hours, employment outlook, advancement, and careers related to this position.

Writers, Artistic and Dramatic

Chronicle Guidance Publications, Inc.
PO Box 1190
Moravia, NY 13118-1190
Toll-free: 800-622-7284

1989. Occupational brief describing the nature of the job, working conditions, hours and earnings, education and training, licensure, certification, unions, personal qualifications, social and psychological factors, location, employment outlook, entry methods, advancement, and related occupations.

Professional and Trade Periodicals

American Cinematographer

PO Box 2230
Hollywood, CA 90078
Phone: (213)969-4333
Fax: (213)876-4973

David Heuring, editor. Monthly. Magazine of the American Society of Cinematographers. Covers film and video production. $24.00/yr.; $3.25/issue.

Animation Magazine

Thoren Publications
5889 Kanan Rd., Ste. 317
Agoura Hills, CA 91301
Phone: (818)991-2884
Fax: (818)991-3773

Rita Street, publisher/editor. 4x/year. $4.95 per issue.

Board Report for Graphic Artists

American Professional Graphic Artists
PO Box 1561
Harrisburg, PA 17105
Phone: (717)774-5413

Editor(s): Drew Allen Miller. Monthly. Serves graphic artists, designers, printers, and advertising agencies. Consists of three publications: The Graphic Artists Newsletter, the Designer's Compendium, and Trademark Trends. Recurring features include results of surveys, news of research, statistics, reviews of fresh designs and trends, and indexed subsections for rapid research.

Career Opportunities News

Garrett Park Press
PO Box 190 C
Garrett Park, MD 20986-0190
Phone: (301)946-2553

Calvert, Robert, Jr., and French, Mary Blake, editors. Bimonthly. $30.00/year; $4.00 sample issue. Each issue covers such things as resources to job seekers, special opportunities for minorities, women's career notes, and the current outlook in various occupations. Cites free and inexpensive job-hunting materials and new reports and books.

Casting Call

Mel Pogue Enterprises
3365 Cahuenga
Hollywood, CA 90068
Phone: (213)874-4012

Biweekly. $36/year, $1/single issue. Lists show business positions.

Designer

University and College Designers Association
210 N. Ironwood Dr.
South Bend, IN 46615-2518
Phone: (219)288-8232

Editor(s): Bill Noblitt. Quarterly. Focuses on different areas of visual communication design, including graphics, photography, signage, films, and other related fields. Reviews communication and design technologies and techniques. Recurring features include information on the Association's educational programs and other activities.

Drama-Logue

PO Box 38771
Los Angeles, CA 90038-0771

Serves as a major source for West Coast theatre, film, and television jobs.

The Hollywood Scriptwriter

162 N. Wilcox, No. 385
Hollywood, CA 90028
Phone: (818)991-3096

Kerry Cox, editor.

Journal of Career Planning and Employment

College Placement Council, Inc.
62 Highland Ave.
Bethlehem, PA 18017
Phone: (215)868-1421

Four issues/year. Free to members. Can be used to provide assistance to students in planning and implementing a job search.

Kennedy's Career Strategist

Marilyn Moats Kennedy Career Strategies
1153 Wilmette Ave.
Wilmette, IL 60091

Twelve issues/year. $89.00/year. Offers job search guidance.

Managing Your Career

Dow Jones and Co.
420 Lexington Ave.
New York, NY 10170

College version of the *National Business Employment Weekly*. Excludes job openings, but provides job-hunting advice.

Occupational Outlook Quarterly

U.S. Government Printing Office
Superintendent of Documents
Washington, DC 20402
Phone: (202)783-3238

Quarterly. $6.50/year; $2.50/single issue. Contains articles and information about career choices and job opportunities in a wide range of occupations.

Corporations recruit actively on college campuses to replace the large number of employees who leave their organizations and to find their future leaders. However, few small companies have the resources to recruit on campus. Therefore, college students must find small businesses on their own or with the help of their career planning and placement offices.

Source: *Planning Job Choices: 1994*

The Off-Hollywood Report

Independent Feature Project (IFP)
132 W. 21st St., 6th Fl.
New York, NY 10011
Phone: (212)243-7777

Editor(s): James Shamui and Scott Macauley. Four issues/yr. Reflects the aims of the IFP, which operates as a support organization for independent film makers. Provides information on upcoming IFP activities and other events in the independent film industry. Features a profile on a distributor of independent feature films in each issue. Recurring features include a calendar of events, filmmaker interviews, and articles on financing.

Pacific Coast Studio Directory

6313 Yucca St.
Hollywood, CA 90028
Phone: (213)467-2920

Contains addresses and phone numbers for

agents, studios, television stations, production companies, special effects people, stunt people, guilds and unions, props suppliers, etc. Frequency: quarterly.

Premiere

PO Box 55387
Boulder, CO 80323-5387

Susan Lyne, editor. Monthly. $12.95/year; $2.95/copy. Entertainment magazine, including interviews with celebrities, movie reviews, and entertainment news.

Ross Reports

Samuel French
7623 Sunset Blvd.
Hollywood, CA 90046
Phone: (213)876-0570

Lists contact people for television shows currently in production. Frequency: monthly.

> **B**y the year 2005, women and minority workers will account for 62 percent of the work force—and about 70 percent of the new entrants.
>
> Source: *U.S. News & World Report*

SMPTE Journal

Society of Motion Picture and Television Engineers
595 W. Hartsdale Ave.
White Plains, NY 10607
Phone: (914)761-1100
Fax: (914)761-3115

Jeffrey B. Friedman, editor. Monthly. $55.00/year. Journal containing articles pertaining to new developments in motion-picture and television technology; standards and recommended practices; general news of the industry.

Spotlight Casting Magazine

PO Box 3270
Hollywood, CA 90078
Phone: (213)462-6775

Weekly. $40/year. Provides help wanted ads for actors, singers, dancers, technicians, and other show business positions.

Video Business

Capital Cities Media Inc.
825 7th Ave.
New York, NY 10019
Phone: (212)887-8400

Bruce Apar, editor. Weekly. $70.00/year.

The Writer

The Writer Inc.
120 Boylston St.
Boston, MA 02116-4615
Phone: (617)423-3157

Sylvia K. Burack, editor. Monthly. $24.75/year; $32.75/year for foreign subscribers. Magazine for free-lance writers. Publishing practical information and advice on how to write publishable material and where to sell it.

Writers Club Newsletter

Jacklyn Barlow
67 Aberdeen Circle
Leesburg, FL 34788
Phone: (904)742-1224

Editor(s): Jacklyn Barlow. Bimonthly. Serves as a forum for writers wishing to share experiences, resources, writing problems, and successes.

Writer's Digest

F&W Publications
1507 Dana Ave.
Cincinnati, OH 45207
Phone: (513)531-2222
Fax: (513)531-1843

Bruce Woods, editor. Monthly. $24.00/year; $2.50/issue. Professional magazine for writers.

Basic Reference Guides

The 100 Best Companies to Work for in America

Signet/NAL Penguin
1633 Broadway
New York, NY 10019

Levering, Robert; Moskowitz, Milton; and Katz, Michael. 1985. $5.95. 477 pages. Describes the best companies to work for in America, based on such factors as salary, benefits, job security, and ambience. The authors base their 'top 100' rating on surveys and personal visits to hundreds of firms.

101 Careers: A Guide to the Fastest-Growing Opportunities

John Wiley & Sons, Inc.
605 3rd Ave.
New York, NY 10158
Phone: (212)850-6000
Fax: (212)850-6088

Michael Harkavy, author. $14.95. 352 pages. Provides listing of the best-paying job prospects. Includes occupational overviews, descriptions of fast-growing areas, salary information, and resource listings.

Academy Players Directory

Academy of Motion Picture Arts and Sciences
8949 Wilshire Blvd.
Beverly Hills, CA 90211
Phone: (213)278-8990

Directory of actors, listing their agents. Information is arranged in categories such as: young leading man/lady; leading man/lady; and character actors and comedians; and children.

ACD Membership Directory

American Center for Design (ACD)
233 E. Ontario
Ste. 500
Chicago, IL 60611
Phone: (312)787-2018
Fax: (312)649-9518

Annual.

Acting From the Ultimate Consciousness

Putnam Publishing Group, Inc.
200 Madison Ave.
New York, NY 10016
Phone: (212)951-8400

Eric Morris. 1992.

Acting Step by Step

Resource Publications, Inc.
160 E. Virginia St., Ste. 290
San Jose, CA 95112
Phone: (408)286-8505

Marshall Cassady. 1988. Includes bibliographical references.

Actor

Warner Books, Inc.
Time & Life Bldg.
1271 Avenue of the Americas
New York, NY 10020
Phone: (212)522-7200

Pamell Hall, editor. 1994.

The Actor and The Text

Applause Theatre Book Publishers
211 W. 71st St.
New York, NY 10023
Phone: (212)595-4735

Cicely Berry. Revised edition, 1992.

> **T**he costume designer begins work early in the pre-production phase and is usually on the set every day in order to check costumes and deal with any last-minute changes. The size and composition of his/her creative team depends on the number and type of costumes that need to be build.
>
> Source: *Getting Started in Film*

The Actor's Book of Classical Monologues

Penguin Books
375 Hudson St.
New York, NY 10014
Phone: (212)366-2000

Stefan Rudnicki, editor. 1988.

America's Fastest Growing Employers

Bob Adams, Inc.
260 Center St.
Holbrook, MA 02343
Phone: (617)767-8100
Fax: (617)767-0994

Smith, Carter. 1992. $14.95. Identifies firms with the most rapid growth in employment opportunities. Provides contact information, recent sales figures, current employees, and a breakdown of common positions sought by the firms profiled.

Annual Report
Actors' Fund of America
1501 Broadway
Ste. 518
New York, NY 10036
Phone: (212)221-7300
Fax: (212)764-0238

Includes membership listing and financial report.

C ooperative education, internships, practicums, and similar programs are designed to provide students with relevant work experience, but they're also an avenue to full-time employment after graduation. Employers often hire those who have co-oped or served an internship with them.

Source: *Planning Job Choices: 1994*

Artist's Market: Where to Sell Your Commercial Art
Writer's Digest Books
1507 Dana Ave.
Cincinnati, OH 45207
Phone: (513)531-2222
Fax: (513)531-4744

Annual, September. $21.95, plus $3.00 shipping. Lists 2,500 buyers of free-lance art work; includes references which could help direct a job search. Covers ad agencies, art studios, galleries, clip art firms, audiovisual firms, television film producers, periodicals, record companies, book publishers. Entries include: Name, address, phone, how to break in, and other information. Arrangement: Classified by type of market.

The Best Companies for Women
Simon and Schuster
Simon and Schuster Bldg.
1230 Avenue of the Americas
New York, NY 10020

1989. $8.95.

Billboard's International Recording Studio & Equipment Directory
BPI Communications
1515 Broadway, 39th Fl.
New York, NY 10036
Phone: (212)536-5025
Toll-free: 800-344-7119
Fax: (212)921-2486

Susan Nunziata, editor. Annual. $40.00. 100 pages. Covers U.S. and international recording studios, equipment and cassette/CD manufacturers, studio designers, and industry service providers worldwide.

The Business of Design
Van Nostrand Reinhold Co., Inc.
115 5th Ave.
New York, NY 10003
Phone: (212)254-3232
Toll-free: 800-842-3636

Ian Linton. 1988. Includes an index.

Cinematographers, Production Designers, Costume Designers, and Film Editors Guide
Lone Eagle Publishing
2337 Roscomare Rd., No. 9
Los Angeles, CA 90077
Phone: (310)471-8066
Fax: (310)471-4969

Susan Avallone, editor. 1991. $49.95. 414 pages.

Contemporary Theatre, Film, and Television
Gale Research Inc.
835 Penobscot Bldg.
Detroit, MI 48226
Phone: (313)961-2242
Fax: (313)961-6241

Annual. $110.00. Covers: In ten volumes, about 5,800 leading and up-and-coming performers, directors, writers, producers, designers, managers, choreographers, technicians, composers, executives, dancers, and critics in the United States and Great Britain. Entries include: Name, home and/or agent or office addresses, personal and career data, writings, awards, other information. Arrangement: Alphabetical. Indexes: Cumulative name index also covers entries in *Who's Who in the Theatre* editions 1-17 and in *Who Was Who in the Theatre*.

The Corporate Directory of U.S. Public Companies

Gale Research Inc.
835 Penobscot Bldg.
Detroit, MI 48226
Phone: (313)961-2242
Fax: (313)961-6241

1991. $325.00. Provides information on more than 9,500 publicly-traded firms having at least $5,000,000 in assets. Entries include: General background, including name, address and phone, number of employees; stock data; description of areas of business; major subsidiaries; officers; directors; owners; and financial data. Indexes: Officers and directors, owners, subsidiary/parent, geographic, SIC, stock exchange, company rankings, and newly registered corporations.

DGA Directory of Members

Directors Guild of America (DGA)
7920 Sunset Blvd.
Hollywood, CA 90046
Phone: (310)289-2000
Fax: (310)289-2029

Annual.

Directing Television and Film

Wadsworth Publishing Co.
10 Davis Dr.
Belmont, CA 94002
Phone: (415)595-2350

Alan A. Armer. Second edition, 1990. Includes a bibliography and an index.

Directors Guild of America Directory

Directors Guild of America
7920 Sunset Blvd.
Hollywood, CA 90046
Phone: (213)289-2000

Lists members of the Guild and their credits. Price: Free to members.

Directory of Corporate Affiliations

National Register Publishing Company
Macmillan Directory Division
3004 Glenview Rd.
Wilmette, IL 60091
Phone: (708)933-3322

Annual. $687.00. Covers: 5,000 parent companies; 500 privately owned companies; and about 45,000 domestic divisions, subsidiaries, joint ventures, and/or affiliates. Entries include: Name of parent company, address, phone, assets, earnings, liabilities, net worth, type of business, approximate annual sales, number of employees, corporate headquarters address, alphabetical listing of subsidiaries, divisions, and affiliates; names, titles, address, phone of key personnel. Arrranged alphabetically by parent company name; geographical; by Standard Industrial Classification (SIC) code. Indexes: Alphabetical, SIC code, geographical, personal name.

For twentysomethings not yet burdened with minivans and mortgages, the risks of signing on with a small company often pale beside the payoff. Small companies, it is true, are far more prone to going under. And one individual's decisions, right or wrong, can weigh heavily—and visibly—on the bottom line. On the other hand, the lack of a bureaucracy forces rapid professional development.

Source: *U.S. News & World Report*

Directory of Leading Private Companies

National Register Publishing Company
Reed Reference Publishing
121 Chanlon Rd.
New Providence, NJ 07974
Phone: (908)464-6800

Annual, March. $529.00, plus $8.75 shipping. Covers: Over 7,800 privately owned companies. Entries include: Company name, address, phone, telex, year founded, financial assets and liabilities, net worth, approximate sales, names and titles of key personnel, number of employees, number of U.S. and foreign offices, and other information. Arrangement: Alphabetical. Indexes: Geographical, parent company, Standard Industrial Classification number.

Dun and Bradstreet Million Dollar Directory
Dun's Marketing Services
Dun and Bradstreet Corporation
Three Sylvan Way
Parsippany, NJ 07054-3896
Phone: (201)605-6000
Fax: (201)605-6911

Annual, February. $1,250.00. Covers: 160,000 businesses with a net worth of $500,000 or more, including industrial corporations, utilities, transportation companies, bank and trust companies, stock brokers, mutual and stock insurance companies, wholesalers, retailers, and domestic subsidiaries of foreign corporations. Entries include: Company name, state of incorporation, address, phone, annual sales, number of employees, parent company name; names, titles, and functions of principal executives; other data. Arranged alphabetically. Indexes: Geogrpahical, product.

Seven Steps to Being the Best

1. Determine the world standards.
2. Use process mapping.
3. Communicate with employees as if your life depended on it.
4. Distinguish what needs to be done from how hard it is to do it.
5. Set stretch targets.
6. Never stop.
7. Pay attention to your inner self.

Source: *Fortune*

Dun and Bradstreet Reference Book of Corporate Managements
Dun's Marketing Services
Dun and Bradstreet Corporation
Three Sylvan Way
Parsippany, NJ 07054-3896
Phone: (201)605-6000

Annual, November. $695.00; $550.00 for public libraries (4 volumes, lease basis). Covers: Nearly 200,000 presidents, directors, vice presidents, officers, and managers in 12,000 credit, personnel, and data processing corporations. Controllers and assistant officers are not listed unless the corporation requests. Entries include: Company name, corporate headquarters address, phone, line of business, names of principal executives, title, whether a director, business and professional occupations and dates, educational data, business affiliations outside the corporation, and other information. Arranged alphabetically by company name. Indexes: Personal name, geographical, and Standard Industrial Classification code.

Feature Filmmaking at Used-Car Prices
Viking Penguin, Inc.
375 Hudson St.
New York, NY 10014
Phone: (212)366-2000

Rick Schmidt. 1988.

Film Actors Guide
Lone Eagle Publishing
2337 Roscomare Rd., No. 9
Los Angeles, CA 90077
Phone: (310)471-8066

Steve LuKanic, editor. 1991, first edition. $49.95. 502 pages. Directory of film actors. Lists actors who are currently active in the industry or have worked during the past 10 years. Directory includes birthdate and birthplace information, contact information, titles, awards, and much more.

Film Composers Guide
Lone Eagle Publishing
2337 Roscomare Rd., No. 9
Los Angeles, CA 90077
Phone: (310)471-8066

Steven C. Smith, editor. 1990, first edition. $29.95. 314 pages.

Film Directors: A Complete Guide
Lone Eagle Publishing
2337 Roscomare Rd., No. 9
Los Angeles, CA 90077
Phone: (310)471-8066

Michael Singer, editor. 1992, first edition. $29.95. 560 pages.

The Film Producer
Saint Martin's Press, Inc.
175 5th Ave.
New York, NY 10010
Phone: (212)674-5151

Paul N. Lazarus, III, editor. 1992.

Film Producers, Studios, Agents & Casting Directors Guide

Lone Eagle Publishing Co.
9903 Santa Monica Blvd., Ste. 204
Beverly Hills, CA 90212
Phone: (310)471-8066

Susan Avallone, editor. Third edition, 1992.

Film Writers Guide

Lone Eagle Publishing
2337 Roscomare Rd., No. 9
Los Angeles, CA 90077-1815
Phone: (310)471-8066

Susan Avallone, editor. 1991, third edition. $49.95. 414 pages. Includes feature film titles (produced and unproduced), cable features and miniseries, and stageplays. Provides a practical reference to screenwriters and their work.

Financial World 500 Fastest Growing Companies

Financial World Partners
1328 Broadway
New York, NY 10001
Phone: (212)594-5030

Annual, August. $3.95. Lists of 500 United States firms showing greatest growth in net earnings for the year. Entries include: Company name, rank, net earnings for two previous years, total assets, other financial and statistical data. Arrangement: Main list arranged by net earnings, other lists arranged by return on equity and other measures and by industry.

Financial World America's Top Growth Companies Directory Issue

Financial World Partners
1328 Broadway
New York, NY 10001
Phone: (212)594-5030

Annual, May. $3.00. List of companies selected on the basis of earnings per share growth rate over 10 year period ending with current year; minimum growth rate used is 5%. Entries include: Company name, current and prior year's ranking, earnings growth rate, and other financial data. Classified by sales and earnings growth rate. Indexes: Company ranked within industry.

Forbes Up-and-Comers 200: Best Small Companies in America

Forbes, Inc.
60 5th Ave.
New York, NY 10011
Phone: (212)620-2200
Fax: (212)620-1863

Annual, November. $4.00. List of 200 small companies judged to be exceptionally fast-growing on the basis of 5-year return on equity and other qualitative measurements. Entries include: Company name, address; biographical data for chief executive officer; financial data. Arranged alphabetically. Indexes: Ranking.

Appear for all interviews, on campus and elsewhere, unless foreseeable events prevent you for doing do. And, if you can't make the interview because of an unforeseeable event, notify your career center or the employer at the earliest possible moment.

Source: *Planning Job Choices: 1994*

Fortune Directory

Time, Inc.
Time and Life Bldg.
Rockefeller Center
New York, NY 10020
Phone: (212)586-1212

Annual, August. $25.00; payment must accompany order. Covers: combined, in a fall reprint, 500 largest United States industrial corporations (published in an April issue each year) and 500 largest United States non-industrial corporations, the Service 500 (published in a June issue). The Service 500 comprises 100-company rankings of each of the largest diversified financial, diversified service, and commercial banking companies, and 50-company rankings each of the largest life insurance, retailing, transportation, and utility companies. Entries include: Company name, headquarters city, sales, assets, and various other statistical and financial information. Classified by annual sales, where appropriate; otherwise by assets. Indexes: Separate alphabetical indexes for industrials and service companies. Send orders to: Fortune Directory, 229 W. 28th St., New York, NY 10001.

FSI Directory of Professional Freelancers

Fastbreak Syndicate, Inc. (FSI)
PO Box 1626
Orem, UT 84059
Phone: (801)785-1300

Annual. Also cited as *Professional American Freelancers.*

Getting into Film

Ballantine Books
201 E. 50th St.
New York, NY 10022
Phone: (212)751-2600
Fax: (212)572-8026

Mel London, author. 1986.

To economize on headhunters' fees and classified advertising, a growing number of companies are now filing the resumes that snow in each year where they might actually do jobseekers some good: in an electronic database.

Source: *U.S. News & World Report*

Getting Started in Film

Prentice Hall General Reference
Rte. 9W
Englewood Cliffs, NJ 07632
Phone: (201)592-2000

Emily Laskin. 1992. Offers advice from leading film producers, directors, cinematographers, actors, designers, writers, and other screen professionals on how to get started in the industry. Price: $16.00.

A Guide to Documentary Editing

Johns Hopkins University Press
701 W. 40th St., Ste. 275
Baltimore, MD 21211
Phone: (410)516-6900

Mary-Jo Kline. 1987. Includes bibliographies and an index.

The Harvard Guide to Careers

Harvard University Press
79 Garden St.
Cambridge, MA 02138
Phone: (617)495-2600
Fax: (617)495-5898

Martha P. Leape and Susan M. Vacca, editors. 1991. $12.95. 222 pgs. Handbook providing information on the career search process from career exploration to writing resumes and interviewing.

Hollywood Art: Art Direction in the Days of the Great Studios

St. James Press
835 Penobscot Bldg.
Detroit, MI 48226
Phone: (313)961-2242
Toll-free: 800-877-4253
Fax: (313)961-6083

Beverly Heisner. 1990. Focuses on the history of art direction in American films, concentrating on the heyday of the Hollywood studios and the American film, 1920-1959.

Hollywood Creative Directory: The Complete Who's What and Where in Motion Picture and TV Development and Production

Hollywood Creative Directory
3000 Olympic Blvd., Ste. 2413
Santa Monica, CA 90404
Phone: (213)315-4815
Fax: (213)315-4816

Contains 2,000 cross-referenced names. Frequency: 3/year.

Hollywood Reporter Blu-Book Directory

Hollywood Reporter
6715 Sunset Blvd.
Hollywood, CA 90028
Phone: (213)464-7411

Contains addresses and phone numbers of production companies, support services, postproduction, film and tape, distribution companies, law firms, and international companies. Also contains phone numbers for actors' agents. Frequency: annual.

Honk If You're a Writer: Unabashed Advice, Undiluted Experience, & Unadulterated Inspiration for Writers & Writers-to-Be

Simon & Schuster Trade
Simon & Schuster Bldg.
1230 Avenue of the Americas
New York, NY 10020
Phone: (212)698-7000

Arthur Plotnik, editor. 1992.

How to Make It in Hollywood

Harper Perennial
10 E. 53rd St.
New York, NY 10022
Phone: (212)207-7000

Linda Buzzell, author. 1992. $10.00. 351 pages. Contains information on how to create and develop a career in Hollywood. Explains how to find jobs in Hollywood, what they are, and possibilities for career advancement.

How to Sell Your Screenplay: The Real Rules of Film and Television

New Chapter Press Inc.
Old Pound Rd.
Pound Ridge, NY 10576
Phone: (914)764-4011
Fax: (914)764-4013

Carl Sautter, author. 1988.

International Documentary Association Membership Directory and Survival Guide

International Documentary Association
1551 S. Robertson Blvd., Ste. 201
Los Angeles, CA 90035
Phone: (213)284-8422

International Motion Picture Almanac

Quigley Publishing Company, Inc.
159 W. 53rd St.
New York, NY 10019
Phone: (212)247-3100
Fax: (212)489-0871

Annual, January. $81.00, plus $5.00 shipping. Covers: Motion picture producing companies, firms serving the industry, equipment manufacturers, casting agencies, literary agencies, advertising and publicity representatives, associations, etc. Entries include: Generally, company name, address, phone. For manufacturers - Products or service provided, name of contact. For producing companies - Additional details. Arrangement: Classified by service or activity. Also includes: *Who's Who in Motion Pictures and Television* section giving brief biographical details and lists of motion picture, television and other performances, and positions and achievements for about 5,000 actors, actresses, producers, directors, etc.

To embed our values, we give our people 360-degree evaluations, with input from superiors, peers, and subordinates. These are the roughest evaluations you can get, because people hear things about themselves they've never heard before.

Source: *Fortune*

International Television and Video Almanac

Quigley Publishing Company, Inc.
159 W. 53rd St.
New York, NY 10019
Phone: (212)247-3100
Fax: (212)489-0871

Annual, January. $81.00, plus $5.00 shipping. Covers: *Who's Who in Motion Pictures and Television and Home Video*, television networks, major program producers, major group station owners, cable television companies, distributors, firms serving the television and home video industry, casting agencies, literary agencies, advertising and publicity representatives, television stations, and associations. Entries include: Generally, company name, address, phone; producing, distributing, and station listings include additional detail. Arrangement: Classified by service or activity, then generally geographical.

International TV and Video Guide

The Tantivy Press
838 Broadway
New York, NY 10003

1986. $13.95. International coverage of the television and video industries.

Jobs '94

Simon & Schuster
Simon & Schuster Bldg.
Rockefeller Center
1230 Ave. of the Americas
New York, NY 10020
Phone: (212)698-7000

Kathryn and Ross Petras, authors. Annual. $15.00. 685 pages. Job guide providing company information, including salaries, working conditions, and job security. Lists the top companies in selected industries. Provides employment forecasts by region and career.

Working closely with the director and integrating the ideas of the cinematographer and the costumer designer, the production designer must translate the director's vision into a reality into which the film can be set. Because this task can be monumental in scope, the production designer often has a large staff and budget and therefore has direct responsibilities to the producer as well.

Source: *Getting Started in Film*

LA 411

LA 411 Publishing
PO Box 480495
Los Angeles, CA 90048
Phone: (213)460-6304

Contains resources for Los Angeles film and tape production. Includes free-lancers such as production assistants and directors of photography. Details where to find equipment, props, and wardrobe; location information; and postproduction. Frequency: annual.

Making a Good Script Great: A Guide to Writing and Rewriting by a Hollywood Script Consultant

Samuel French, Inc.
45 W. 25th St.
New York, NY 10010
Phone: (212)206-8990
Fax: (212)206-1429

Linda Seger, author. 1987.

Making Movies

Dell Publishing Co.
1540 Broadway
New York, NY 10036
Phone: (212)354-6500

John Russo. 1989. Includes bibliography and an index.

Music Business Handbook & Career Guide

Sherwood Co.
PO Box 4198
Thousand Oaks, CA 91359
Phone: (805)379-6820

David Baskerville. Fifth edition, 1990.

National Directory of Addresses and Telephone Numbers

Omnigraphics, Inc.
2500 Penobscot Bldg.
Detroit, MI 48226
Phone: (313)961-1340

Annual. Covers about 223,000 corporations, federal, state, and local government offices, banks, colleges and universities, associations, labor unions, political organizations, newspapers, magazines, television and radio stations, foundations, postal and shipping services, hospitals, office equipment suppliers, airlines, hotels and motels, accountants, law firms, computer firms, foreign corporations, overseas trade contacts, and other professional services. Entries include company, organization, agency, or firm name, address, phone, fax, toll-free phone.

National Directory of Minority-Owned Business Firms

Gale Research Inc.
835 Penobscot Bldg.
Detroit, MI 48226
Phone: (313)961-2242
Fax: (313)961-6241

January, 1990. $195.00. Covers: Over 35,000 minority-owned businesses. Entries include: Company name, address, phone, name and title of contact, minority group, number of employees, description of products or services, sales volume. Arrangement: Alphabetical. Indexes: Standard Industrial Classification (SIC) Code, geographical.

National Directory of Women-Owned Business Firms

Gale Research Inc.
835 Penobscot Bldg.
Detroit, MI 48226
Phone: (313)961-2242
Fax: (313)961-6241

January, 1990. $195.00. Covers: Over 20,000 women-owned businesses. Entries include: Company name, address, phone, name and title of contact, number of employees, description of products or services, sales volume. Arrangement: Alphabetical. Indexes: Standard Industrial Classification (SIC) code, geographical.

New York Theatrical Sourcebook

Broadway Press
12 W. Thomas St.
PO Box 1037
Shelter Island, NY 11964-1037
Phone: (516)749-3266
Toll-free: 800-869-6372
Fax: (516)749-3266

David Rodger, publisher. Annual, November. $30.00. 560 pages. Covers over 2,500 suppliers of products and services for film, television, theater, designers, and craftspeople.

Non-Profit's Job Finder

Planning Communications
7215 Oak Ave.
River Forest, IL 60305-1935
Phone: (708)366-5200
Fax: (708)366-5280

Daniel Lauber, editor. 1992. $14.95. 306 pgs. Provides over 1,001 sources of job, internship, and grant opportunities.

NPPA Membership Directory

National Press Photographers Association (NPPA)
3200 Croasdaile Dr.
Ste. 306
Durham, NC 27705
Phone: (919)383-7246
Fax: (919)383-7261

Annual. $35.00.

The Official Southwest Talent Directory

Cobb-Rendish Publishing
2908 McKinney Ave.
Dallas, TX 75204
Phone: (214)754-4729

Annual. $25.00/single issue.

Peterson's Job Opportunities for Business and Liberal Arts Graduates

Peterson's
PO Box 2123
Princeton, NJ 08543-2123
Phone: (609)243-9111

Compiled by the Peterson's staff. 1993. $20.95 paperback. 300 pages. Lists hundreds of organizations that are hiring new business, humanities, and social science graduates in the areas of business and management. Explores how to match academic backgrounds to specific job openings. Provides information about opportunities for experienced personnel as well. Includes data on starting locations by city and state, summer jobs, co-op jobs, internships, and international assignments.

Often what stops people from pursuing a particular job is the feeling that "I'm not good enough to apply for that job." They imagine the other applicants to be more qualified. However, you need not ever be the perfect candidate for a certain job or career. In fact, there is no such thing as the perfect candidate. Seldom does anyone have all of what the job calls for. There is only the imperfect person—YOU—the individual who has some of what is needed for the job and can learn the rest on the job or get additional schooling.

Source: *Planning Job Choices: 1994*

The Practical Director

Focal Press
80 Montvale Ave.
Stoneham, MA 02180
Phone: (617)438-8464
Fax: (617)438-1979

Mike Crisp, editor. 1993.

The Producer's Master-Guide
330 W. 42nd St.
16th Fl.
New York, NY 10036-6994
Phone: (212)465-8889
Fax: (212)465-8880

Annual, in November. $89.95/single issue.

The Producer's Masterguide Year: The International Production Manual for Motion Pictures, Broadcast Television, Commercials .
New York Production Manual, Inc.
611 Broadway, Ste. 807
New York, NY 10012-2608
Phone: (212)777-4002

Shmuel Bension, editor. Thirteenth edition, 1993. Contains information about laws and unions in the film industry.

> **T**hose with a bachelor's degree in the arts and letters often become marketable in alternative careers when they have chosen the proper electives and obtained career-related work experiences. Two or three courses in an area of specialization, such as computer science, marketing, finance, or personnel administration, can enhance one's chances for employment considerably.
>
> Source: *Planning Job Choices: 1994*

The Production Assistants' Handbook: How to Break into the Film Business
Players Press, Inc.
4264 Fulton Ave.
PO Box 1132
Studio City, CA 91614
Phone: (818)789-4980

Jeff Alves, author. 1991. Guides the beginner and aids the professional through the ins and outs of the movie production business and outlines the information needed to start work, find work, and remain employed.

Screenwriting: The Art, Craft and Business of Film and Television Writing
New American Library/E.P. Dutton
PO Box 21766-A
Columbia, SC 29221
Phone: (803)772-6919

Richard Walter, author. 1988. $9.95. 224 pages.

Special Effects and Stunts Guide
Lone Eagle Publishing
2337 Roscomare Rd., No. 9
Los Angeles, CA 90077
Phone: (310)471-8066

Tassilo Baur and Bruce Scivally, editors. Second edition. $39.95.

Standard and Poor's Register of Corporations, Directors and Executives
Standard and Poor's Corporation
25 Broadway
New York, NY 10004
Phone: (212)208-8283

Annual, January; supplements in April, July, and October. $550.00, lease basis. Covers: Over 55,000 corporations in the United States, including names and titles of over 500,000 officials (Volume I); 70,000 biographies of directors and executives (Volume 2). Entries include: For companies - Name, address, phone, names of principal executives and accountants; number of employees, estimated annual sales, outside directors. For directors and executives - Name, home and principal business addresses, date and place of birth, fraternal organization memberships, business affiliations. Arranged alphabetically. Indexes: Volume 3 indexes companies geographically, by Standard Industrial Classification number, and by corporate family groups.

Successful Scriptwriting: The Art and Craft of
Writer's Digest Books
1507 Dana Ave.
Cincinnati, OH 45207
Phone: (513)531-2222
Fax: (513)531-4744

Jurgen Wolff and Kerry Cox, authors. 1991. $14.95.

The Technique of Acting
Bantam Books
666 5th Ave.
New York, NY 10103
Phone: (212)765-6500

Stella Adler. 1990.

The TV and Movie Business: An Encyclopedia of Careers, Technologies, and Practices
Harmony Books
201 E. 50th St.
New York, NY 10022
Phone: (212)572-6120

Harvey Rachlin, author. 1991.

UFVA Membership Directory
University Film and Video Association (UFVA)
c/o Donald J. Zirpola
Loyola Marymount University
Communication Arts Dept.
Los Angeles, CA 90045
Phone: (213)338-3033
Fax: (213)641-3964

Biennial.

U.S. Employment Opportunities: A Career News Service
Washington Research Associates
7500 E. Arapaho Plaza
Ste. 250
Englewood, CO 80112
Phone: (303)756-9038
Fax: (303)770-1945

Annual; quarterly updates. $184.00. List of over 1,000 employment contacts in companies and agencies in the banking, arts, telecommunications, education, and 14 other industries and professions, including the federal government. Entries include: Company name, name of representative, address, description of products or services, hiring and recruiting practices, training programs, and year established. Classified by industry. Indexes: Occupation.

Variety Who's Who in Show Business
R.R. Bowker
121 Chanlon Rd.
New Providence, NJ 07974
Phone: (908)464-6800
Fax: (908)464-3553

1989. Details short biographies and lists credits for notable industry professionals of all areas.

Ward's Business Directory of U.S. Private and Public Companies
Gale Research Inc.
835 Penobscot Bldg.
Detroit, MI 48226
Phone: (313)961-2242
Fax: (313)961-6241

1991. Four volumes. Volumes 1-3 lists companies alphabetically and geographically; $930.00/set. Volume 4 ranks companies by sales with 4-digit SIC code; $655.00. $1,050.00/complete set. Contains information on over 85,000 U.S. businesses, over 90% of which are privately held. Entries include company name, address, and phone; sales; employees; description; names of officers; fiscal year end information; etc. Arrangement: Volume 1 and 2 in alphabetic order; Volume 3 in zip code order within alphabetically arranged states.

Job availability by geographical region is highly variable. While most of the country is not in a hiring mode, certain regions offer more opportunities than others. According to Dr. Patrick Scheetz of the Collegiate Employment Research Institute, the better areas are the southeastern and northcentral, followed by the southwestern regions. On the lower end of the scale are the southcentral, northwestern, and last is the northeastern region of the country.

Source: *Planning Job Choices: 1994*

What a Producer Does: The Art of Moviemaking (Not the Business)
Silman James Press
c/o Samuel French Trade
7623 Sunset Blvd.
Hollywood, CA 90046

Buck Houghton, author. 1991. $14.95. 200 pages. Explores the creative concerns of the movie making process, from the screenplay to postproduction laboratory work.

Who's Who in American Film Now
New York Zoetrope, Inc.
838 Broadway
New York, NY 10003
Phone: (212)420-0590
Fax: (212)529-3330

Irregular; latest editions April 1987 (cloth) and

May 1988 (paper). $19.95. Covers: Over 4,700 persons in the film industry, including writers, producers, directors, actors, production designers, art designers, costume designers, cinematographers, sound technicians, choreographers, stunt personnel, musicians, special effects designers and technicians, and film editors. Entries include: Name, affiliation, address, phone; names and release dates of films with which associated. Arrangement: By activity.

Who's Who in the Motion Picture Industry

Packard Publishing Co.
PO Box 2187
Beverly Hills, CA 90213
Phone: (310)854-0276

Rodman Gregg, editor. Annual. $21.95. 260 pages. Lists about 1,200 cinematographers, directors, producers, writers, and studio executives in the theatrical and television motion picture industries.

The salary range for a screenwriter varies widely and depends on whether or not screenplays include treatments or are first drafts with options for final drafts or whether the writer is only handling a rewrite or polish. For the various categories compensation ranges from $5,000 to $53,000. A screenplay in great demand by the production companies may sell for over $1,000,000.

Source: *Getting Started in Film*

Women in Broadcast Technology Directory

Women in Broadcast Technology (WBT)
c/o Susan Elisabeth
2435 Spaulding St.
Berkeley, CA 94703
Phone: (415)540-8640

Annual.

Working Actors: The Craft of Televison, Film, & Stage Performance

Focal Press
Butterworth Publishers
80 Montvale Ave.
Storeham, MA 02180
Phone: (617)438-8464
Fax: (617)438-1479

Richard A. Blum. 1989.

Working in Hollywood: 64 Film Professionals Talk About Moviemaking

Crown Publishing Group
201 E. 50th St.
New York, NY 10022
Phone: (212)572-2100
Fax: (212)572-6192

Alexandra Brouwer and Thomas Lee Wright, authors. 1990.

Writer's A-Z

Writer's Digest Books
1507 Dana Ave.
Cincinnati, OH 45207
Phone: (513)531-2222

Kirk Polking, Joan Bloss, and Colleen Cannon, editors. 1990. Includes a bibliography.

The Writer's Handbook

The Writer's Magazine
120 Boylston St.
Boston, MA 02116
Phone: (617)423-3157

Sylvia K. Burack, editor. Revised edition, 1993. Annual. Contains information on getting published, writing techniques, and working with agents and editors. Describes specialized writing markets and lists publishers, writers' organizations, and literary agents.

Writer's Market: Where to Sell What You Write

Writer's Digest Books
1507 Dana Ave.
Cincinnati, OH 45207
Phone: (513)531-2222
Fax: (513)531-4744

Annual, September. $25.95, plus $3.00 shipping. Covers: More than 4,000 buyers of books, articles, short stories, plays, gags, verse, fillers, and other original written material. Includes book and periodical publishers, greeting card publishers, play producers and publishers, audiovisual material producers, author agents, and others. Entries include: Name and address of buyer, phone, payment rates, editorial requirements, reporting time, how to break in. Arrangement: Classified by type of publication.

Writing Effectively with Your PC: Computer Tools, Tips, and Tricks for Modern Writers

Random House, Inc.
201 E. 50th St.
New York, NY 10022
Phone: (212)751-2600

Larry Magid, editor. 1993.

Writing Screenplays that Sell

Harper Collins Inc.
10 E. 53rd St.
New York, NY 10022
Phone: (212)207-7000

Michael Hauges, author. 1991. $12.00.

The Young Performer's Guide: How to Break into Show Business

Betterway Publications, Inc.
PO Box 219
Crozet, VA 22932
Phone: (804)823-5661

Brian A. Padol and Alan Simon, authors. $14.95. 309 pages. Provides information on aspects of show business including how to enter the field and how to understand its potential for success and failure. Describes the roles of agents, managers, and tools of the trade.

MASTER INDEX

Master Index

The Master Index provides comprehensive access to all four sections of the Directory by citing all subjects, organizations, publications, and services listed throughout in a single alphabetic sequence. The index also includes inversions on significant words appearing in cited organization, publication, and service names. For example, "Ward's Business Directory of U.S. Private and Public Companies" could also be listed in the index under "Companies; Ward's Business Directory of U.S. Private and Public."